Bucking the Railroads
on the Kansas Frontier

Bucking the Railroads on the Kansas Frontier

The Struggle Over Land Claims by Homesteading Civil War Veterans, 1867–1876

JOHN N. MACK

McFarland & Company, Inc., Publishers
Jefferson, North Carolina, and London

All photographs used by permission of the Kansas State Historical Society.

LIBRARY OF CONGRESS CATALOGUING-IN-PUBLICATION DATA

Mack, John N., 1963–
    Bucking the railroads on the Kansas frontier : the struggle over land claims by homesteading Civil War veterans, 1867–1876 / John N. Mack.
    p.   cm.
    Includes bibliographical references and index.

    ISBN 978-0-7864-7029-7
    softcover : acid free paper ∞

    1. Railroads — Social aspects — Kansas — History —19th century. 2. Railroads — Economic aspects — Kansas — History —19th century. 3. Land settlement — Kansas — History —19th century. I. Title.
    HE2771.K2M33 2013
    333.3'178109034 — dc23   2012043792

BRITISH LIBRARY CATALOGUING DATA ARE AVAILABLE

© 2013 John N. Mack. All rights reserved

No part of this book may be reproduced or transmitted in any form or by any means, electronic or mechanical, including photocopying or recording, or by any information storage and retrieval system, without permission in writing from the publisher.

Front cover: *background* Eastman's map of Kansas and Nebraska territories showing the location of the Indian reserves according to the treaties of 1854 (courtesy Kansas State Historical Society); *photographs from left* loading cattle at MacCoy's stock yard, Abilene, Kansas, 1867; section men at Salina, Kansas, 1867; depot at Junction City, Kansas, 1867 (all Library of Congress)

Manufactured in the United States of America

McFarland & Company, Inc., Publishers
  Box 611, Jefferson, North Carolina 28640
    www.mcfarlandpub.com

To the veterans of the Civil War who first immigrated to Kansas, their descendants who continue to live there, and to all those who have fought and continue to fight for the ideals of personal responsibility and self-government

TABLE OF CONTENTS

Acknowledgments	ix
Preface	1
Introduction: The War That Had No End — Veterans as Settlers	7
1. The Battle Begins (1866–1867)	31
2. Vigilance Committees and Settlers' Clubs (1868–1870)	59
3. The Transformation of Settler Society (1870)	92
4. Challenges to Public Order (1871–1874)	110
5. Settlers Triumphant (1875–1876)	137
Epilogue	161
Appendix: The Osage in Neosho County (1825–1865)	163
Notes	181
Bibliography	199
Index	209

Acknowledgments

Many authors will tell you that writing acknowledgments is difficult, and in my experience, they are most certainly correct — especially because it is almost impossible to look back and remember all of the people who were influential in my life, professional studies, and career path. It is also extremely challenging to convey in a few words the debt of gratitude that I feel towards those whom I do remember and mention below.

I want to begin by acknowledging the critical role played by the advisor of my graduate studies at the University of Kansas, Jonathan Earle. I remember the first time I met Professor Earle — I was finishing my master's degree in Modern Russian and Eastern European history and was in the process of making a decision about what to do next. I was in the hall of the old history department wing and noticed that Professor Earle was in his office. With no appointment and really not knowing what I wanted to say, I quietly knocked on his door. His enthusiastic smile and warm welcome invited me in. His words of encouragement and guidance were deeply appreciated as was his ability to appreciate the unique circumstances facing this a-typical student and father of four. Looking back on my years of dissertation research and writing, I realize that it is these same qualities that have provided me with the necessary strength to finish my dissertation, successfully defend it, and finally revise it to book format. Throughout each stage of the process, Dr. Earle remained positive, supportive, and encouraging. Above all, he never questioned my belief that the study of the settlement of a little researched geographical region in the state of Kansas would yield a valuable return by making a significant contribution to our historical understanding of the political worldview and cultural mindset of Civil War veterans who settled the American west in the decade following the War and of the reasons for their struggle with the railroads which sought (in their minds) to deny them their basic right to self-government.

I also want to acknowledge the role played by other members of the

University of Kansas history faculty. Professor Norman Saul never wavered in his support of my scholarship. In fact, it was Professor Saul who first suggested that I consider Kansas history as a subject for serious academic research. Professor Saul has been both a mentor and an example of true scholarship and civic responsibility. Professor Luis Corteguera provided much needed encouragement at those moments in graduate study when I felt like quitting. Professor Theodore Wilson consistently exercised himself on my behalf. I am in awe of his scholarship and humbled by his consideration of my needs. Professors Paul Kelton, Donald Worster, and John Alexander also provided much needed insights into the methodology utilized by historians in researching the past as well as providing much valued examples of true scholarship.

I would be remiss if I did not also recognize the important role played by Vice-President Joe Burke of Labette Community College when I was employed there as a professor of history during the years of my initial research. Living in southeast Kansas, Joe supported my attempts to pursue excellence as both a researcher and professor. I also want to thank the members of the Senior Citizens' Center in Parsons, Kansas, for their insatiable thirst for information and willingness to share the stories of their families' past with me as I sought to understand the cultural history of southeast Kansas. Professor Otto Burniake, chair of the Social Science department at Georgia Perimeter College where I am now employed, has also been supportive, and I want to make sure I recognize how important that support continues to be. Dave Wilson and Jane Live, of the Osher Institute of Kansas, have supported my desire to share my research with others, and I thank them, together with the many members of the institute who attended the lectures I gave, who through their enthusiasm for learning about the settlement of southeast Kansas, have reinforced my conviction that this book and the stories of individuals, families, and communities it contains have value for both academic scholars and the more general public. In addition, Virgil Dean, editor of the *Kansas History Journal,* and Professor Bruce Kahler of Bethany College, together with my fellow members of the Kansas Historical Association, have offered both positive support and constructive criticism in response to the early editions of this research presented at conferences and in manuscript form that have helped to refine and strengthen my argument in critical areas of the text. I especially want to thank the editors and anonymous reviewers of the *Kansas History Journal,* the *Little Balkans Review,* and the *Catholic Historical Review* who were willing to support my initial efforts to formulate my research into material worthy of publication and were gracious enough to publish some of the material contained in this book in their journals.

Finally, I want to thank my children, Nathan, David, Jacob, and Michaela, for their support of my academic pursuits. When I decided to return to school and embark on a new career in my late 30s, they were among the very few who did not question my sanity! Their unflagging belief in me continues to be a gift I can never repay.

Preface

The story unveiled in this text begins at the end of the Civil War as thousands of Union veterans turned their gaze towards Kansas as a place where they could make a new beginning in an attempt to heal from the emotional and physical wounds they bore as a result of their military service. Many of these veterans immigrated to the southeastern corner of the state in the late 1860s. Buoyed by their recent success over the forces of rebellion and inspired by the dedication of their fellow soldiers, they came with a fierce commitment to the political principles that had motivated their enlistment as soldiers and their dedication to defend the cause of the Union. Upon arriving in southeast Kansas, they threw themselves into the labor of improving their individual claims even as they worked together to build lawful, ordered communities.

It was perhaps inevitable that their labors would bring them into conflict with the railroads that were intent on building lines through southeast Kansas to reach warm-water ports in Texas. To the settlers the railroads represented both a promise and a threat. Through linking the farmers and entrepreneurial businessmen with eastern markets, the railroads guaranteed the prospects of economic gain. However, by assuming title to the land already claimed by settlers, the railroads threatened not only the viability of their families and farms but also their independence and freedom. The settlers, who had not shied away from defending their liberty in the Civil War, responded to this challenge aggressively. Refusing to be cowed into submission, they banded together, formed associations and committees, and worked both locally and nationally to defend themselves and their rights in the halls of public opinion and the corridors of political power. Ultimately, their efforts were crowned with success when the Supreme Court ruled in their favor in 1876.

The first article to announce the decision appeared on April 13, 1876, in the *Chanute Tribune*. The leading article proclaimed in bold letters:

"TRIUMPH AT LAST!!" Other papers had similar headlines. The *Parsons Eclipse* led with the biblical phrase, "Gloria in Excelsis!" The *Oswego Independent* proclaimed "Jubilate!" And the *Southern Kansas Advance*, not to be outdone by its competitors, heralded "The Hour of Triumph."[1] Each article told the same story — the settlers had triumphed! For the first time in the history of the American west, the Supreme Court had ruled against the railroads in favor of the settlers who were guaranteed the right to purchase their land from the United States government at $1.25 per acre.[2]

The *Chanute Times* reported, "The decision secures the homes of three thousand families. Three hundred guns have been fired, bells are ringing, bonfires are burning, and flags are flying."[3] Victory celebrations were held in every village, town and city throughout Labette and Neosho Counties as the settlers celebrated their success. Although the settlers' chief concern had been the defense of their land, they believed that their victory had secured much more. The *Parsons Eclipse* explained, "The Osage Ceded Land case is one of the most remarkable instances where truth and equity has [*sic*] triumphed over fraud and wrong."[4] As this book will demonstrate, this understanding of the supreme importance of their victory resonated with the thousands of settlers who had risked much in their struggle against the railroads. Although to modern readers, their rhetoric may seem "over the top" and exaggerated, it is important to understand that these men (and women) believed that their struggle was essential to the survival of the republican experiment of self-government that defined the American political system and had engaged both the original founders of the nation and their own engagement on the bloodied fields of war in the struggle to preserve the Union intact.

According to a Westlaw database, the case brought by the southeast Kansas settlers to the Supreme Court has been examined, cited, or discussed in 259 Supreme Court cases, two Interior Board of Land Appeals decisions, and five U. S. Attorney General Opinions as well as 45 State Court decisions.[5] Legal scholars have explored the import of these cases in three primary areas: Native American–U.S. government relations, public lands, and statutory legislation. As scholar Stephen Williams has argued, the case brought by the settlers against the railroads and the final decision of the Supreme Court in 1876 established important legal precedents and principles.[6] In addition, in his ground-breaking investigation of the land policy of the United States government in Kansas, historian Paul Gates argued that the victory of the settlers over the railroads in 1876 was of "significance not only for Kansas but also for the history of public land policy on a national scale."[7] Kansas historian Craig Miner also noted that "of all the complex struggles between settlers and railroads for Indian lands in Kansas, with the government and the courts in the middle," it was the one that occurred in the Osage Ceded Lands that "achieved the greatest publicity and aroused the greatest public passion at the time."[8] Furthermore, the victory of the settlers, as Miner and Unrau asserted, "represent[s] a definite change of direction in the precedents set for the transfer of Indians lands in Kansas" and "did have an impact upon the later history of Indian Territory, where the pattern of railroad purchase of Indian reserves never obtained."[9]

However, in spite of its historic importance and the testimony of these leading scholars, the story of the legal triumph of Civil War veteran settlers over the railroads and their struggle to attain it have yet to be examined and analyzed. The purpose of this book is to fill this gap in historical knowledge by uncovering the role played by Civil War veterans in the settling of the American west and, in so doing, to give voice to the thousands of men, women and children whose refusal to give in to the demands of the railroads changed the course of American history.

Like Hansel and Gretel's father following a trail of bread crumbs, I have sought to trace the behavior of southeast Kansas settlers through the 1860s and '70s by observing their words and actions. Even though these men and women were primarily focused on the intense struggle to survive in an unfamiliar clime, they left behind a rich collection of sources that have allowed me to enter into their lives and thoughts and, by so doing, come to understand how they perceived themselves and the world around them and how they defined themselves in relation to the world and their time. The fruits of this in-depth study have indeed been rewarding as I recovered a story of community struggle and triumph that had been all but lost to the historical record.

My intent has been to hear and understand the settlers' own words and (as much as I can) thoughts. This has required me to adopt a multi-disciplinary approach and has produced a study that spreads out in several directions. To understand their choices, I have relied upon the insights of political, economic, cultural, and social historians. Some historical research projects are like rifle shots. They fly straight towards their target and are united by a singular theme. However, research projects such as this one are more like shotgun bursts which head in a singular direction but spray out along the way.

There are at least two ways to begin researching important historical topics. The first begins with a central question and then pursues the answer to that question by seeking out the appropriate sources. The second begins with a collection of sources and then seeks to determine a unifying question that will help to uncover their meaning. My approach in this book follows this second route. My journey began when I was appointed associate professor of history at Labette Community College in Parsons, Kansas. As I came to know my students, I discovered that many of them were the descendants of original settlers. To my surprise, these students knew little about the history of their families and communities. When I turned to find articles and books to use in bridging this gap, I found that hardly any resources (beyond a few local histories written by local residents) existed. This is the genesis of the project that ultimately produced this manuscript. Undoubtedly, the discovery process that attends every probe into the past is rewarding for the scholar. And there is no doubt that this research project was doubly so for me. I found that as a result of my studies I understood my students better and was better able to teach them "from the past into the present." In short, it helped me become a better teacher. I also believe that the argument I present, with its supporting material, sheds light on the important role fulfilled by Civil War veterans in the post-bellum settling of the western frontier and helps to explain in greater detail the reasons for the widespread opposition to railroad expansion by settlers throughout the west.

In researching the story of the settlement of southeast Kansas from 1867 to 1876, I relied on local newspapers published in Labette and Neosho counties. My reasons for employing this methodology are two-fold. The first is practical — quite literally they are frequently the only sources available. All of the documents related to this time period possessed by the Missouri, Kansas, and Texas and the Leavenworth, Lawrence, and Galveston railroad companies were destroyed by fire in the first decades of the 20th century. (My investigations into the collections of the various railroad clubs and organizations associated with each railroad confirmed the lack of source material from this early period.) The Kansas State Historical Society possesses a small collection of private papers, letters, and documents from this time period that I have utilized, but as the reader will note, these are both small in number and fragmentary in content. I have visited each local historical society in Neosho and Labette counties to discover what "treasures" might be found in their archives. Unfortunately, with the exception of a few early land-deeds, one reconstructed log cabin (at the Osage Mission Historical Society), and an interesting collection of early apothecary instruments (at the Chetopa Historical Society), I found no documents from the time period I was studying. The library of Parsons does possess an interesting and informative photocopy of the papers of Robert S. Stevens, the first general manager of the Missouri, Kansas, and Texas Railroad Company, which I relied upon in Chapter 5 to provide the perspective of the railroads. Thus, the paucity of additional primary source material forced me to rely heavily upon the writings of newspaper editors.

Fortunately, newspapers did not prove to be hard to find! In fact, twenty-eight newspapers were published (for varying lengths of time) between 1867 and 1876. The following papers were published in Neosho County: *Chanute Times* (Chanute); *Erie Ishmaelite* (Erie); *Thayer Headlight* (Thayer); *Neosho County Dispatch* (Erie); *Neosho County Journal* (Osage Mission); *Neosho County Record* (Erie); *Neosho Valley Eagle* (Jacksonville); *New Chicago Times* (New Chicago); *New Chicago Transcript* (New Chicago); *Osage Mission Transcript* (Osage Mission); *Osage Mission Journal* (Osage Mission); *People's Advocate* (Osage Mission); *Thayer Criterion* (Thayer); *Tioga Herald* (Tioga); and the *Weekly Anti-Monopolist* (Osage Mission). The following newspapers were published in Labette County: *Anti-Monopolist* (Parsons); *Chetopa Advance* (Chetopa); *Chetopa Herald* (Chetopa); *Kansas Democrat* (Oswego); *Labette Sentinel* (Labette); *Oswego Independent* (Oswego); *Oswego Register* (Oswego); *Parsons Eclipse* (Parsons); *Parsons Surprise* (Parsons); *Parsons Weekly Herald* (Parsons); *Parsons Sun* (Parsons); *Western Enterprise* (Parsons); and the *Southern Kansas Advance* (Chetopa).[10]

More importantly, however, I have chosen to utilize newspapers in the construction of this story because I believe that they are essential sources that can be mined with great benefit. Today, when television and the world-wide Web dominate cultural dialogue, it is sometimes difficult to remember a time when the newspaper was supreme or when a small community supported so many papers. Never was this truer that in the mid-19th century when, as Brayton Harris has noted, "intersecting technologies ... put newspapers at the forefront of social activity."[11] In a day and age far removed from our own when large corporations own most news outlets, local editors operated frequently on their own reconnaissance and were often solely dependent upon the good graces of their local readership for their livelihood. As Craig Miner has remarked, "It is hard to fool local readers about yesterday's events in their own town."[12]

Perhaps even more importantly, newspapers were an important intellectual and social "meeting place" for the local citizens. Historian David Dary explained the central role played by newspapers in the settlement of the western frontier by noting that small-town newspapers "reflected the total image of their towns and cities" by providing "community life with cohesion and direction and purpose." The editors of local newspapers rebuked social ills and/or demanded social reform. In so doing, they were important in the establishment and preservation of "standards of public morals." Because small-town editors were local men — often printing papers out of their living rooms and parlors on small printing presses that they had brought with them in wagons or on the backs of pack animals, they were in touch with their communities and became the voice through which local opinions were expressed. The pages of local newspapers thus provide "a written record of the lives of their communities."[13] Professional historians have sometimes neglected these newspaper sources. Historian Jeffrey Pasley argues that this is a mistake—instead, according to Pasley, "newspapers and their editors need to occupy a place in accounts ... as central as the role they actually played."[14] Although newspapers must be approached, as with any source, with care by historians, it is nevertheless true that they remain an invaluable source of information for Kansas historians. Indeed, they are indispensable to the telling of the story. This is especially true in the case of the settlement of southeast Kansas.

Finally, I think it is important to emphasize that my goal in discovering the history presented in this book has to been not only to recover the "what" but also to comprehend (as much as I can from the vantage point of the present) the "why." The settlers discussed in this manuscript could have made other choices. Nearby Cherokee and Crawford counties erupted in violence as settlers took up arms to confront the railroad. The residents in these counties turned on each other, as some settlers chose to settle with the railroads and some did not. The violence and civic discord which followed earned this region the epithet of "the Kansas Balkans." The struggle of the citizens of Labette and Neosho counties, however, did not take this path. Instead of descending into a fight of settler against settler, the men (and women) in Neosho and Labette counties managed to remain remarkably unified in their opposition to the railroad claims. As this book will reveal, their unified opposition to the railroads ultimately changed the course of American history, the nature of western settlement, and laid the foundation for the evolution of political thought in Kansans and the American west.

Introduction

The War That Had No End — Veterans as Settlers

Ever since Dorothy was caught up in a tornado that transported her from the drab, dreary, and gray landscape of Kansas to the imaginative, colorful, and fascinating Land of Oz, the state of Kansas has been associated primarily as a place from which to escape in the minds of many Americans. It seems that many Americans would agree with the Scarecrow's response to Dorothy's description of her home, "I cannot understand why you should wish to leave this beautiful country and go back to the dry, gray place you call Kansas."[1] Dr. Karl Menninger noted in 1939 that Kansans "meekly endure the opprobrium and ridicule of other states."[2] In 1986, scholar Thomas Fox Averill observed that Kansas is frequently depicted in both literature and popular culture as a "bleak, harsh, flat, boring land from which anyone would do well to be removed, even by a tornado."[3]

To this day, Kansas continues to be the brunt of jokes in both print and on the silver screen — the proverbial "black hole" from which educated and talented people wish to escape and in which the lesser talented and poorly educated are condemned to remain. Of course, modern Kansas has not helped its image as it became known for a time as the state that outlawed the teaching of evolution and is still known as the home of the radically fundamentalist Phelps clan, which protests soldier funerals all over the country in order to proclaim their message that "God hates" both "fags" and "America."

It may thus come as a surprise to contemporary Americans that, in the middle of the 19th century, Kansas was a prime location for men and women wishing to establish new lives for themselves in the American west. Although today Kansas is solidly in the "mid-west," in the 1850s and '60s

Kansas was on the edge of the western frontier, functioning as a beacon of opportunity and possibility in the minds of many who wished to escape the economic and geographical limits of life in the land east of the Mississippi River by beginning afresh in the American west.

Although many today think of Kansas as flat and monotonous with few differences in its geographical features, in reality Kansas has a great diversity of terrain, climate, and soil as well as a variety of indigenous plants and animals. The southeastern corner of Kansas lies on the fringe of the Ozark Plateau. The northeastern portion of the state is characterized by rolling hills and bluffs shaped by glacial activity hundreds of thousands of years ago. West of the 100th meridian, the geography changes as the hills and tall grasses of the eastern region of Kansas are replaced by the flatter, short grass and level plateau of the High Plains.

The state is drained by two major river basins, the Kansas and the Arkansas. The Kansas River, part of the larger Missouri River system, and its many tributaries and streams water the northeastern region, while the Arkansas, part of the larger Arkansas-Red-White system, originates in the Rocky Mountains and meanders through southwestern and south-central Kansas before crossing over the southern border of the state and continuing eastward. It too is connected to an extensive series of tributaries and streams, many of which have created both soil and topography conducive to productive farming. Significantly, two of the rivers connected to the Arkansas-Red-White system, the Verdigris and the Neosho, flow through southeast Kansas and were a key element in the reason the area was attractive to would-be settlers in the post–Civil War period. These river systems also helped to support an abundant animal life that helped to sustain the Native Americans who first inhabited the area and then the early immigrant population. Grouse, prairie chicken, wild turkey, ducks, and geese were found in abundance. White-tailed and mule deer as well as large herds of buffalo (until their numbers were decimated by over-hunting in the 1870s) ranged for food in Kansas and provided much needed protein for both native peoples and early settlers.

Originally inhabited by the native peoples of the midwestern portion of the North American continent, after European exploration the area now known as Kansas was claimed by no fewer than six non-indigenous nations. The Spanish conquistador Francisco Vasquez de Coronado was the first European to visit Kansas and to claim it as belonging to the Spanish crown. England was next to claim the region as it advanced the theory that the original Virginia and Carolina land grants extended from ocean to ocean. France then claimed Kansas with the rest of Louisiana, and eventually "sold" the territory to the United States as part of the Louisiana Purchase in 1804. In 1819, the United States agreed that the land west of the 100th meridian was officially under Spanish sovereignty; however, when Mexico declared its independence, the southwestern portion of Kansas fell under its jurisdiction. Then, when Texas declared its independence from Mexican authority, it claimed all of the land belonging to Mexico to the north as its own; finally, in 1848 when the US-Mexican War ended with the signing of the Treaty of Guadalupe Hidalgo, the land of Kansas was again returned to the United States.

As Robert W. Baughman has noted, the first "use" of Kansas by the United States government was to turn it into a "dumping ground for Indians of the Upper Mississippi valley."[4] Initiated by President Andrew Jackson and passed by Congress in 1830, the "voluntary removal" of eastern indigenous peoples to Kansas (and Oklahoma) took place in the 1830s and '40s. For the most part, native peoples from south of Ohio were "given" land in the area that became the state of Oklahoma, while those who lived in the north were assigned to live in Kansas. By the conclusion of the removal process in 1846, approximately twenty-seven different indigenous people groups (or fractions of people groups) were settled in Kansas.[5]

Within 8 years, however, the rights of the removed tribes to the land of Kansas were negated by the passage of the Kansas-Nebraska Act, which officially opened the area for white settlers. The area that would become the state of Kansas had first been explored by Americans in 1804 as part of the famous Lewis and Clark Expedition sponsored by President Thomas Jefferson. Lewis and Clark were soon followed by both explorers and trappers — chief among these men were Zebulon Pike (1806), Stephen H. Long (1819–20), Jacob Fowler (1821–22), Sylvester Pattie (1824), Jedediah Strong Smith (1824–31), and John Charles Fremont (1842–44). However, it was the discovery of gold in California in 1849 that brought a large number of Americans to and through Kansas on their way to the land of promise and opportunity. This migration greatly influenced the history of Kansas. As Miner notes, it was the "realization that prairie lands, though barren of trees, could have soil rich enough to grow abundant crops" that led to a change of attitude about Kansas.[6] Whereas Kansas was first seen only as a place to travel "through," the more people were exposed to its pristine beauty and agricultural possibilities, the more plausible the idea of Kansas a place in which to settle became. Edward Everett Hale was among the first to advocate settlement in Kansas in his work, *Kanzas and Nebraska* (published in 1854), when he quoted from a journal of a friend who had visited the area now known as Kansas City, Kansas: "The land ... is immensely rich and very beautiful. All this region ... is superior to any I ever saw for civilization, and if it were occupied by New England society, I would never think of visiting California."

The publication of Hale's book in 1854 coincided with the passage of the Kansas-Nebraska Act in 1854 which made possible the vision articulated by the journal entry which he quoted. This act, which organized the territories of both Nebraska and Kansas, was signed into law by President Franklin Pierce on May 30. The initial import of the Kansas-Nebraska Act was to open two territories for settlement. Divided by the 40th parallel, the territory to the North primarily contained the area now circumscribed by the borders of the state of Nebraska; the southern territory originally included a geographical region much larger than the present area of Kansas.[7] According to the act of organization, the territory known as Kansas included all that land lying within the following limits — "beginning at a point on the western boundary of the State of Missouri, where the thirty-sevenths parallel of north latitude crosses the same; thence west on said parallel to the eastern boundary of New Mexico; thence north on said boundary to latitude thirty-eight; thence following said boundary westward to the east boundary of the Territory of Utah, on the summit of the Rocky Mountains; thence northward on said summit to the fortieth parallel of latitude; thence east on said parallel to the western boundary of the State of Missouri; thence south with the western boundary of said State to the place of beginning."[8]

All in all, the Kansas territory encompassed approximately 126,283 square miles (i.e., all of the present state of Kansas plus most of present-day eastern Colorado). When Congress officially established Kansas as a land district on July 22, 1854, it provided for the establishment of official land offices where settlers could register their claims.[9] John Calhoun was commissioned as the first surveyor general of the territory on August 4th, and also ex officio register of filings for the land offices soon to be established. The first land office was established in 1855 in Lecompton, which had been chosen as the temporary seat of territorial government. By May of 1856, over 3,000 filings had been received at this office.[10]

On February 11, 1859, a proposal was presented to the territorial assembly to divide Kansas into 38 counties (one of which was in the present state of Colorado).[11] By the time the state constitution was adopted by the convention in July that number had been increased to 40.[12] In 1860, when Kansas officially requested to be received into the Union as a state, the boundaries were revised and the state of Kansas was admitted into the Union as the 34th state on January 29, 1861. The eastern, southern, and northern borders were kept as they were originally defined in the Kansas-Nebraska Act but the western border was set at the 25th meridian in relation to the nation's capital, effectively separating Kansas from the land that would become part of the state of Colorado.

The Kansas-Nebraska Act was a controversial political move organized by Stephen Douglas, the senator from Illinois. The establishment of the territories not only put under the direct control of the federal government the largest area of unorganized land remaining in the American west, the act also effectively ended the unofficial truce over the issue of slavery which had been established by the Missouri Compromise of 1820, that limited the introduction of slavery north of the 20th parallel. In proposing the Kansas-Nebraska Act, Douglas had proposed to replace the compromise with the concept of "popular sovereignty" — an idea which stipulated that each territory should be able to choose whether it would enter the Union as a slave or free state.

Douglas sincerely believed that adopting the principle of popular sovereignty would help to defuse the growing schism over the issue of slavery by removing the focus of the debate from the halls of Congress to the meeting places of the territorial assemblies. He was convinced that much of the bitterness aroused between the North and the South was rooted in the belief that Congress had the power to determine the status of slavery in the territories. Once this authority was taken away and given to the people living in the territories, members of Congress would no longer be divided over the issue of slavery but could return to working together to promote the overall good of the nation. Unfortunately, as later events revealed, Douglas and his supporters were wrong; the violence that erupted in "Bleeding Kansas" in the 1850s, as Craig Miner has demonstrated, heightened the national focus on the divisive issue of slavery and thus served to further alienate the opponents of slavery from its supporters.

This fact, however, should not obscure the significance of the Kansas-Nebraska Act as a significant step in the evolution of a politically independent American west. The supporters of popular sovereignty believed that they were embracing a concept deeply embedded in the American theory of self-government: that the best government is local and that people should be free to determine what kind of government they desired. They pointed to Thomas Jefferson's original plan (proposed in 1784) for western territories in which Jefferson had sought to grant full self-government to those who settled the frontier areas. Even though Jefferson's plan was ultimately superseded by the passage of the Northwest Ordinance of 1787, which established control of the governments of newly established territories by federally appointed authorities and limited the freedom of frontiersmen to govern themselves, because of opposition from representatives from the already established states, for those living in the American west it established an important political precedent.

After the passage of the Northwest Ordinance, territories established by Congress were administered from Washington. The president appointed the territorial governor and arranged for the election of a congressional delegate as well as the territorial assembly. The president was also responsible for certifying the results of any election that took place. To the majority of those who immigrated to the western frontier, the territorial system of government was a violation of the basic principles of the American political system. Those on the frontier frequently argued that the territorial system denied them their constitutional rights as Americans to self-government and repeatedly urged that it be replaced by a new political system that guaranteed them "self-rule." As Jesse Applegate, an early settler in the territory of Oregon, expressed it in a letter to the editor of the *Oregon Statesmen*, the strong desire of those living in frontier region was for Congress "to restore to us our birth-right — the privilege of making our own laws, and electing our own judges and rulers, and to be freed from charlatans and strangers that are neither with us nor of us."[13]

Historian Robert Johannsen noted that, in advancing the principle of popular sovereignty, Stephen Douglas was drawing "upon the long tradition of frontier discontent when he drafted the Kansas-Nebraska Act."[14] From the time he first entered Congress in 1847, Douglas forcefully and frequently articulated his belief that the system of federal control over territories violated the spirit of the founders who had set forward "the great and fundamental principle of free government, which asserts that each community shall settle ... all ... questions affecting their domestic institutions by themselves, and in their own way."[15]

It was their support for what Douglas called the "inherent and inalienable" right of self-government that led members of Congress and President Pierce to adopt as a new principle of Territorial management in passing the Kansas-Nebraska Act: "the right of the people of an organized Territory, under the Constitution and laws of the United States, to govern themselves in respect to their own internal polity and domestic affairs."[16] As Douglas wrote, in defending the act to a group of clergymen who opposed it because it would potentially open new areas to slavery that had been previously closed, "The principle of the Nebraska bill is purely a question of self-government, involving the right and capacity of the people to make their own laws and manage their own local and domestic concerns.... It is the principle upon which the thirteen Colonies separated from the imperial government. It is the principle in defense of which the battles of the Revolution were fought. It is the principle to which all our free institutions owe their existence, and upon which our entire republican system rests."[17]

In his defense of the Kansas-Nebraska Act, Douglas was joined by other prominent senators who reiterated his contention that a basic principle of republican government was at work. Senator Isaac Toucey from Connecticut argued that the act upheld "the right of the people to govern themselves in an independent, separate, distinct community."[18] William Dawson of Georgia asked his colleagues in the Senate if they could deny that "that the principle of the bill is not the American principle — the principle upon which our whole system of government is based — the right of people to govern themselves."[19]

The reaction to the passage of the Kansas-Nebraska Act was passionately divided along partisan lines. Abolitionists and other free-labor northerners believed that the act was a barely concealed power play by aristocratic southern slave owners to gain political control of the newly opened territory in the west. As Craig Miner has noted, "It was widely assumed that under such a system Nebraska, which was clearly too far north to support agriculture based on slavery, would enter the Union as a free state, but that Kansas, contiguous as it was to slaveholding Missouri, might well be added to the salve South."[20] Henry Ward Beecher spoke for many in the North when he commented, "If the South inoculates the State with her leprosy, the plains of Kansas are fairer and richer to-day as a wilderness, than they will ever be again."[21]

However, there were others who applauded Douglas' efforts. As one Indianan explained to a friend, he had vigorously supported passage of the Kansas-Nebraska Act because "we did understand the K[ansas] and N[ebraska] Bill ... as guaranteeing to all future Territories perfect sovereignty and independence in reference to all municipal questions and matters."[22] In a letter discussing his acceptance of the Democratic nomination for President, James Buchanan echoed the beliefs of many settlers when he wrote: "This legislation [the Kansas-Nebraska Act] is founded upon principles as ancient as free government itself.... The Kansas-Nebraska Act does not do more than give the force of law to this elementary principle of self-government."[23] This is exactly what Douglas himself had declared on the floor of Congress when he said, "I believe that the peace, the harmony, and perpetuity of the Union require us to go back to the doctrines of the Revolution, to the principles of the Constitution, ... and leave the people, under the Constitution, to do as they may see proper in respect to their own internal affairs."[24]

As scholars have explained, it is difficult (if not impossible) to disentangle the myriad motivations of Douglas in supporting the Kansas-Nebraska Act.[25] Undoubtedly, his motivations involved more than concern for settlers' rights or Constitutional principles and included advancing his own political career and financial interests. However, this fact should not obscure the fact that for Douglas and his supporters, the rights of settlers to determine their own political future was an important concern. Historian Robert Johannsen explained, "A frontiersmen himself, he was cognizant of the needs and desires of other frontiersmen and regarded his bill as an important step in the direction of territorial self-government."[26] As Douglas later remarked in an article written for *Harper's Magazine* in 1859, the fundamental political principle he had adopted in proposing the Kansas-Nebraska Act was "that every distinct political Community, loyal to the Constitution and the Union, is entitled to all the rights, privileges, and immunities of self-government in respect to their local concerns and internal polity, subject only to the Constitution of the United States."[27]

Interestingly, while in both northern and southern States, reactions tended to follow already drawn partisan lines, the act was received in the west with almost universal acclaim regardless of party affiliation or opinions about slavery. The editor of the *Oregon Statesman* hailed the act as a "democratic step forward, enlarging the rights of American citizens in the Territories, admitting them to be, at once, competent and equal to self-government."[28] One frontiersman wrote, "The glorious Nebraska bill, involving the principle of Self-Government, has passed, thanks to God first and then to the fearless band of Patriots who voted for it — second only to the signers of the Declaration of our Independence, well may they feel proud of their position." He even went so far as to paraphrase a well-known biblical passage in praise of Douglas and the other supporters of the act, "after generations will yet rise up and call them blessed."[29]

Significantly, in the Kansas territory, settlers interpreted the act in a similar way — as guaranteeing them the right to govern themselves in all respects. As one observer, Henry Bragg, noted, popular sovereignty was a "principle they [the Kansas settlers] hold quite as sacred as their lives."[30] The noted concern of the settlers in Kansas was not with the principle of popular sovereignty itself but with the loose interpretation of it that allowed members of nearby states to claim residency and vote in elections without actually settling in the territory. As one editor wrote, "We are for the principles of the Nebraska act, and wish to see them fully carried out — we want to see the question of slavery and all other questions determined by the people of this Territory without any interference from abroad, either from Massachusetts or Missouri, or any other people not from Kansas."[31]

Even the more virulent and vocal opponents of slavery, who had immigrated to Kansas shortly after the territory was open for settlement, endorsed the Act because it supported the rights of settlers to govern their own affairs. In a petition to Congress, drawn up by members of a prominent free-state group in Lawrence (Kansas), an appeal was made "for rights — not for trivial rights, but for the dearest rights guaranteed to us by the Declaration of Independence — by the Constitution of the Union — by the law of our organization — by the solemn compact of the States, and which you pledged to us as the condition of our coming here."[32] As the editor of the *Lawrence Republican* explained, "The Kansas Act purported to leave the 'people free to form their domestic institutions in their own way.' Its spirit, as expounded by its authors, was that not only the question of slavery, but all other local matters, should be left to the unbiased decision by the people."[33]

The history of Kansas in its territorial period (1854–1861) has been amply discussed by historians, and it is not the purpose of the author of this book to repeat information that can be found elsewhere.[34] However, it is important for the reader to understand the fundamental importance attached to the principle of local self-government by those who settled in the state of Kansas in the years both preceding and following the Civil War. It is this commitment which lies at the very heart of the struggle of post-bellum immigrants to southeast Kansas to build lawful communities, claim their land as their own, and protest the claims of the Railroads described in the following pages. As the Republican editor of the *Anti-Monopolist* exhorted his readers in its inaugural edition, "Be kind enough my friends to reflect that you are a citizen of the United States. Then follow me to that important epoch in the history of the Republic, when the concentrated wisdom of ages culminated in giving birth to that immortal instrument, the Constitution for the United States. Its authors had but recently emerged from a bloody struggle, waged for the purpose of defending their doctrine of the capacity of a people for self-government."[35] The Democratic editor of another southeastern Kansan newspaper agreed, "It will ever be our aim as a citizen of the United States to fully recognize the doctrine of political equality as the true basis of our society."[36] Although they disagreed on many points, both Republicans and Democrats were united in their allegiance to the fundamental political doctrine expressed in the concept of popular sovereignty as articulated in the act which had made settlement in Kansas possible.

The first immigrants to the Kansas territory chose to live in the northeastern region and established Kansas' oldest cities and towns (e.g., Topeka, Lawrence, Manhattan, Atchison, and Leavenworth). As these settlers struggled to define both the political and cultural identity of Kansas, the central issue they confronted was that of slavery. The decision, finally arrived at in 1859, to reject slavery by entering the Union as a "free state" played a key role in the process of creating both the image (and reality) of what it meant (and means) to be a Kansan. These early immigrants believed that they had triumphed over the repeated attempts of a powerful slave-owning aristocracy to deny them their right to self-government. Missouri and its pro-slavery ruffians became the "other" over against which Kansans created their own identity as law-abiding and freedom-protecting men and women.

In the post–Civil War period, as thousands of Union veterans made the trek to establish homes and build communities in southeast Kansas (the second region to be settled in the State), this identity was assumed by the new immigrants who saw themselves as the heirs of the original settlers and believed that it was their duty to continue the struggle against outside forces they believed were intent upon robbing them of their Constitutional right to determine their own futures and to govern their own lives.

In his essay, "America's Golden Midcentury," western historian Robert W. Johannsen argued that that "no real understanding of nineteenth-century America can be achieved without at some point coming to grips with what the people of the time called the 'spirit of the age.'" He further recommended that historians engage in "a study of perception, of how Americans perceived themselves and the world around them, how they defined themselves in relation to their world and their time." While noting that some scholars would label this approach as "hopelessly old-fashioned," Johannsen insisted that "the results are rewarding" even though the "effort" is "neither easy nor simple."[37]

I am convinced that my argument in this book validates Johannsen's basic assertions. To understand the actions of the settlers it was been necessary first of all to understand their political presuppositions. I had to "begin at the beginning." The roots of their story must be sought in the 1840s and '50s, when they came to age politically and began to form the attitudes that would sustain them through the rest of their lives.[38] Joel Sibley explains, "Whatever the Civil War did or did not do, the behavior of America's leaders and its electorate remained rooted in other times and the values and ways of engaging in politics of those times. As the years passed, the memories of the war were to affect the political world more directly and powerfully. But even those events were always rooted in the continuing strength of the earlier forces still at play."[39]

In other words, although the Civil War was undeniably the central and defining event in their lives, both their reasons for entering the war and their understanding of its significance afterwards were shaped by the beliefs they had absorbed during the pre war years. As Earl Hess has written, "The war's successful close reinforced the values of liberty ... as no other event did. It insured that continuity would be the theme of popular ideology throughout the mid-nineteenth century: continuity of rhetoric, belief, and of self-image."[40]

In the political world of nineteenth century Kansans, certain words were infused with special meaning. Single words or phrases connoted complex sets of values, creating a kind of conceptual shorthand readily understood by those who were speaking or writing as well as those in the intended audience. Familiar patterns of thought manifested the prevailing assumptions of the "speakers" and the particular problems that concerned them.[41] For settlers in southeast Kansas, these key patterns revolved around the concepts of "liberty" and "freedom." Thus as they expressed their hopes and defended their actions throughout their decade long struggle with the railroads, they consistently utilized a shared political language, in which key words functioned as a "political shorthand."

A good example is the headline "The Republic Is in Danger," which appeared in the December 20, 1872, edition of the *Osage Mission Transcript*. For settlers, allowing monopolies like the railroads to control unlimited control of land, money, and power threatened to create a social order destined to follow the course of tyranny: namely, the economic and political system fostered by the railroads bred habits and relations that generated moral vice, sanctioned concentrated power, thereby threatening the basis of liberty. As the *Transcript* explained, the railroads' attempt to seize "the birthright of the people" was a first step leading towards the total subversion of "the ballot box" and the "corruption" of the Republic. Looking back to earlier examples of failed Republics, the editor reminded his readers of a time when "a vile, mercenary rabble" sold "their votes for bread and the theaters." The end result of the current situation, he concluded, would also parallel that of ancient Rome unless the settlers stood together to oppose the "deep-seated treachery to our democracy" that was inspired by "a thirst for the downfall of liberty and the establishment of tyranny on this continent."[42]

By reminding his readers of ancient Rome, and by repeating the words "corruption," "tyranny," and "liberty" the editor of this local paper was making essential connections between the current struggle in which the settlers were engaged and the longer narrative of republican history. He argued that the critical problems that had been manifested in British tyranny at the time of the Revolutionary War and had re-emerged in the slave system were once more apparent in the plans of land-grabbing railroad magnates. Thus, even as it had been in 1776 and 1861, these settlers believed that the future of the republic was at stake in their struggle. The forces of subversion had altered their form but were waging their ever-constant paradigmatic war against liberty. The confrontation with railroad monopolists was thus of a piece with the elemental struggle of free people against corruption and tyranny; it was part of the unfolding narrative of the common "every-day American's" fight for the right to self-government against the collective aristocratic designs of the rich and powerful. In fighting the railroads, southeast Kansas settlers consequently believed they were responding, not just to the personal threat of losing their homes and farms, but also to a much larger perceived risk of losing the very Republic they had defended with their lives as soldiers in the Civil War.

By consistently framing their struggle in this manner, southeast Kansans convinced themselves that their campaign against the railroads was a defining moment in the nation's history of equal importance to both the Revolutionary and Civil Wars. The *Parsons Eclipse*, a settlers' paper published in the 1870s, declared, "Such wide spread and universal distress never pervaded our country before as does ours at the present time. There is no mistaking the cause of it; the money-kings have a death-grip upon the throats of the people ... If the country would save itself they have no time to slumber but must be up and doing."[43] Another small newspaper published in a small Neosho County town, the *Osage Mission Journal*, assured its readers that "two years will not pass before the organization of a great national party, having the cause of the people on the Osage ceded lands as one of the most prominent planks of its platform."[44]

Settlers repeatedly insisted that the continued presence of railroad monopolies was inconsistent with the founding principles of the nation, arguing that if railroads were allowed to increase their power by seizing the property of ordinary citizens the principles by which the liberty of nation was maintained would be destroyed. Thus, by insisting that their cause was not new—that their campaign was an act of renovation rather than innovation — settlers self-identified themselves with the "spirit of 1776" — they understood their actions to be reclaiming and re-establishing the ideals of freedom and liberty that had inspired their forefathers to wage war against the British in 1776 and their own involvement in the struggle against tyranny in the recently concluded Civil War.

Their sense of responsibility for the future of the republic was intensified by their service as soldiers.[45] As historian Earl Hess has written, Civil War "veterans saw a close relationship between their military and civilian lives. They had learned to be alert and vigilant in the army and they carried those traits home."[46] Veteran soldiers in southeast Kansas were proud of their military service. The comments of John Hill, a wounded veteran who settled in Labette County after the war, are typical. As he explained in an open letter to his hometown paper, the *Oswego Independent*, "We are proud of those broad, ugly scars and deformities, they are indelible seals that we carry on our bodies of our fidelity and loyalty to our country."[47] Service in the Civil War as a Union soldier was critically important in certifying a man's reliability and establishing bonds of trust and friendship. For example, the editor of the *Labette Sentinel* in 1870 expressed his confidence in the Republican candidate for state representative who, although young and relatively inexperienced in politics, was qualified to serve admirably in the State House according to the editor solely because "he has borne an honorable part in the late struggle of Freedom against Tyranny. He has shared his blanket on the tented field with his soldier friends who were periling their lives for the support of the cause of freedom. He is true to his promise, a faithful friend to his party and an undaunted friend to the settlers' cause."[48] A similar endorsement can be found on the pages of the *Osage Mission Journal* in 1868, where the editor argues that he is confident in the Republican field of candidates. The people can trust that the nominee for state representative, Capt. Enoch Haynes, is "one upon whom the people can rely without fear of being sold out or sacrificed to railroads or monopolies" and that he "will not fear to proclaim the right in the halls of the legislature" because he "served his country three years in the army." Likewise, the editor was certain that Col. W.H. Williams, nominee for probate judge, could also be trusted by the voting public because he "served his country for three years with honor to himself and his regiment." Similarly, the editor was certain that Col. James M. Harvey, Republican candidate for governor, deserved the support of settlers as "one of the truest men in the country—able but unassuming." Again, his proof was military service—Harvey, he wrote, "gallantly served his country in the field, as true and brave a soldier as ever battled for a good cause." Finally, the editor assured his readers that the candidate for state treasurer, George Graham, was "one of the best men in Kansas" because "he went into the army as a private, and, refusing office, went through the war as a private, while promotions were tendered him."[49] These political endorsements, linked to service in the Civil War, are a small representation of literally hundreds of such ads and editorials found in newspapers published in southeast Kansas. Significantly, in each case, the primary qualification for office was not political acumen, or even party affiliation, but rather exemplary service as a Union soldier during the war.

To these early settlers, service in the war was a badge of honor that legitimized their struggle against the railroads. It was precisely because they had sacrificed so much to defeat the Rebellion that they were uniquely qualified to both discern the contemporary threat to the Republic and to defeat it. The Civil War was never far from their minds or pens. Milton Reynolds of the *Parsons Sun* boasted, "We freed the slave. We proclaimed freedom in all the land. The doctrine of equal rights, of perfect equality before the law, is enthroned and established."[50] A similar argument was advanced by a group of settlers who gathered in Ft. Roach in December of 1868 to craft an open petition to Congress opposing a proposed Treaty with the Osage (the "Sturges Treaty").[51] Among the "reasons" given for their boldness in "call(ing) the attention of Congress to their condition, feelings and desires," they emphasized their military service and the honor it bestowed upon them: "The great majority of us are soldiers, who have faithfully served our Government through her great trials and times of danger—many of us scarred and crippled—we feel that the government is indebted to us and our comrades in arms for her very existence and therefore we are entitled to a respectable hearing and consideration."[52]

Veterans felt a common bond—even though most settlers had come to southeast Kansas alone, they recognized a reciprocal willingness to sacrifice all for the sake of the Union and sought to build their communities on the basis of this shared commitment.[53] Service in the war was a key requirement for public service—and those who had not fought in the war were generally mistrusted. Military service was a badge of "right" character; "the willingness to offer life, health, and property as a possible sacrifice to the common good had become a test of dedication to liberty."[54]

Military service had also taught them the necessity of continual vigilance. Bernard Bailyn has shown that a deep suspicion (bordering on paranoia) formed the foundation of early American political thought: "fear of a comprehensive conspiracy against liberty ... lay at the heart of the Revolutionary Movement."[55] This fear and the attendant responsibility to be ever alert to the danger of a conspiratorial corruption was an essential part of the worldview of the veteran settlers; they believed it was their responsibility to defend the liberty they had so recently purchased with their blood.

In fact, the Civil War had reinvigorated their commitment to vigilance. As Michael Holt has argued, "Opposition to the Slave Power conspiracy provided a cathartic opportunity to restore to political activity its basic purpose, to regain a sense that vigilant citizens could save republican government."[56] William Gienapp likewise asserts that Union veterans were shaped by a "political culture" that emphasized "mass involvement and the widely shared belief in the necessity of safe-guarding the experiment of popular government."[57]

The numerous local newspapers of southeast Kansas, published in cities and towns throughout the late 1860s and '70s, insisted that settlers heed this call to battle. In laying down their arms, they could not relax their vigilance. The *Labette Sentinel*, published in the small town of Labette by a local farmer turned part-time newsman, cautioned its readers not to become complacent. Warning that "the yeomanry of our land" could be caught off-guard by "pursuing their honorable calling, improving our country, paying their assessments, and laying down their lives in defense of the nation's honor," the *Sentinel's* editor argued strongly that "they should not neglect their own private rights and privileges." The paper further asserted that, as veterans, the settlers had a special duty to defend the Republic against the foes of liberty — be they "rebels or railroads." For, as the editorial declared, "when land sharks seek to devour them" and "monied monopolies endeavor to over power them" it was the bounden duty of veteran farmers to "rise up in the might of their anger, defend their homes — their alters and their fires" by denouncing "corruption" and uniting to defeat "combined corporations and railroad kings."[58]

In southeast Kansas, this call to action reverberated in the speeches of local leaders, the editorial columns of small-town newspapers, and on the streets and alleys of their villages and towns. Settlers viewed the railroads as the embodiment of corruptive, conspiratorial, and passionate tyranny. They saw monopolies as another form of the arbitrary authority that had threatened liberty and freedom in earlier times. Each year, as the settlers gathered to commemorate the Fourth of July, they rehearsed (in both speech and ritual) the historical narrative of the nation's struggle against tyranny.[59] Utilizing rhetorical skills honed in earlier battles with slavery, settlers relied on a "strategy of provocation through invocation, exhorting citizens to action by appealing to the familiar values of the republic."[60] They worried about the corrosive effects of power; they believed that tyranny was a direct result of the abuse of power. And they self-consciously cast themselves as ardent defenders of the Republic waging war against the corruption and tyranny by envisioning a transformation of the way in which the nation was being governed.

For many veteran settlers, however, the struggle to reconcile the central tenets of their political beliefs with the reality of their economic situation presented a difficult conundrum. On the one hand, they desired above all to be independent of reliance on outside sources, yet the reality of their situation as small farmers separated from the large markets of Chicago and the East was that their only hope for economic survival lay in a cooperative arrangement with the very forces they believed were undermining their freedom. Undoubtedly, this too was a cultural inheritance brought with them from the 1840s and '50s. Historian William Barney notes: "Throughout the nineteenth century, Americans engaged in an ongoing debate over how best to reconcile the emerging market society with their political culture of republicanism."[61] What made the effort so difficult was that in the everyday experience of the settlers, commerce and corruption seemed to go hand in hand. It appeared that personal sacrifice and community service (the hallmark of authentic republican societies) were in danger of being overcome by the avarice and greed that followed in the train of commerce. Kansas Governor Charles Robinson, in a speech to southeast Kansas settlers gathered in Erie on July 19, 1873, expressed this fear directly by reminding his hearers of a glorious republican past when "the blood of the nation was warmed by the fire of stern necessity" and "iron men, with sterling integrity, were sent to the front." However, according to Robinson's lament, "that time and those men have passed into history." The danger confronting Kansans today, he concluded, was that "the fires of Avarice are burning with intense heat, and Mammon is the god of the nation."[62]

Republicans of the eighteenth century had argued that the best safeguard to the abuse of power was the virtue of the people. As historian Ruth Bloch observed, "Throughout the Revolutionary period, virtue was the most valued quality defining individual commitment to the Republican cause."[63] Early Americans had also believed that prosperity constituted one of the most serious threats to virtue.[64] These beliefs were challenged by the emergence of what Charles Sellers has called "the market revolution."[65] The growth of market capitalism, ("an evolutionary process with deep roots in the colonial past") was a conspicuous feature of American life in the 19th century.[66] The prosperity motive that had been viewed with such alarm by traditional republican thought was gradually accepted as both normative (for the individual) and necessary (for the nation).

Acceptance of this compromise, however, remained perpetually irksome to settlers in southeast Kansas. Undeniably, the promise of markets for their agricultural goods, increased immigration, and rising land values quickened the pulse of many. They understood the central role of the railroads in the fulfillment of their hopes; at times, they could even be eager to outdo other villages and towns in their efforts to "court" the railroads to their locale by pledging bonds and other financial incentives. Yet, even in their most exuberant expressions of hope, doubts persisted. As John Horner, former president of a Methodist school (Baker College) in Baldwin City, Kansas, and first superintendent of schools in Labette County, explained in a column in his newspaper, the *Chetopa Advance*, corruption inevitably followed the path laid down by Railroad tracks. "These facts are simply appalling," he asserted before listing a litany of evils brought by railroads: "The public schools are robbed.... Senators are bought like oxen.... The homes of the hardy pioneers are relentlessly wrested from them." All of these evils, he stated, could be attributed to the "rapacious monopolist" and "soulless corporations." [67]

In his analysis of the Grange movement, Sven Nordin has argued that post–Civil War farmers "were torn by two contradictory forces — Jeffersonian agrarianism and a new industrial urbanism."[68] As the corporation emerged as the dominant form of economic organization, corporate industrial capitalism dissolved old foundations of power and status and created new ones.[69] The livelihood and self-reliance of small farmers became more precarious and increasingly dependent upon wage labor while the existing moneyed aristocracy, both mercantile and agrarian, discovered that their traditional bases of power (i.e., kinship and participation in civic, political, and religious organizations) were gradually being supplanted by the power of the purse. In short, the settlers experienced the "new order" as a "force from outside."[70] Thus, in their fight against railroads settlers reacted not only to the existential challenge to their land but also to a perceived threat to the social order they were attempting to construct.

A critical part of this social order was the correct place of women in a properly ordered society. Once again, this was not new to post-bellum America but was rooted in past experiences. Politics and gender were intertwined in early America and throughout the 19th century. Ruth Bloch has argued that "conceptions of sexual difference underlay some of the most basic premises of the Revolution and shaped important ideological changes in the early Republic."[71] Women's historian Barbara Welter declared that patriarchy was merged so tightly with the prevailing republican ideology in the early American Republic that "if anyone, male or female, dared to tamper with the complex of virtues that made up True Womanhood he was damned immediately as the enemy of God, of civilization, and of the Republic."[72]

In the years between the Revolution and the Civil War, the gendered meaning of virtue and its implications for the political life of the nation were contested as a role for "Republican mothers" was constructed.[73] However, even as society debated the proper function of women within a "Republican America," they all agreed that "a woman belonged in the home."[74] Thus, the ideal of womanhood which developed in the late eighteenth and nineteenth centuries complemented an earlier republican image of an active virtuous male with that of an equally virtuous passive female. According to Paula Baker, woman, "selfless and sentimental, nurturing and pious," was seen as "the perfect counterpoint" to man as aggressive and controlling."[75] The Civil War reinforced and intensified these preexisting gender constructions.

The identification of masculinity and virtue was never more clearly demonstrated than in the role of the male as soldier. As soldiers men were active — defending the nation against tyranny by taking up weapons and aggressively engaging in battle. In refusing to allow women to participate actively in the war effort, however, female virtue was constructed along vastly different lines. Women played a supportive role — ever submissive, they prayed for their fighting men, worked to bandage their wounds, and remained supportive by writing letters and engaging in other passive activities that communicated faithfulness and loyalty to their men. In this way, as Michael Barton has written, the Civil War reinforced traditional gender categories: "Men had to be brave and assertive and work for a living, but women had to be submissive, gentle, and domestic."[76]

This conceptual framework guided the work of the male leaders of the nascent southeast Kansas communities. As noted Kansas historian C. Robert Haywood demonstrated in his acclaimed history of Kansas cowtowns, the settlers who came to Kansas brought with them the cultural values of the east and were radically conservative in their approach to community building. Significantly, in the 1867 election, the male voters of Labette and Neosho Counties rejected the proposal to allow women to vote by a margin of nearly 3 to 1.[77] It was the man's responsibility to actively defend his home and hearth — to protect his wife and family. Women were important but they were to play a secondary, supportive role. As the *Neosho Valley Dispatch* instructed its readers, "Let the wife only understand and have faith in her true position — that of woman 'the helper.'"[78]

To their dismay and consternation, however, the male setters discovered that their patriarchal vision of an ordered community would not remain unchallenged. Men found themselves confounded by the physical environment of southeast Kansas as the prairie refused to accept demurely their assertions of manly domination. Male settlers also found themselves confronted by female settlers who refused to abide within the limitations foisted upon them by the male leaders of their communities.[79] An early correspondent to a small newspaper, the *Neosho County Dispatch*, signed herself "M.A.D." as she exclaimed in an open letter to the community: "Women of Neosho! I want you to so rule your lives in your families, so improve your minds in regards to the past history of your country, and the whole world's present condition that each husband and father, son and brother will think it the most useful hour of his life when he shall be permitted to cast a vote that shall make you, at least so far as the human mind can see, one step higher."[80]

Another woman, who signed herself "Lady Labette," remarked on her expectations in immigrating to Kansas: "We thought when we emigrated to Kansas that we would find a home in one spot on the globe where a woman was (for the first time since she was banished from Paradise) considered equal to the lords of creation." To her dismay, she had discovered that her expectations were not to be realized: "But in that we were mistaken." Lady Labette however notified the male leaders of the community that she (and the women for whom she spoke) would not be content to sit by and allow the men to continue their patriarchal domination unchecked. Strikingly, her strident stance was fueled by the same political language used by the men in their struggles against the railroads: "The women of Kansas, like all other States, have no more power to contend for the laws that are to govern her and her children than had the poor slave when he labored and lived to support his master in idleness and ease who rightfully had no authority over him."[81] This linkage of slavery and gender subordination, of course, reaches back to the contentions expressed in the Seneca Falls Convention in 1848. That Lady Labette wanted to extend the notion of Kansas as a "free state" to include both an anti-slavery and a pro-suffrage plank shows clearly that at least some of the women in southeast Kansas were not content to accept the passive role that the men of their communities wished to ascribe to them.

The ensuing struggle over the construction of gender in southeast Kansas must also be analyzed against the backdrop of the awesome power and kinetic energy of nineteenth century railroads. As Maury Klein has observed, "to 19th century Americans the locomotive was a wondrous machine.... Its raw power enchanted starry-eyed dreamers and hard-nosed businessmen alike." It is thus little surprise that these same Americans found themselves fascinated by "the dramatic thrust of its presence upon bands of steel."[82] The boundless energy, the raw phallic power, of the railroads both excited and frightened southeast Kansans.[83] The railroads promised prosperity, but to reap its rewards the settlers were forced to assume a dependent role. The "thrust" of the railroad threatened to rape them of the very land upon they claimed and to reveal to the world their own impotence.[84] Simply put, railroads constituted a threat to the ownership of their lands, the political independence of their communities, and (on a deep, subconscious level) the virility of their masculinity.

That all of these complex concerns revealed themselves in a struggle over land ownership does not surprise anyone vaguely familiar with the history of the United States. From the earliest days of exploration and subsequent colonization, land-ownership featured as a prominent feature of the Euro-American self-identification as "civilized" human beings and thus equal to those who lived in "Great Britain" and the rest of Europe. As a result, the struggle over land ownership has been a frequent subject of scholarly research. This is especially true of historians of the American west who have often connected the desire of Euro-Americans for "free land" with the rising pulse of western settlement in the 19th century.[85] It should be noted, of course, that the land that these settlers desired was not "free" nor was it "virgin territory" but the ancestral homelands of America's indigenous peoples. This fact helps to explain why, as Europeans colonized the west and claimed the lands historically possessed by Native peoples, the land passed from the Natives directly to individual settlers only rarely. Instead, by exercising its right to make treaties, the transfer of land became an exclusive right of first the British Crown and/or colonial governments and finally the federal government of the United States.[86] In each case, the state functioned as an intermediate custodian in the transfer of title to actual settlers.[87]

Of special importance to this study of settlement in southeast Kansas was the policy of the federal government in making land grants to veterans. As James Oberly observed, the tradition of land grants for military service was a key factor in the post–Civil War expectations of veterans vis-à-vis their government.[88] This fact helps to explain the oft-repeated assertion of settlers that the land was their reward for military service and that their claims to it were worthy of special consideration — they were historically and culturally conditioned to associate cheap or free land with military service. As a group of settlers explained to the editor of the *Osage Mission Journal*, "The great majority of us are soldiers, who have faithfully served our Government through her great trials and times of danger — many of us scarred and crippled. We feel that the government is indebted to us and our comrades in arms for her very existence and therefore we are entitled to a respectable hearing and consideration."[89]

Congress did not, however, give all of the western lands it controlled to the veterans. Significantly, with the passing of the Public Debt Act in 1790, Congress envisioned the public lands as a resource to be sold in order to pay off the massive debt it had accrued by fighting the British in the Revolutionary War. The use of public land sales as a method of raising much-needed funds, as Paul Gates has noted, featured prominently in the plans of nineteenth-century social reformers; "aware that donations of land would be much easier to get from Congress than money," they "brought forward many schemes for sharing the lands with the states for colleges, seminaries, and institutions for the care of the blind, the insane, and other unfortunates as well as for a host of miscellaneous purposes."[90] Most of the land granted in this way went to schools — as the Land Ordinance of 1785 had mandated, the sixteenth section in every township was set aside for this purpose. Other grants were given for religion, for earthquake sufferers, for Polish exiles, for an asylum in Kentucky, and similar projects. Thomas Donaldson has estimated that over a thousand land grants for such purposes were administered by Congress in the antebellum period.[91]

In the 1820s Congress added a third use to public lands policy when it began to experiment with the granting of alternative sections of land for transportation purposes. Roads were first, followed by canals and railroads.[92] In the 1850s and '60s, as railroads became the primary mode of transportation, grants were made to the corporations that promised to build them. In southeast Kansas, land grants were made to the Lawrence, Leavenworth & Galveston Railroad and to the Missouri, Kansas & Texas railroads. These land grants were the primary source of the conflict between the settlers and the railroads. Settlers came to southeast Kansas believing that the rubrics laid out in the Homestead Act of 1862 would apply — that they would be able to purchase the land from the Federal Government for $1.25 an acre; railroads on the other hand believed that the land grants to railroad corporations superseded the stipulations of the Homestead Act and that, because the land had been given to them to sell in order to raise the funds necessary to build the railroad systems, the settlers would be required to purchase the land from them at a "fair market value" instead of the significantly reduced amount stipulated in the Homestead Act. At its core, the debate was over competing interpretations of law and treaties; however, the fact that the settlers saw the debate as essentially a political question — of republican self-government versus the tyrannical rule of a small well-entrenched, wealthy, aristocratic elite — reveals a great deal about the manner in which veteran settlers viewed the struggle over land and the political identity of their communities through the prism of republican principles and their service as soldiers in the Civil War.

At this point, it is probably necessary to define the geographical focus of my research because, like many geographical regions, the region identified as "southeast Kansas" can mean different things, depending on the context and circumstances. For the purposes of this work, the area under discussion is the region encompassed in the modern period by the political areas known as Labette and Neosho Counties, an area approximately thirty by fifty miles.

Originally home to the Osage indigenous peoples, the region was first officially organized as a political unit in the state of Kansas as Dorn County. After the Civil War, it was renamed Neosho County and split into two (Neosho in the north and Labette in the south) in 1867. This region was known as the Osage Ceded Lands, and was the area in the state of Kansas first transferred to the United States government by the Osage peoples. It is this transference and the subsequent legal battle over land title that ensued that sets both the geographical and chronological boundaries for this book.

This work explores the multifaceted struggle of settlers to established lawful, ordered communities of freedom in five thematic and roughly chronological chapters. Chapter 1 introduces the reader to the veteran settlers who came to southeast Kansas in the years following the Civil War. Since southeast Kansas was not "virgin" territory but instead the ancestral winter home of the Osage Native peoples, in this chapter I also discuss the relationship which developed between the Osage peoples and the settlers. (The historical background to this relationship is discussed in greater detail in the Appendix.) By the time the settlers arrived, the Osages had already entered into negotiations with the United States government for the sale of their land. Thus, contemporary accounts reveal that the relationship between settlers and natives was cordial and, at times, friendly. The conflict, from the very beginning, was with the railroads. Even though the railroads had not yet begun to lay tracks, the settlers were aware of their intentions. Chapter 1 therefore discusses the interpretive conceptual grid through which the settlers interpreted the threat of the railroads.

In Chapter 2, I examine the initial development of social networks so essential to community organization. Unlike other areas in Kansas, the vast majority of settlers came on their own to southeast Kansas–with no preexisting network of friends or family. Confronted with a hostile environment, unknown surroundings, and an uncertain legal framework, the chapter describes their efforts to form Vigilance Committees and Settlers' Clubs in an attempt to bring order to the perceived chaos. These committees and clubs, which initially functioned as extra-legal agencies, played an important early role in the creation of social capital.

Chapter 3 discusses the stabilization of social networks throughout the villages, towns and cities. These networks created the institutional structure around which active opposition to the railroads formed. As settlers developed the infrastructure of their communities, the villages, towns and cities they had established assumed a permanent character. Chapter 3 highlights the significant role of religious institutions in the social evolution of southeast Kansas. As communities were founded and churches built, settlers were able to establish a network of relationships around which their struggles could coalesce.

In Chapter 4 I discuss two challenges to communal unity that developed in the early 1870s. The emergence of the Liberal Republican Party and its cooperation with a newly established Democratic Party challenged the hegemony of the Republican party. Bound together both by their experience in the Civil War and by their struggle to survive the difficult first years of settlement, the settlers had initially united in support of Republican office-seekers. However, by 1872, the settlers found themselves confronting new experiences and the unity which had been so painstakingly created was beginning to fray. At the heart of this struggle lay the question of the meaning of the Civil War. Was the struggle against the rebellion the defining moment in their lives, or was that struggle one in a long series of struggles against tyranny and corruption? Was the past the determinate factor or was the future? Similar questions were forced upon the settlers by the emergence of the temperance movement. Was the active role being played by women consistent with their vision of lawful ordered communities? Settlers found themselves divided as both politics and gender were contested.

Chapter 5 discusses the impact of the railroads on settler society and describes the re-emergence of a unified social movement: the Settlers' Protective Association. This bi-county association coordinated the settlers' opposition to the railroads. Confronted by large corporations intent on denying them the land that they had developed, settlers put aside their differences in order to work together. Through a strategic use of public and private meetings, the association successfully kept the settlers united and focused. Chapter 5 discusses the manner in which the association skillfully utilized both public opinion and the legal system to challenge the claims of the railroads to their land.

I have chosen to end my account with this legal victory. On a practical level, this is because all stories must have an ending and eventually research has to be concluded (if only for a time before it is begun again). However, on a more substantive level, the struggle against the railroads was a galvanizing force in the early years of settlement and every action and event within the nascent communities was framed by this effort. Early settler society was characterized by a remarkable unity of purpose and resolve. The victory of the settlers in 1876 brings the initial post–Civil War era to a close and is thus a fitting conclusion to the story this book aims to tell.

1

THE BATTLE BEGINS
(1866–1867)

In 1861, as the news of the firing upon Union troops in South Carolina spread throughout the old Northwest, young Samuel Van Sandt hurried to enlist. Born in Hamilton County, Ohio, on August 9, 1842, he had moved with his parents to Michigan while he was still an infant. When he was five, his father, John Van Sandt, died and his mother moved to live near relatives in Indiana. When Samuel turned 16, he left home for Kentucky where he worked at several odd jobs before moving back to Michigan. It was in Michigan that he heard of the southern rebellion and, as he would later tell his children and grandchildren, inspired by the memory of his father, he immediately enlisted in Company D of the Second Michigan Infantry.[1] As a member of the regiment, he fought at Bull Run, Yorktown, on the Peninsula and was also engaged at Williamsburg, Frazier's Farm, Savage Station and Malvern Hill. When his regiment was transferred from the command of General Heinzelman to General Burnside's corps, he took part in the campaign around Vicksburg and in the battle of Jackson, Mississippi. Transferred again, Van Sandt marched with his regiment back to Kentucky and crossed the Cumberland Mountains into east Tennessee, where he participated in the engagements at Campbell's Station and London and finally the battle of Knoxville, that included the assault on Fort Saunders. In the waning days of the war, he marched again with his regiment to Virginia, where they rejoined the Army of the Potomac, and participated in the victory march through the streets of Washington, D.C.

When the war ended, Van Sandt returned to Indiana where his mother was living; however, within months, he left Indiana for Iowa, where he worked in the town of Clarinda before taking a job freighting goods for the government from Iowa to its forts in Nebraska. In 1867, tiring of working for others, he married a young woman he had met in Clarinda, purchased a team of horses and a prairie schooner, and (with his young wife in the schooner and, as he explained later in life, with only a few dollars in his pocket) left Iowa to journey to southeast Kansas, where he staked his claim on a farm in Neosho County, just outside the present day city of Chanute. In Neosho County, this frequent traveler, who had marched across much of the south and the old northwest, put down permanent roots, raised a family and worked with fellow veterans to build ordered communities of liberty in southeast Kansas. When he died on August 19, 1920, he had lived in the Chanute region for over 50 years and was buried with his compatriots in historic Elmwood Cemetery.[2]

Historians have identified three major waves of immigration to Kansas in the latter half of the 19th century. As we have seen, the first wave came with the passing of the Kansas-Nebraska Act in 1854 and the official opening of the territory to settlement. Most of these people settled in the northeastern section of the state. The second wave came in the mid-1860s in response to the end of the Civil War and the sale of the remaining "Indian" lands. The majority of these settlers took up their claims in the southeast section of the state. The third wave came in the 1870s and '80s, when, in response to massive recruitment efforts by both the State Board of Agriculture and representatives of the various (and competing) railroad companies, thousands of immigrants flocked to the state from Europe. As an abundant corpus of scholarship has shown, the vast majority of settlers from Europe settled in the central and western sections of the state. Significantly, of these three waves of immigrations, the first and the third have received much scholarly attention.[3] With the exception of a few published articles in *Kansas History*, however, the second has been almost neglected.

Part of the reason for the neglect is that, unlike those who came in the first and third waves, the settlers who came to Kansas in the years immediately following the Civil War came in small units, either as single young adults or as members of young families. In the settlement of northeastern Kansas in the 1850s and the central and western sections of the state in the 1870s and 1880s, most (although not all) immigrants came in groups and established colonies that struggled to maintain (with varying degrees of success) their own internal social structure. In the southeast, however, few "transplant" colonies were established. As James Shortridge has noted in his analysis of frontier settlement patterns, southeast Kansas is unique in

> the near absence of formal or informal colonies by any Anglo-American groups. Such group enterprises traditionally have been a way for people from distant places to pool knowledge and resources in order to survive in a new

environment. The concept had been important in the settlement of northeastern Kansas in the 1850s and was to be again in the central and western sections of the state in the 1870s and 1880s. New Englanders, Southerners and Europeans all participated. In the southeast, though, the early, pervasive and individualistic presence of veterans from nearby north-Midland states precluded the possibilities for a rich mix of culture groups and settlement forms.[4]

The story of Samuel Van Sandt told at the beginning of this chapter is typical of the experience of thousands of Union veterans who journeyed to the west after the Civil War. Many, like Samuel, chose to settle in the fertile lands of the Neosho Valley (present-day Labette and Neosho counties), which were watered abundantly by the many streams and tributaries of the western Verdigris River and eastern Neosho River. In the late 1860s and early 1870s, thousands came to stake claims, build homes and establish communities based on (what they perceived to be) the ideals of the republic for which they had fought.

Like Van Sandt, most came to southeast Kansas with few financial resources; as early settler C.E. Cory remembered in an address to the 28th annual meeting of the Kansas State Historical Society in 1903, "We were all poor alike."[5] An article in the *Southern Kansas Advance* advanced the same opinion in 1870 by stating that "hitherto we have been poor in pocket."[6] Lacking money and political connections, these young settlers traveled to southeast Kansas with limited resources and an even narrower number of known acquaintances and friends. Because they were young and were seeking to leave behind their memories of war and loss, they immigrated without the established network of friends and acquaintances that age and maturity often bring. Yet, they came with a determination to build ordered, prosperous and unified communities. As a founder of the new city of Jacksonville (Neosho County) explained in an open letter to the readers of the *Osage Mission Journal*: "The great anxiety of our people is to build up a town in our midst where we can have school houses, churches, lyceums, in short all of the moral, social, educational and religious advantages incident to the progressive civilization of the age."[7]

The migration of these veteran settlers transformed southeast Kansas. A correspondent to the *Neosho Valley Eagle* in 1869 explained the change he had witnessed:

> Two years ago it was a vast wilderness, with here and there a small cabin, the wild grass knee deep in the door yards and scarcely a cow pen built in the way of improvements, dependent upon northern Kansas and western Missouri for our bread....But I am happy to congratulate our friends here and elsewhere that large farms have been opened up and put under cultivation.[8]

The *southern Kansas Advance* gave an analogous report in 1870:

Where only six months ago nothing but the boundless expanse of prairie could be seen, you will now see the cabins of the settlers thickly spread about and the cattle quietly grazing on the rich grass which the country affords. And here and there enterprising villages have sprung up as if by magic, but looking really like old established towns of the east.[9]

The *Western Enterprise* reported a similar transformation, noting that while southeast Kansas was "an unbroken wild, inhabited only by the savage dweller in his wigwam" in 1867, by 1872 it had become "a densely populated country, with highly cultivated farms, accompanied with all the improvements, arts and sciences of thrifty civilization at whose touch the deep, rich soil is made to yield its fruit, some sixty and some an hundred fold."[10] Census reports confirm the substance of these reports. In 1865, 628 people resided in the region; by 1870 that number had swelled to 20,179.

Even though the *Enterprise* presented southeast Kansas as a region sparsely inhabited in 1867, the reality that confronted the veteran soldiers was not an "unbroken wild" but a land that had been settled for centuries. It is true that the Neosho Valley was largely uninhabited by white settlers prior to 1865, but this did not make it "virgin" land. In fact, it was a vital part of the ancestral homeland of the Osage, indigenous peoples who, each fall and winter, lived in villages along the Neosho and Verdigris rivers while the younger men of the tribe traveled further west to hunt the buffalo that ranged in the area around present-day Wichita. Although they had allowed French traders to marry and raise mulatto children in their villages, and had been supportive of the establishment of a Roman Catholic Mission near Flat Rock Creek, the Osages had been adamant in opposing the wholesale settlement of whites in their territory.[11] A few "white men" had illegally settled on the northern end of their land before the Civil War but most had been removed by federal troops. The few that had remained were effectively chased off the land during the war as Confederate and Union troops alternatively burned settlements to the ground.[12] William Cutler, one of the earliest to research and record the history of Kansas in the post–Civil War period, maintained that "from 1860 to 1865 there were only two white men living within the limits of the county, during any part of this period, so effectually did the disorder produced by the Rebellion destroy the embryo settlements."[13]

However, as the presence of white settlers in northeastern Kansas grew and began to press southward into land previously controlled by the tribe, the Osage chiefs changed their minds and entered into negotiations to sell a section of the easternmost portion of their land in 1863. The Osage

1. The Battle Begins (1866–1867)

This carte-de-visite photograph of three unidentified Osage Indian chiefs was taken sometime between 1860 and 1869.

Ceded Land, as this section came to be known, was a strip approximately thirty by fifty miles comprising all of present-day Neosho and Labette counties as well as small portions of Cherokee, Crawford and Allen counties.[14] The final form of the treaty granting the land to the federal government in return for a promised governmental stipend to the tribe was signed by the Osages and federal representatives at Fort Smith, Arkansas, in September 1865. The signed document was forwarded to President Andrew Johnson in 1866. After the Senate ratified the treaty on January 21, 1867, President Johnson signed it into law.

Significantly, since the signing of the treaty coincided with the end of the Civil War, word of the treaty quickly spread among Union veterans. These veterans believed that the distribution of land grants in this newly opened land would be governed by the stipulations of the Homestead Act, which had been signed into law by President Abraham Lincoln on May 20, 1862.[15] The Homestead Act had established a reasonably straightforward process by which any U.S. citizen, or intended citizen, over the age of 21 and/or head of a household, who had never borne arms against the U.S. government, was given the right as land opened for settlement to file an application and lay claim to surveyed government land. For 5 years, the settler was required to both live on the land and improve it. In an effort to discourage speculators, the act stipulated that the settler had to build a rudimentary dwelling, and most importantly, put the land under the plow, plant crops, and harvest them before the 5-year period had expired.

With proof of residency and improvement, at the end of the 5-year period, the settler could file for his deed of title at a locally established land office. Local land offices forwarded the paperwork to the General Land Office in Washington, DC, along with a final certificate of eligibility. The case file was examined, and valid claims were granted patent to the land free and clear, except for a small registration fee. The act also allowed settlers to claim title to the land in a shorter period of time (6 months) if they established proof of intent to settle and improve the land and were willing to pay the government $1.25 per acre. In a significant addition to the act, after the Civil War, Union soldiers were allowed deduct the time they served from the residency requirements.

With a firm conviction that the land transferred from the Osage to the federal government would be treated according to these stipulations, settlers began to flood onto the Osage Ceded Lands from the north and west as soon as the treaty had been signed. Stephen Beck recalled his arrival in the territory in July of 1866, "We were passing Humboldt when the people were assembling there to celebrate the Fourth of July 1866 and to jointly celebrate the ratification of the Osage treaty."[16] In his report to the

1. The Battle Begins (1866–1867)

Missouri legislature about settlement patterns in the newly opened Osage land, the geologist C.B. Wilber explained in 1870: "Long trains of covered wagons are daily seen crossing the Missouri River, bearing south and west until they reach these promised lands."[17]

From all accounts, the Osages were initially ambivalent to the presence of white settlers. Even though the treaty took two years to make its way through the Senate and finally receive the signature of the president, once they had signed the document the Osage peoples considered the land to be no longer their own and stopped their opposition of white settlement.[18] Settlers reported occasional "sightings" of native peoples; early settler Margaret Plummer reminisced that "occasionally one stopped and asked for a drink, or a group or more, dressed as Americans, passed by." She also added, "There was no fear of them."[19] Francis Dinsmore agreed, "Sober Indians were very peaceable, but when two or three got drunk they usually had a fight but seldom bothered the settlers."[20] The Mission School, run for girls by the Sisters of Loretto and for boys by the priests and lay brothers of the Osage Mission Church, admitted white children who attended alongside Osage children.[21] The Native people were open to the influx of settlers and peaceably accepted their intrusions.[22]

Thus, when John Horner, editor of the *Chetopa Advance*, was asked by an inquirer, "Are you properly protected from the assaults of the Indians?" he responded, "Eastward and northward there is not a hostile Indian for a thousand miles."[23] And, when news of a rumor circulating in Ft. Scott about a recent attack on Chetopa reached the editor's ears, he responded with a quick and fervent denunciation: "We delight to assure these imaginative Bohemians that their bald heads are safe from the Tomahawk and so is Chetopa and her people. The 'dreaded' Osages are one hundred miles away on the Arkansas hunting buffalo."[24]

This is not to say that there was cultural understanding between settlers and the remaining Osage peoples who still inhabited villages along the Verdigris and Neosho Rivers; as evidenced by the comments of the *Western Enterprise* previously cited, incoming settlers brought with them the usual set of 19th-century Anglo-American ethnocentric assumptions about the superiority of white civilization. They quite literally did not "see" the Native peoples as equals or recognize them as possessing a legitimate claim to the land. In the minds of the settlers, the Osages always remained the savage "other" against which the civilized "us" was configured. One story in the *Neosho Valley Eagle* highlighted the perceived differences between the "savages" and the settlers by relating the following juicy gossip: "An enterprising Lo came into our town a few days ago and tried to persuade a prominent lawyer to go with him and be their legal advisor. The inducements offered were the speaker's sister and 'lots of whiskey, corn and them things.' The legal gentleman 'couldn't see it.'"[25] Another story in the *Eagle* revealed that (at least) some settlers conceptualized Native peoples as the enemy that had to be opposed in every way possible: "The sooner white men commence taking scalps the better and show they can make themselves proficient in taking the top-knot off a lo!"[26] Others advocated a more peaceful approach, but one that was nonetheless rooted in the same spirit of ethnocentrism. The following editorial on the state of "Indian affairs" by editor John Horner is a good example of this second approach—"If our Indian policy is to be such as becomes a Christian civilization, then in the management of the civilized Indians especially, let the military influence be removed as far as possible from them, and instead of the soldier with his bayonet, send the missionary of the Cross, with the Bible in one hand and the plow in the other, and through these instrumentalities, make them feel that the Government is their best and truest friend and not a treacherous enemy."[27] Even though Horner is clearly less violent than the editor of the *Eagle*, his basic approach is rooted in the same otherization of native peoples that characterized both the language used by settlers and the cultural perspective that undergirded it.

In short, most settlers would have agreed with Horner's advice to the government: "Make citizens of the civilized Indians and control the wild ones by military force. Put them on reservations, train the young in schools, and compel the old ones to work or starve."[28] They most certainly would have applauded Horner's assertion that the "weak fabric" of indigenous "nationalities" could "not stand up against the march of Anglo-Saxon civilization."[29] In short, settlers prided themselves on their cultural supremacy. This was exactly the conclusion drawn in an editorial published by the editor of the newspaper, *The Headlight*, who argued that "several years of experience on the frontier has given us the following judgment upon the subject: it is evident that civilization must in a few short years cover this land.... The indications of Providence, as manifested in the great natural resources of this country, the blessings attending the development of the same by a civilized race, speak too plainly the words, 'go down and possess the land.' Still plainer is this command when we reflect that the Indian is not, in the true sense, using but abusing (if not the land) themselves; banded together a set of idle, roving thieves and murders, a barrier to civilization and progress."[30]

Incoming settlers brought with them the standard 19th-century stereotypes of "Indians." Seen through the cultural prism of 19th-century ethnocentric assumptions, settlers concluded that Native people were dirty, uneducated, prone to drunkenness, lazy, and so on. In other words, native peoples were uncivilized — significantly, almost all of these prejudicial observations emphasized the reversal of traditional gender categories in native society that was (to the settlers) the final proof of the backward nature of native peoples. As Horner explained in his description of the life-style of the Osages, "women tend the ponies, do the cooking, pack the baggage, tend the babies, do all the drudgery and keep strictly within their 'Sphere' while 'free male citizens' tend to politics, support the family [?] and get drunk."[31]

To further cement this perspective, editors frequently reported stories of interactions between settler communities and Osage peoples that showed the Osages in a negative light. The following story, told by John Horner, is typical:

> Quite a company of Osages were in town last week with poultries and ponies for sale. As a whole, they are not quite up to the type of aboriginal loveliness portrayed by Cooper in his Leather Stocking tales. The warriors do not impress you, to any alarming extent, with the action of their prowess or bravery. They ought to patronize Hayes and invest largely in his soap. Father Schoenmaker, who has had them under his tutelage for some thirty years, ought to have taught them the use of water as a beverage. Those of the female persuasion are not charming. They wear no bonnets.[32]

Interestingly, as studies of the history of the Osage people have repeatedly shown, throughout their long history of interactions with whites, the Osages repeatedly demonstrated their remarkable ability to use the prejudices of the whites to their own economic advantage. They continued this tradition in dealing with the newly arriving settlers. Some Osage men, primarily Métis, hired themselves out as laborers to help the newly arriving settlers construct their first homes.[33] Others attempted to profit from the legal ambivalence of the situation between the signing of the treaty and its ratification by the Senate by charging settlers "rent" and/or by offering to "sell" them their lands. Still others offered to sell or trade goods with settlers. In this last arrangement, settlers often found themselves outmaneuvered; as Dinsmore explained, "The Osages were great traders. One Indian would trade a pony or sell it to a settler for $5 or $6. In a few days, another Indian would come and claim it was his."[34] Although Dinsmore does not explain how these scenarios were settled, there is no report of violent conflict between Native peoples and the incoming settlers in the early years of settlement in the Osage Ceded Lands. The lack of conflict was not due to restraint shown by settlers but must be attributed instead to the judicious conduct of the Osages who perceived that fighting the whites would not be to their advantage, economic or otherwise.[35]

Contrary to the conclusion drawn by Horner, the Osage men had not lost their ability to wage war, as evidenced by their continued success in hunting buffalo and chastising their Native adversaries. Rather, the Osages decided to continue their condition of trade and negotiated relationships with the whites. The Osages were astute in these relationships, as evidenced by the comments of Dinsmore who noted, "Practically all of the Indians could read and speak English, but often they would not talk or answer questions."[36] Undoubtedly, this behavior was part of an overall attempt on the part of the Osages to retain some degree of control over their own destinies by controlling the flow of information.

The Osages realized that it was in their best interest not to appear too docile or manageable; an examination of their behavior in the years they coinhabited the Neosho Valley region settlers shows that they carefully maintained an image of restrained violence to keep the settlers from becoming too comfortable with their surroundings. As reported in numerous newspapers, the Osages routinely made a public display of their athletic prowess and physical strength within sight and earshot of settlers. A classic example of this transpired on July 4, 1869, when sixty Osage braves danced in front of an awe-struck crowd in Osage Mission. Although this appearance had been carefully scripted after lengthy negotiations to emphasize the control that the white settlers had over the warlike behavior of the Osages, the Osages co-opted the celebration for their own purposes. The original contract had called for fifty braves; the Osages brought sixty. And, when the Osage Chief, Little Beaver, began to dance, he did so wearing the scalp of a Kiowa chief, Black Kettle, who had been taken at the Battle of Washita. The story was reported in both the *Osage Mission Journal* and the *Neosho Valley Dispatch*.[37] A group of twenty Osages set up camp outside the city. After wandering through the city announcing their presence and inviting the residents to a "war-dance," they proceeded to give a "demonstration" at five o'clock in the afternoon. As all of the residents of the city gathered to witness the spectacle, six men beat drums while the rest of the Osages (the *Dispatch* reported that they were "hideously disfigured by paint and feathers") danced around a central pole. While the dance was being conducted, the *Dispatch* noted, "Big Elk, the gentleman in charge, sat himself down at ease with his honors, his eye proudly glancing at a Cheyenne scalp which ornamented a pole he had in his hands." The display had its desired effect — for, after recording that the Osages had departed towards the Verdigris, the *Dispatch* concluded the story by expressing the sincere desire of city residents that "it is hoped they will remain [there] for some time to come."

The not-so subtle message sent was that the settlers should not mistake peace for weakness. Little Beaver also surprised the settlers by asking to speak; in his speech, he showed remarkable political acumen by linking the concerns of the Osages to those of the settlers. As the *Chetopa Advance* reported, "He took a still higher ground against monopolies than did Clarke and Hoyt, and opposed not only railroads but also saw mills, because they eat up the timber and the whistles scare away the buffalo."[38]

Even as individual relationships were being negotiated, however, both the settlers and the Osages knew the outcome of settlement had already been determined. When they signed the Treaty in 1865, the Osages had agreed to leave the ceded land and to allow the settlers to stay. Of far greater concern to the early settlers therefore was the threat to their claims inherent in the declared intention of railroad companies to lay tracks through southeast Kansas in their drive to connect the markets of the north with the warm-water ports of Texas. Rumors and premonitions that the claims of the settlers would be disputed and/or denied by railroad lawyers circulated. In 1868, as men, women and children were pouring in large numbers into Neosho and Labette Counties, the *Allen County Courant* succinctly warned the would-be settler:

> Something is terribly amiss in the settlement of these lands, we said once before, and as attending circumstances are developing themselves we are reminded of the assertion's stern reality. The truth is that bona fide settlers are failing to secure rights to their homes. Men went on to these lands with the full faith that after complying with certain regulations that had generally governed the settling all government lands, heretofore, they would be given a title to their homes at one dollar and twenty-five cents per acre and under homestead. But they were woefully mistaken and are left in a greater quandary than ever. Reports well authenticated state that not one settler in forty will be able to secure a title and that under rulings of the land office a man, no matter how many improvements he may have made, and what other rights guarantees him a title, he cannot get a title if he be an unmarried man. The whole procedure is wrong.[39]

To understand the reaction of the settlers in southeast Kansas to this warning and the nature of the dispute over land ownership that ensued, it is important to remember that, like Van Sandt, the vast majority of the men who came to southeast Kansas in the 1860s and '70s were veterans of the Civil War. Although Census reports from the late 1860s reveal that some women immigrated by themselves and/or as heads of household, the vast majority of immigrating households were "headed" by men. For example, according to the 1870 census, there were 516 more males than females in Labette County out of a total of 9,976 residents.[40] As the *Neosho Valley Eagle* informed would-be immigrants, "The population is composed of energetic, enterprising men from almost every State in the Union. A large majority of the men served in the army during the great Rebellion."[41] The

Neosho County Dispatch likewise insisted that "four-fifths of the settlers in this and Labette counties are honorably discharged soldiers who, upon the termination of the war, came to southern Kansas with the view of making it their future home."[42] Geographer James Shortridge has confirmed the substance of these reports by documenting that veterans "constituted the dominant group" among the early settlers and by stressing that "the emerging character of southeastern Kansas was shaped primarily by Union veterans from the northern and north-Midland states."[43] As early historian Cory recollected,

> After the great Civil War had ended and a million sturdy, vigorous young fellows found themselves out of employment, they very naturally decided to go into new fields. And so it came to pass that they went to their old homes and gathered up their few possessions and brought their wives and babies with them to the new west. These were the people who really settled in southeast Kansas. Within ten years after the close of the Civil War a man in that region who had not an army record was something of a curiosity.[44]

In 1912, William Calderhead, a local historian, reported to the Kansas State Historical Society that "for forty years after the war closed the men who fought the battles for the preservation of the Union did the work of its civil life. In every school district the school board were old soldiers; in every township the township board was composed of old soldiers; in every county the county commissioners and most of the other officers were old soldiers."[45]

Like Van Sandt, few veterans came directly to southeast Kansas upon their release from the military. Most went home first and tried to resume their old lives. However, finding it difficult (if not impossible) to reenter the society they had left, some felt themselves drawn to the west. Noted Civil War social historian Phillip Paludan explained, "Soldiers brought home war memories and were different men because of what they had seen and done."[46] Undoubtedly, they experienced what many (if not most) soldiers go through upon their return to civilian life: an inability to fit in, a feeling that the people who stayed behind did not and could not understand their experience of war. This was certainly true of the Civil War veterans. Gerald Linderman has written, "Soldiers in any case were reluctant to look back, for at home they found difficulty enough in contending with the problems of the present....Almost all experienced disorientation in various degrees. Some felt that they had returned from another world or another plane of existence."[47] The historian Reid Mitchell agrees, arguing that Civil War veterans "brought home whatever lessons might be learned from the war, whatever patriotism, brutality or cynicism it might have created, and whatever memories that might be self-consciously celebrated or half-unconsciously repressed."⁴⁸ To cope, many soldiers moved on with their lives by moving west. This is a phenomenon that has not been adequately noted by historians. Historian Larry Logue has argued, "Analysts of postbellum American society would do well to pay more attention to the behavior of ex-soldiers....Veterans comprised several distinctive classes in modernizing America and ... had a noteworthy, if varied, impact on postbellum life." ⁴⁹ As Dean May has remarked, "The war ... drove many away from their homes in search of haven and a fresh start."⁵⁰

Although wounded by their own experiences of war, these men had lost neither their idealism nor their commitment to the political principles that had inspired their engagement as soldiers and their dedication to defend the cause of the Union.⁵¹ For soldiers, the war to save the Union was at its root a defense of their own personal freedom. Historian Earl Hess explains, "Northerners believed that the conflict was a grand struggle to preserve free government in north America, a struggle which had implications for the preservation of political freedom."⁵² Northern soldiers had opposed the southern rebellion because, in their minds, secession was the harbinger of disorder and social anarchy and was fueled by a general disrespect for democratic government. As the social historian Randall Jimerson has written, "The southern rebellion posed a clear, immediate threat to the Union, which was the strongest bulwark of liberty and independence. Danger to the Union, moreover, jeopardized the entire system of republican government, which Unionists viewed not as a mere abstract principle but as the foundation of American freedom."⁵³

Nothing they had experienced in the long years of war had challenged this basic assumption. As James McPherson notes, "The conviction of northern soldiers that they fought to preserve the Union as a beacon of republican liberty throughout the world burned as brightly in the last year of the war as in the first."⁵⁴ This explanation is matched by the words of Cory, who explained that "thousands of stout young fellows, just from the army, had settled over the Ceded Lands. They had come west to make homes for themselves. Their four years of training in the greatest army of history had made them aggressive and fearless."⁵⁵ This fearless aggression was dedicated, as the *Neosho Valley Eagle* explained, to the defense of freedom: "the *Eagle* screams in advocacy of justice and right; it screams for true and wholesome Union principles; it screams for the rights of settlers in opposition to rail road monopolies and land sharks."⁵⁶

On February 6, 1869, the *Neosho Valley Eagle*, noting that "anything in relation to our land would be interesting to our readers," carried the complete text of a speech given to Congress by Representative Sidney Clarke on its front page. In this speech, Clarke expressed the political philosophy held by the majority of veteran settlers in southeast Kansas who had overwhelmingly elected him to office. To these settlers their fight to own the land was as essential to the future of the Republic as had been their fight to defeat the rebellion. Clarke asserted

> Our public land system is one of the best safeguards of the Republic. Whoever owns the land of a country, be they many or few, will in the end control its politics....Where the masses of the people own the soil that country is strong to resist all external foes, and to overcome much of the internal dissension. Where the land is controlled by a minority poverty will surely abound and the national vitality will be destroyed.

This cabinet card shows Sidney Clarke (1831–1909), an abolitionist from Lawrence, Kansas, and supporter of the Free Soil Movement. Clarke was elected in 1864 to the U.S. House of Representatives as a Republican. He was re-elected in 1866 and 1868. In 1878, he was elected to the Kansas House of Representatives. In the 1880s, he moved to Oklahoma and became an advocate for settlement and statehood in the territory.

According to Clarke, the entire republican experiment of "a free government upheld by willing obedience to law" depended on the fact that "each family could own its own home and where the soil should be in the possession of those who cultivated it." It was the principle of land-ownership by the masses, which Clarke described as the "grand ideal of the Anglo-Saxon brain," that the "yeomanry of the mother country" brought with them when "they were transferred to these shores" and it was this principle that had animated the war for independence and the subsequent expansion of the "American Union" in fulfillment of its "continental destiny." But, Clarke warned, at the present time, the United States was in great danger: "In our midst we have had fearful examples of land monopoly. No portion of our country has escaped its destructive influences."

For Clarke as for the veteran settlers who had elected him to represent them, the danger posed by land monopolies was a continuation of the threat posed by the slave system—"The old slaveholders understood well the truth of this political axiom. They therefore steadily sought to obtain entire control of the soil in their own States and as persistently hindered the development of that homestead policy in which the genius of our free institutions has molded our land system." In fact, Clarke reminded his hearers (and readers),

> Look for a moment at these two great facts: the gun at Fort Sumter had hardly woke a continent to arms ere their Representatives passed the acts by which the nation, pledged itself to span the continent by the Pacific railroad and bind two oceans together in bonds that should never be severed. Within the eventful year that passed, the Republican party passed the first homestead bill, and thus sealed the Republic forever, as with blood, to its highest hope and best ideal."

The conclusion of this matter (for Clarke) was self-evident: Just as the masses had risen to defend the Union and crush the power of the slave aristocracy, so too they must come together to defeat the power of the land aristocracy. If they did, Clarke promised, "The land, like the slaves, will pass from their grasp. It will become the home of freemen, and the land oligarchy, which is only a remnant of the slave system, will pass away forever."[57]

Jean Baker has argued that for Northerners the republican vision of liberty constituted a single "collective expression of American civic life" that not only "expressed, emerged or reflected the United States" but was "a part of that reality and had public meaning."[58] Nothing reveals this more clearly than the festive Independence Day celebrations held each year in settlements, villages and towns throughout southeast Kansas. The editor of the *Neosho Valley Eagle* called his readers to celebration by reminding them of their civic responsibilities and hopes on the occasion of Jacksonville's first official celebration of the 4th of July:

> Let us fondly hope that our own bright Ark of Liberty may successfully breast every billow and breaker of discord or anarchy, and that each returning anniversary of our nation's birthday may find our people more firmly united, happy and prosperous, and the world may say of us and our institutions: they are "Like Nature's bulwarks built by Time, Against eternity to stand."[59]

In the early years of settlement, the largest of these gatherings was held in 1870 in the city of Oswego where over 5000 people gathered to celebrate the 94th anniversary of the Republic.[60] As the *Kansas Democrat* reported, the crowds were both large and enthusiastic: "Early in the morning our streets were thronged with the people of the surrounding country. Old and young; fair ladies and gallant swains, all determined on a good, old fashioned Fourth."[61]

After it had assembled, the crowd was led in procession to the center of the town where, after an opening prayer and the singing of the national anthem "America," the Declaration of Independence was publicly read. The guest of honor, Judge Adams from Leavenworth, was then asked to give a keynote address. Adams' speech (which was, according to the *Oswego Register*, extemporaneously delivered) expressed in summary format the political perspectives of the veteran settlers; the *Democrat* observed, "The oration was of the Fourth of July order, recounting the trials of our patriot fathers and the struggles of the infant colonies."[62]

Adams began by remembering the Pilgrims who, he claimed, had been inspired to come to the shores of the New World by "the spirit of Liberty." Surrounded by "vast forests ... teeming with thousands of hostile Indians," having "left all that was dear to them, save their love for their Maker, behind them forever, and feeling the full sense of their helplessness," they still "thanked God above for the liberty they enjoyed." When this liberty was sorely tested by England's desire to tax them unlawfully, Adams rehearsed, "the Pilgrim Fathers after having had a taste of liberty could not endure tyranny longer and resolved to throw off the British Yoke." Facing incalculable odds, "surrounded and outnumbered by almost countless dusky foes," they had persevered and triumphed because of their dedication to the "spirit of liberty."

It was this spirit, "born of heaven and implanted in the breasts of the Pilgrim Fathers," Adams reminded his hearers, which had inspired the writing of "that immortal instrument, the Declaration of Independence, just read in your hearing" and had sustained "the self-sacrificing heroism of the Patriots of this country." And, it was the same spirit, Adams asserted, which had manifested itself in the recent struggle in which the vast majority of his hearers had been engaged. For, as he instructed them, although "the same spirit of liberty has passed through every generation to the present time, the war of the great rebellion has no parallel in history." It was because "the cornerstone of the rebellion was American slavery" that the battle against it was "a combat for liberty." In this combat, each of his hearers had played their part: "The merchant left his goods, the farmer his plow, and rushed to the defense of the stars and stripes, followed by the prayers of mothers, wives and sweethearts." The cost of defending their liberty had been frighteningly high —"the five years of war cost 600,000 lives." Yet, Adams concluded in celebratory zeal, "Passing by all the horrors of the rebellion, let us rejoice today that peace is restored." It was because of their sacrifices (he assured his hearers) that the future of the country was bright —"The time was when Rome was the center of the civilized world. Today the American nation is the strongest, most powerful nation on the globe. To be an American citizen is to claim a higher prerogative than of any other nation. All through this vast country there is not a slave."

The vision presented by this oration is striking. In Adams' mind, as he rehearsed what he called "history familiar to all," those who waged war against the southern rebellion were cut from the same cloth as the early Pilgrims and the Revolutionary generation. Veteran settlers were part of the triumphant story of war-waging, freedom-seeking, frontier-settling white men and supportive sacrifice-facing, pious-praying white women. Their battle against the power of the slave aristocracy was of a piece with the Revolutionary generation's battle against English tyranny. Both wars had been inspired by the "same spirit of liberty." And, as they labored to build homes and communities in southeast Kansas, it was important for them to understand that they were continuing their work in the same "spirit of liberty." As Adams triumphantly announced in his closing exhortation, "Let us go forward as American citizens. Let us advance. The resources of our great county are not fully developed."[63]

Some scholars have argued that in the years immediately following the Civil War, Americans were exhausted by a "dominant war-weariness" which led them, as Gerald Linderman has suggested, "to thrust into shadow all things military."[64] This is not validated by the experience of the veterans who came to southeast Kansas; instead, they envisioned their struggle to build ordered communities as a continuation of their struggle to save the Union. They had exchanged their swords for plows, but they had not abandoned either the vocabulary or mindset of war. Veterans considered their struggles to build communities in southeast Kansas to be a continuation of their effort to preserve the Union. They had marched to victory over the forces of rebellion; now they were advancing as pioneers to wage war on the disorder and disarray of the Kansas prairie. In the words of the *Labette Sentinel*, settlers to southeast Kansas self-identified themselves as "strong-minded, big-hearted, enterprising, persevering and muscular people, afraid of nothing but wrong."[65] A correspondent to the *Osage Mission Journal* agreed; commenting on the character of the new settlers who were arriving, he wrote, "We are proud to say that the 'new comers' are of the better class of society — intelligent, industrious, moral, progressive and respectable. In short, just such men and women as are needed to develop the resources and material interests of southern Kansas — those who will turn the tide of human affairs and improvement into the common sense channels of progress."[66] Another correspondent concurred: "No trash or scum is found here, but live, energetic men, who attend to business, and thus benefit themselves and their town."[67]

Military language and imagery occurred frequently in the letters, articles and newspaper editorials of early settlers. A salient example is found in the response of the editor of the *Chetopa Advance* to an inquiry from Wales about the nature of pioneer life in southeast Kansas. In his published reply, Editor John Horner described the settlers as "the advancing army of civilization" in which "the sick, gouty and decrepit fall to the rear. The bold, stalwart, enterprising young and energetic are in the van."[68] Using similar imagery in other editorials, Horner frequently impressed upon his readers the importance of cooperation by comparing them to military units: "Communities, like armies, must be disciplined and learn to act in concert."[69] A correspondent to *The Kansas Democrat* in Oswego (Labette County) made a similar correlation between soldiers and settlers by noting that "if tact, talent and energy are needed anywhere it is in a new country, to open up and develop it, and he who succeeds with a small capital is as good a soldier as ever followed Sherman to the Atlantic."[70] A group of veterans, meeting in 1869, revealed their own understanding of the connection between their former actions as soldiers and their current labors as farmer-pioneers by arguing: "Many of these veterans of the late war for the Union wear the memorable scars, and some are mutilated, showing the extent of their suffering in its behalf; they are here struggling for life to gain a foot hold upon the soil that they make homes for themselves, their wives and their little ones."[71]

Military language was ubiquitous and could be applied to almost any activity in which the settler was engaged. For example, when the editor of the *Neosho Valley Eagle* announced that the District Clerk, Capt. J.L. Denison, had recently married, he described it using the imagery of a military campaign:

> Startling news from the front! Grand strategic move by ye fighting Editor. He proposes to fight it out on this line if it takes all winter. Once more in our capacity as faithful chroniclers of passing events, we are called upon to record one of the most brilliant and successful strategetic [*sic*] movements known to modern history. The facts as we have learned them are substantially as follows: On the 27th our daring and energetic District Clerk and ex official fighting editor on the staff of the Eagle broke up his camp, and in light marching order moved rapidly on the village of Iola. So rapidly and skillfully and withal, so secretly was the movement conducted that all hostile forces remained in a state of most profound ignorance in relation to the movements of the salient Captain until late on Sunday evening when he descended upon the astonished natives like 'a wolf on the fold' and succeeded in carrying off the fascinating prize.[72]

Other used similar language to describe even more mundane activities. "Our associate Editor," announced the *Advance*, "has declared a war of extermination against rabbits."[73] Frank Hudson, City Marshall for the city of Chetopa, warned his fellow Chetopans, "I have declared war against the dogs. Owners of dogs are required, by Ordinance No. 13, to have them registered at once."[74] A correspondent to the *Kansas Democrat* used analogous imagery to describe his fruitless struggle to evade the bed-bugs that plagued early settlers: "We have scratched for mortal hours, tearing blood enough out of us for any decent army of bed-bugs, but all to no purpose. We have attempted strategey [sic], tried to surprise and cut off their retreat, have dug dutch-gap canals around us, but all in vain. No sooner do we light a liglit [sic], but they are off to their mountain fastnesses (to-wit: in the shingles and rafters) where they lay so close that finding them is out of the question."[75] "The Army worm," warned the *Oswego Register*, "is now

Shown here in his Union military uniform, John Horner came to Kansas and served as president of Baker University (Baldwin City) from 1866 to 1867 before moving to Chetopa to establish the *Chetopa Advance* newspaper.

invading this country, making sad havoc in wheat fields."[76] The *Allen County Courant* alerted its readers: "As we go to press we learn that a large fire has been in progress all day, destroying much property. Fences, orchards, barns, haystacks and wood piles seem to have been willed alike to the devouring element."[77]

The forces of nature, like the forces of the rebellion, could be active agents of harm against which the settler had to be prepared to defend himself. In nature, the settler would find not only a friend but also a deceptive foe: "We can see from our office window the prairie fires raging to the north of town. They look beautiful, fanned by the calm night breeze; but these fires are as destructive as they are beautiful and we advise those who are not prepared against their destructive effects to do so at once."[78]

As this warning illustrates, a deep and pervasive fear characterized the veteran settlers as they sought to build farms and communities in southeast Kansas. Appearances could often prove to be deceiving; surrounded by danger the veteran settler had to remain perpetually vigilant. In her analysis of the cultural values undergirding the efforts of 19th-century settlers, geographer Julie Wilson has perceptively argued that "ideologies of conquest permeated the social consciousness of Kansas settlers and altered their perception of the possible."[79] This insight is applicable to the veteran settlers of southeast Kansas; however, it must be modified by the recognition that alongside this triumphant ideology was a more ominous fear that their freedom and liberty would be snatched away from their grasp. Ironically, even as they were expanding the Republic, they believed they were fighting a defensive war. Infused with republican ideals, settlers believed that liberty and freedom were precarious, power was dangerous and corruption through licentiousness a constant threat.[80] As a correspondent to the *Osage Mission Journal* reminded his fellow settlers: "It is the nature of men (when trusted with positions of power) to let their selfish and ambitious passions over rule all their finer and more virtuous principles."[81]

The editor of the *Labette Sentinel* gave voice to these deeply rooted fears in an editorial entitled, "The Yeomanry of our Land." After charting the history of the "bold and defiant" settler who has "pushed his course westward" by placing the "broad domain from the Atlantic to the Pacific within the grasp of civilization through the indomitable energy, severe toil and hard earnings of the laboring community," he proceeded to give the southeast Kansas settler a strong warning:

> While the yeomanry of our land are pursuing their honorable calling, improving our country, paying their assessments, and laying down their lives in defense of the nation's honor, they should not neglect their own private rights and privileges. When their homes are invaded either by rebels or railroads; when land sharks seek to devour them; when monied monopolies endeavor to overpower them, or unprincipled demagogues desire to become their rulers; then they should rise up in the might of their anger, defend their homes — their alters and their fires — denounce corruption, fight against combined corporations and railroad kings, hurl from power those profligate debauchees who have crept into our legislative halls under the guise of honest representatives of the peoples' interests, but only to sell themselves and their constituents to the highest bidder.

For the editor of the *Sentinel*, if farmers were not vigilant, they might find that all of their labors would be in vain. The danger to the Union and thus to their own private rights had not been eliminated; the money power of slavery had been replaced by the money power of railroads and other monopolies. The threat of a new kind of "slavery" hung over the heads of the settlers — their freedom was in danger. As the editor of the Parsons

Anti-Monopolist warned, "Thousands of the readers of the *Anti-Monopolist* put in life honor and fortune to save the republic — in the terrible ordeal a race of four million slaves were incidentally enfranchised. It would be a terrible comment upon the power of that Great Instrument if while our servants were creating citizens of the United States out of four million colored slaves, it was engaged in enslaving twenty million free white citizens of the United States."[82]

To these editors and to thousands more of their readers, politicians were more interested in maintaining their own personal power than they were in defending the rights of the powerless. The fight must therefore go on–the War had not ended and the newly immigrated farmer must not cease being a soldier even as he sought to build a home for his family. For if he did, the *Sentinel* prophesied, "the land you have inherited, which you have fought and bled for, which you have undergone untold privations and hardships to seek out for a home, and which you have improved" will "be taken from you by the ruthless hand of soulless corporations or railroad kings." The challenge then was apparent: "The people should rise up at once as one man and contest their rights in these lands to the bitter ends."[83]

It was not enough, the *Labette Sentinel* warned its readers, to build a prosperous farm. All of their work could be lost if they failed to see the threat of "land monopolies" and the "corruptive power" of big money. It was against these that the veteran settler had to be most vigilant. As they had fought the "slave power," so now, asserted the *Sentinel*, they must fight the power of money, landed monopolies and corrupt politicians.

The *Sentinel*'s call found its mark. Settlers were prepared to fight for their perceived rights; as the *Neosho Valley Eagle* warned: "Thousands of our pioneer boys have been 'under fire' on many a blood ensanguined field in defence [sic] of the Union. They know their rights, and dare maintain them."[84] A similar argument was advanced by Congressman Sidney Clarke in his letter of April 13, 1868 to N.G. Taylor, Commissioner of Indian Affairs, "In behalf of these hardy pioneers, many of whom fought for the defence [sic] of the government whose protection they now ask from all systems of land monopoly, I earnestly appeal that ... the lands be opened up to actual settlers free from all schemes of speculation and monopoly."[85]

Veteran settlers were especially attuned to this call to action because it fit their preconceived sense of justice. Bruce Kahler explains, "The crucible of war had transformed them into comrades who for the rest of their lives shared a deeply felt appreciation for each other and they expected to be honored by all Union-loving Americans."[86] As one veteran immigrant asserted in a letter to the editor of the *Neosho Valley Eagle*, "For the service we did our country, for rolling back the huge wave of anarchy that threatened to swallow our Capitol, our freedom and our government—for scattering the forces of treason, it would be our privilege, if we chose to come west to government lands, to enjoy such privileges as government had before extended to settlers and pioneers." In the same edition of the paper, after discussing the plans of railroad monopolies to claim the settlers' lands, a correspondent bitterly notes: "Our labor in the South must have been of little value if this is our due."[87]

A similar attitude was manifested in Osage Mission on January 18, 1869. Meeting together to discuss the rumors and assert their right to the land, a group of veterans passed a series of resolutions in which they asked the pointed question: "Was it the capitalist or laboring man that bared his breast and stood a living wall of adamant between our late domestic foes and the threatened disruption of our country, and which prevented the realization of that disastrous fate?" The answer was clearly: "the laboring man." As the settlers then went on to explain, "Many of these veterans of the late war for the Union wear the memorable scars, and some are mutilated, showing the extent of their suffering in its behalf; they are here struggling for life to gain a foot hold upon the soil that they make homes for themselves, their wives and their little ones."[88]

An interesting story that illustrates this sense of entitlement appeared in the *Sun*. As the newly established city of Parsons prepared to celebrate its first 4th of July, one of the town's successful businessmen, a local grocery merchant by the name of Oliver Duck, decided to present the city with its own flag. When the 4th arrived, the mayor, Colonel Willard Davis, received the flag from Duck and raised it in an official ceremony. Davis' story is interesting. A South Carolinian by birth, he had left his prosperous business and his slaves behind when South Carolina declared its intention to secede from the Union. Immigrating to Illinois in 1860, he joined the army and fought with Union forces against the rebellion. Like many others, upon his discharge, he wandered for a few years before immigrating to southeast Kansas where he bought land in the new city of Parsons. To Milton Reynolds, the editor of the *Sun*, Davis' sacrifice was great — he had jeopardized life and forfeited property.[89] Because of this, he deserved to be rewarded. Thus, according to Reynolds, it was fitting that Davis would receive the gift of a flag and the privilege of raising it over the new city of Parsons. He editorialized:

> With the first firing upon Sumter, he had determined to live, as he had always lived, breathing only love for the Union of the States and devotion to the flag and if need be die in its defense. For a united country he had to some extent jeopardized life and sacrificed property, and it was with peculiar satisfaction he could now, in behalf of the growing, vigorous and prosperous city of Parsons, accept such a gift.[90]

A collage from *Harper's Weekly*, November 8, 1873, showing life in southeast Kansas.

Like Reynolds, settlers in southeast Kansas believed that their sacrifices during the War had earned them a reward. And, of all the rewards to which they believed they were entitled, the most fundamental was the land itself.[91] As Paul Gates made clear in his classic study of 19th century land settlement patterns, settlers believed that they possessed "a settlement right" enabling them "to get the land either as a free homestead or as a pre-emption right for $1.25 an acre when the Indians were removed."[92] Ownership of the land was at the very heart and soul of the republican principles of individual liberty and equal opportunity; James Oakes has explained that the two fundamental convictions that underlay republican political thought in the mid-nineteenth century (i.e., "a powerful commitment to individual independence and a conviction that the virtue of the citizenry depended upon the widespread, though not necessarily equal, diffusion of property") were dependent upon the possibility of cheap, available land.[93] Therefore, according to the political logic that sustained their settlement, land was central to the thousands of incoming Veterans. Private ownership guaranteed their liberty while the availability of cheap land ensured that financial opportunities would remain open for all settlers, not just the wealthy and well-connected. As the *Parsons Sun* explained to its readers:

> A landed aristocracy is a curse to a free government; and a *landless people* have an uncertain hold upon the rights secure to American freeman. To make a man secure in his rights, in this or any country, plant him firmly in the soil! Let him rest upon his own broad acres; and with God's genial skies above him, the promise of "seed time and harvest shall not fail him."[94]

A correspondent urged the editor of the *Neosho Valley Eagle* to spread the news far and wide:

> Dear EAGLE, fly away to the north, east and South, and say to houseless, homeless starving thousands, come to the Great west, to our enchanting Valley, by the hundreds; aye, by thousands, there is room for all and more too. Kansas can feed the world in a few years! Then, why drag out a miserable existence in pent up cities? When you come to our own lovely west, be as free as the wind that sweeps over our beautiful prairie homes, and in a few years become opulent.[95]

According to this letter-writer, by immigrating to southeast Kansas men and women would find freedom (i.e., "be as free as the wind") and prosperity (i.e., "in a few years become opulent"), thus preserving and guaranteeing to their children the two characteristics of a republican democracy that the Rebellion had threatened and that they had fought to preserve! For these settlers, as long as the opportunity of cheap land remained open to them, the resources offered by the land were limitless (i.e., "Kansas can feed the world in a few years!").

The *Neosho County Dispatch* expressed a similar sentiment in an editorial entitled "southern Kansas and its Prospects." After printing an article from the *New York Tribune* decrying the plight of "one hundred thousand families in houses or parts of houses they do not own, paying a better part of their incomes weekly, monthly or quarterly to landlords or their agents ... ceasing to pay rent only when they cease to live," the *Dispatch* proclaimed, "If this evil is ever remedied, it will be when these unfortunate beings break the chain that binds them to such slavery, come to the wide, free country of the west, and become land holders."[96] The enemy of slavery of any kind was land ownership — the key to defeating it was making sure that land remained available and inexpensive enough for ordinary people to purchase.

Early settlers boasted that southeast Kansas was the land of choice for the poor and less-advantaged. The *Neosho County Dispatch* avowed that "nearly all of our citizens who are in the most independent circumstances came here poor, and by diligent labor made for themselves a home and a competency."[97] The *Southern Kansas Advance*, in its 1870 "booster edition," promised would-be settlers, "The settler with very little means can go on and in a very few years have a home, which for fertility of soil cannot be equaled in the world."[98] The *Neosho Valley Eagle* assured its readers, "Undoubtedly if one section of our State presents a better field for poor men than another, it is that portion commonly known as southern Kansas. Here may be expended a few dollars for improvements and a rich reward awaits the adventurer."[99] In an editorial promoting southeast Kansas as the destination of choice for European immigrants, Milton Reynolds of the *Sun* announced, "If they are poor and out of money, they can turn in their muscle and brain toward the wealth of the nation; for here they will find wages better and food abundant and all their civil and political rights placed under the protection of the fundamental law and beyond the reach of party or faction."[100] The *Labette Sentinel* likewise guaranteed its readers that there was plenty of "room to grow rich" in southeast Kansas; in fact, there was so much opportunity for "capitalist farmers" that "millions of acres of rich farming land" were literally "wasting their riches for the want of more people and money."[101]

In their letters to friends and family, settlers often emphasized the opportunities for wealth that were awaiting the poor but hard-working immigrant. As a correspondent to the *Osage Mission Journal* explained in 1869:

> Mr. Editor: And still they come! That is to say, we of the Upper Labette, we continually are receiving accessions to our population.... The great Architect of our Universe made our country after the most beautiful sublunary fashion and reserved its occupancy by tillers of the soil for that generation which is

"weaker and wiser." ... Although we hold that God and all of His works are perfect, we also hold that He has endowed the mind of man with faculties for progress and improvement, and that He has created nothing terrestrial so perfect or beautiful that does not allow and even encourage the arts and sciences of men to improve upon. With these views we hail with delight every progressive element that infuses itself into our frontier society.[102]

In a similar vein, new arrival R.C. Davis wrote to his friend, John Farel, in Brooklyn, "Here I am in the southern part of Kansas near the Indian Territory line; I have a claim of 160 acres. The lands now belong to the Osage Indians but the country is settling up rapidly and all are sure that the land will be in market by next spring....The country here is decidedly the best in Kansas. Don't you want to come out here? You could make it pay by taking you a good claim. The land is first rate and will be mighty high as soon as it comes in market and gets settled."[103]

Like the editor of the *Osage Mission Journal*, settlers sang the praises of the "rich and productive soil" and, with the editor of the *Neosho Valley Eagle*, proclaimed the region to be "one of the most fertile and beautiful prairie valleys in the west."[104] Even the "experts" added their voices of confirmation; as the geologist C.B. Wilber explained in his analysis of southeast Kansas and southwest Missouri: "We positively declare that no man can suggest a substantial good that this country does not possess. For soil, climate, water, drainage, stone, timber, coal, grasses, grazing and general farming, these portions of Kansas and Missouri are unrivalled and, we believe, unequalled."[105]

Early editors seized on almost any indication of fertility to convince themselves and their readers of the advantages of southeast Kansas. When the *Osage Mission Journal* announced the birth of twins to two families, it presented their births as "evidence of the richness and productiveness of southern Kansas."[106] A correspondent to the *Neosho Valley Eagle*, noting that the city was inhabited by "a large number of educated, refined and handsome ladies," concluded that "it is not strange the Providence should design that a land created so beautiful should be inhabited and beautified by some of the fairest and best of His creatures."[107] Local newspapers frequently reported the size of tomatoes and other home-grown vegetables to indicate the possibilities stored in "the treasures of the soil which now lie hidden from view."[108] No praise it seems could be too high; the editor of the *Parsons Sun* assured his readers that "if G. Washington was now living ... his shrewd business judgment, and good common sense would at once see that it is a good point and he would say, 'Martha, this is the place for us to plant our stakes.'"[109]

Settlers frequently employed biblical imagery to describe the "garden" to which they had come. The *Neosho Valley Eagle* invited "Wolverines, Suckers, Pukes, Leather-heads, Hoosiers, Corn-crackers, and Buckeyes" to come to "the land of milk and honey."[110] The *Western Enterprise* proclaimed, "The grass is so luxuriant, the skies so brilliantly bright and the atmosphere so delicious, it seems almost too good to work in, and about as near a paradise as the west can show."[111] Editors possessed the ability to twist even the most obvious negative into a shining example of the positive qualities of southeast Kansas. Noting the flood-like conditions caused by heavy rains, the *Labette Sentinel* taunted would-be critics: "The creeks are now running like rivers, and many streams are temporarily impassable. How is this for drouthy Kansas?"[112] When the temperature turned unusually hot, going over the 100 degree mark each day for over a week, the *Kansas Democrat* jeered: "Think of that ye shivering chaps who live in arctic regions."[113] And, when detractors remarked that southeast Kansas had too much wind and not enough timber to sustain an endless population boom, a correspondent to the *Osage Mission Journal* vehemently responded,

> I believe that these so-called objections will ultimately prove the greatest most beneficial blessings that Kansas enjoys. I believe that they constitute a part of God's providential instrumentality to reserve this favorite garden spot of His footstool from sacrilegious desecration. The wind, you know, blows away the chaff and leaves the sound wheat.[114]

Like Van Sandt, many veteran settlers refused to be blown off course. Convinced that their ability to endure the winds which had blown so fiercely during the Civil War proved their ability to endure any wind that might blow in southeast Kansas, they settled down to build homes, plow fields and raise families. In doing so, they believed that the fruits would justify the labors. Like Van Sandt, the vast majority came to put down roots, and to work towards the establishment of vibrant, prosperous and well-ordered communities. They were prepared to work hard, to sacrifice ease and leisure, to obtain them. Possessed by a heady sense of what they had accomplished even as they were tormented by fears of what they could lose, they had put down the sword, but had not ended the fight.

Thus, it is no surprise that they resonated to the speech of their newly elected congressional representative, Sidney Clarke, which was printed in full in the *Osage Mission Journal*. In his acceptance speech, Clarke had urged his listeners to "rally to the conflict" so that they might "route the cohorts of treason at the ballot box as they were routed by our soldiers on the battlefield." Clarke had also warned his hearers: "That which was won by blood, and on the battlefield, must not be surrendered at the ballot box. The best government God ever gave man now demands the support of all who would guard, with zealous care, the interests of liberty and mankind."[115] Although we know now that Clarke was a clever politician who worked behind the scenes to support the railroads against the interests of the settlers, this was unknown at the time in southeast Kansas. The settlers believed that Clarke was on their side, and Clarke did everything he could to maintain this illusion.[116] Many of these farmers had marched with Grant and Sherman; they had slept in open fields, been wounded in battle and persevered to the end in order to see the Union preserved. They thus enthusiastically accepted Clarke's challenge to show that same perseverance, dedication and loyalty in conquering the prairies and establishing communities of ordered liberty in southeast Kansas.

2

VIGILANCE COMMITTEES AND SETTLERS' CLUBS (1868–1870)

It was one story too many and the editor of the newspaper the *Neosho Valley Eagle,* B.K. Land, had heard enough. The news of another assault on a farmer's wife on a lonely homestead in Neosho County had just filtered into his office. The good news was that this time the woman had managed to escape by running into the fields; but her husband, who had come running in, had not been able to apprehend the assailant. The culprit was still at large; perhaps he was roaming the countryside looking for new victims. His frustration mounting, Land quickly laid out the words which would appear in his weekly newspaper: "Crime seems rife, and if the society cannot be revenged under the law, decent men ought to turn out, hunt down such vile whelps of the Devil and administer summary punishment."[1] It was a bold and forthright call for action. But something had to be done; the future of the newly forming communities in southeast Kansas was at stake.

Veteran settlers who flocked to southeast Kansas brought the anxieties of post–Civil War America with them. These fears were heightened by the initial illegality of their settlement and the very real danger that the railroad monopolies might conspire to wrest the land title away from them. Thus, as they worked to improve claims and establish communities based on republican principles, settlers in southeast Kansas were forced to confront their fears. Living on land that was not legally their own, surrounded by swirling rumors and dire warnings that their efforts might prove to be in vain, settlers turned to each other for support and found strength in their solidarity as veterans of the Civil War.[2] As the *Neosho Valley Eagle* assured them, "The majority of the Northern people sympathize with us, and soldiers in particular share our feelings, for more than three-fourths of us are ex-soldiers."[3] Settlers rejoiced in the words of General Ulysses Grant (whose farewell address to the army was printed in full in the *Eagle*): "By your patriotic devotion to your country in the hour of danger and alarm, your magnificent fighting, bravery and endurance you have maintained the supremacy of the Union and the Constitution, overthrown all armed opposition to the enforcement of the laws and the proclamations forever abolishing slavery — the cause and pretext of the rebellion — and opened the way to the rightful authorities to restore order and inaugurate peace on a permanent and enduring basis on every foot of American soil."[4] They took comfort in the oft-quoted assurances of unnamed "correspondents" in Topeka and Washington, D.C.: "Much interest is felt here in the treaty now being consummated with the Osages. There is a strong sympathy predominant for the protection of the settlers. It should be the first object of the government to protect and defend the hardy pioneers who are advancing civilization upon the frontier."[5]

Faced with an uncertain future, settlers channeled both their anxiety and hope into action by forming clubs, committees, and organizations to advance their claims and build their communities. The first recorded mention of this activity is 1867, when several meetings were held throughout Neosho and Labette counties. In Canville, a group of settlers met to petition Congress to pass a bill to secure the rights of the settlers by enabling them to receive valid grants for their lands. They prepared a petition containing the names of many settlers and sent it to Congressman George Julian of Indiana who was a personal friend of one of the settlers, D.T. Mitchell. As meetings continued to be held throughout the year, money was raised and Judge Solomon Markham was sent to Washington to represent their interest. On December 28, 1867, a group of veteran settlers gathered in Old Erie "for the purpose of selecting a Central Committee whose duty it should be to organize the different townships for the purpose of petitioning the Congress of the United States for the right of Pre-emption and Homesteads upon lands commonly known as the Osage Indian Lands."[6]

In the fall of 1868, on September 14, the labors of this committee brought about a large convention of settlers in Ladore with delegates present from both Neosho and Labette counties. Other meetings followed in Jacksonville, Erie and Oswego. As the newspaper editor W.W. Graves commented in his *History of Neosho County*, "Here was a population of more than 25,000 people engaged in building homes, in a constant and rigorous struggle for food, and with no law concerning their property. And yet the community was peaceable, orderly, and well-governed then as it is today.

2. Vigilance Committees and Settlers' Clubs (1868–1870) 61

The American love for self-government was never more beautifully exhibited."⁷

Although Graves' quixotic description passes over much of the struggle and conflict of the early years of settlement, he is nevertheless correct in emphasizing the commitment to "community action" on the part of early settlers. For even as the legal status of their claims was being debated in the halls (and backrooms) of Congress, the settlers were struggling to improve claims, feed their families and build communities together. As John Horner of the *Chetopa Advance* editorialized, "Organized effort and associated enterprise are characteristics of the progressive age in which we live. Cooperative labor constructs bridges, constructs railroads, establishes banks, and builds cities; rears churches and founds colleges, lays the electric cable along the oceans' beds and sends the fiery leviathans of commerce on missions of civilization around the globe. Individual isolation is barbarism."⁸

In another edition of the *Advance*, Horner clarified his beliefs: "Let these social gatherings be continued." As he explained, "the more we know of our neighbors, the better we shall love them, as a rule."⁹ Whatever the challenge, settlers in southeast Kansas believed that they could best confront it together. Settlers networked to sustain each other in the fight to obtain legal title for their claims; they also depended on each other in their efforts to establish lawful, ordered communities. In this, they were living out the realities of their republican ideology which, as Jean Baker has argued, believed "civic virtue never emerged from individual interest but rather required collective action."¹⁰ Settlers looked to each other for help in their commitment to enacting justice by defending their families and homes and by punishing the lawless. As the *Parsons Sun* proclaimed, "There is no sublimer spectacle that can be witnessed in this or any other country than the triumph of law and order."¹¹

This proved to be a Herculean task. One of the earliest problems confronting the settlers was the lack of provisions, which was compounded by the difficulty of transporting them through southeast Kansas, given the large number of creeks and rivers which had to be forded. John Horner complained, "We have been compelled to import the supplies for our people and transport them a hundred miles or more by wagon. This has been a constant drain on our resources. Labor and living have been high and everything expensive."¹² Another settler recalled, "At that time Humboldt and Fort Scott were the nearest points at which we could obtain provisions or goods of any kind, save a meager trading post on Canville Creek."¹³

As a result, prices for food were very high. The *Western Enterprise* noted, "So new was the country at that time that nearly all the supplies were brought from Kansas City or Lawrence in wagons.... Corn readily sold at $2 per bushel to the immigrant, and was very hard to get, even at that price. Fruit and vegetables were out of the question and anything like comfort an impossibility."[14] Nelson Case remembered an early time when the prices were even higher: "There was necessarily a great amount of suffering. Provisions had to be hauled from so great a distance that the price continued very high all the time for several years, flour was frequently $15 a hundred, corn $3 a bushel, meal $6 a hundred, bacon 25 cents a pound, and other things in the line of living in proportion."[15]

The fall and winter of 1866 were especially difficult; rain fell constantly and the mild weather did not allow the rivers to freeze. Transportation was minimal; many settlers fell ill because of the lack of provisions. There was not enough feed for the stock; as a result, most of the cows died either of starvation or disease. The summer of 1867 brought additional troubles: an infestation of grasshoppers. Their arrival was first noted by the *Humboldt Union*: "Billions of grasshoppers were seen high in the air, on Tuesday; traveling in a northeasterly direction. Where will they stop seems to be one of the vexed questions. We are satisfied that they will do the crops no injury in this vicinity."[16] The *Union* was wrong. As an early settler recollected, "One day in the summer of 1867 when corn was in roasting ears, while we were eating dinner we heard something like hail hitting the house. Looking out, we saw millions of grasshoppers. In 15 minutes we could not see the sun, the hoppers were so thick in the air."[17] The grasshoppers ate the blades off the stalks and the grains off the ears of corn. When the settlers tried to save the vegetables they had planted in the garden by tying rags around them, the grasshoppers ate the rags before consuming the vegetables.

In the early years, settlers concentrated on subsistence farming. Without effective transportation, they were cut off from lucrative Eastern markets. And, without adequate milling facilities, they were unable to fully use the grain they grew. As the *Chetopa Advance* bewailed, "The people on the upper Labette have fine crops of wheat but no machine to thresh it. Who will supply them?"[18] In the early years, most settlers concentrated on growing their own vegetables and experimenting with various kinds of fruits.[19] Margaret Plummer recalled that the first summer they planted potatoes and garden vegetables, the second summer they added corn and in the third summer they planted wheat.[20] Settlers also adapted to local fruits, as noted by a correspondent to the *Neosho Valley Eagle* who explained that "wild fruit has been plenty here this summer and the grapes, hickory nuts and walnuts that we will have this fall will be the most astonishing thing of all."[21] According to Cory, the settlers learned to improvise:

Melon rinds and sorghum molasses made a preserve which was fine. The ordinary prickly pear was made into a conserve to tickle the palate of any one. Persimmon jam and persimmon preserves were food for kings. They took cubes and triangles of carrots, tomatoes, melon rinds, cantaloupes, cabbage, sweet potatoes, and I don't know what else, and put them in a jar and turned out piccalilli.... And sorghum! You should have seen what those women did with sorghum. Every possible food, from fruit preserves to hoe-cake, made a call for sorghum; and really, a good flap-jack, with home-made sorghum, is not bad eating even now. But the finishing marvel, the final coup, as it were, of these artists was sheep-sorrel pie. They picked the common sorrel from the prairies and treated it somewhat as they would have treated rhubarb, if they had had it, only that they used sorghum instead of sugar. It was really a good pie.[22]

Cory's positive spin notwithstanding, life was difficult for the first settlers. In the early years, food was expensive and difficult to come by. As the *Neosho Valley Eagle*

This humorous cartoon illustration depicts a grasshopper standing upright with a crutch, eye patch, and a sling holding his left arm. By his side is a small suitcase. The countryside in the background has been completely stripped of all greenery, with only tree trunks and twigs surviving.

warned would-be settlers, they would certainly hear "hob-goblin stories about starvation."[23] The *Eagle* reported an engagement, but sadly noted that the wedding would have to wait because the groom-to-be "says he would get married in a minute were it not that being a very sensitive and conscientious youth, don't like the idea of gradually starving anybody's sister."[24] One settler remembered, "The only stomach trouble we heard of then was the trouble to get something to fill the stomach with."[25] The editor of the *Neosho Valley Eagle* was forced to make a public appeal to meet his family's needs: "WANTED — Butter, eggs, lard, potatoes and chickens at the *Eagle* office. We must live. Market price paid for anything that will 'fill up.'"[26] It was not until the growing season of 1869 that the settlers were able to feed themselves, without having to import large quantities of food from Missouri and northern Kansas counties. The *Neosho County Dispatch* joyfully announced, "We also have the satisfaction of recording that there was a larger scope of country planted, and from its extensive yield will probably be sufficient to supply the entire wants of the population."[27]

To supply their protein needs, settlers relied on the milk provided by their cows, the eggs laid by their chickens, fish that could caught in nearby streams and rivers, and any meat that could be obtained by hunting resident wildlife. As an example of the kind of game that could be found in the region, the *Osage Mission Journal* offered the following list in its report on the hunting expedition led "last week by Sheriff Leahy": "5 Deer, 3 Geese, 48 Ducks, 13 Prairie Chickens, 149 Quail."[28] Even as late as 1870, people were still buying locally killed meat at open air markets: "Prairie Chickens are very plentiful in this section. They sell alive for 20 cents, dressed 15 cents each. Venison is very plentiful in this market. One man sold 443 pounds last Saturday at twelve and a half cents per pound."[29]

Early settlers were hampered by the lack of accurate knowledge about their immediate environment. Many coming from northern climes were unacquainted with the serious danger posed by the brown recluse spiders. Other risks were more well-known, but no less serious. Rattlesnake bites were frequent, and settlers reported a constant battle with bed-bugs and lice. Advice and remedies circulated constantly. The *Osage Mission Journal* reported that B. V. Harris, who had been bitten while hunting near the Neosho River, was saved "by prompt use of good whiskey, *ad libitum.*"[30] The *Neosho Valley Eagle* told of a mother who, upon a rattlesnake biting her child in his crib, "killed the snake and then poured whiskey down the child till it was made drunk, which neutralized the effects of the snake poison and saved the child."[31] Others adopted a less intoxicating approach; the *Osage Mission Journal* told the story of Mrs. James Tharp who was bitten while walking from the house to the garden. According to the report, "Mrs. Tharp killed the reptile; and then with equal presence of mind, bound the limb tightly and thus prevented the rapid absorption of the virus."[32] For other pests, the cure often proved to be more perilous than the disease! The *Chetopa Advance* recommended the use of "quicksilver" to control inside pests and an ample sprinkling of "sulphur mixed with coal dust" to keep them from eating garden vegetables![33]

Settlers constantly debated among themselves what crops should be planted, and when they should be planted. The *Neosho County Dispatch* revealed some of the nature of this debate when it admitted, "It has been generally supposed and in fact conceded by those who ought to have known better that Southern Kansas was not adapted to the raising of corn." As might be expected, the *Dispatch* was quick to dispute this commonly accepted opinion by noting, "In many instances we have been shown stalks of corn fourteen feet high, with three well formed ears and four shoots on the same stalk. In examining some of the fields we found, in almost every instance, two well formed ears to each stalk."[34] The *Chetopa Advance* took a different approach, arguing instead that,

> There no longer exists any doubt in the mind of any intelligent reader or observer, but that Kansas and especially the Southern portion of it, is destined to become famous for its fruit producing capacity. The wild grape grows here in unwonted luxuriance and fortunes have already been made in raising the improved variety. Since the first settlement of the country, there has been no failure in the peach crop of Southern Kansas.... Our soil and climate are also equally adapted to the cultivation of the apple.[35]

By far, however, the most challenging feature of the new environment was the weather. As the settlers soon discovered, in southeast Kansas it was anything but predictable! Immigrant Solomon Kious noted wryly in a letter to his hometown paper in Illinois, "I would advise all who wish to emigrate not to come if they do not want to see changeable weather."[36] Settlers were shocked by the sudden appearance of storms accompanied by extremely high winds. The *Neosho Valley Eagle* reported, "We have had for the past week severe wind and rain storms. One house, belonging to Mr. J.F. Allison, was blown down. It was not quite finished, and undoubtedly the wind took a better hold, not being thoroughly enclosed."[37]

The most lethal of the weather patterns were the violent explosions of lightning that came in the late fall and early winter. Unaware of the danger, as the *Chetopa Advance* ruefully noted, settlers frequently failed to take adequate precautions,

> We are surprised to see in riding over the country that the farmers have as yet taken no precautions to protect their stacks of hay and grain, fences and buildings from prairie fires which within the next two or three weeks will sweep the whole area of our country. Let there be no further delay. Already the fires have commenced. One or two frosts and, unless prompt measures are taken, thousands of dollars worth of property will be swept away with the fiery besom of destruction.[38]

Many farmers apparently failed to understand and/or heed the warning. In November, the *Advance* reported,

> Nearly the entire area of our county has been swept clean by the prairie fires. On the open divide in the central portions of the county we travel miles and miles without ever seeing so much as a blade of grass — only cinders and ashes. From Chetopa westward along the line as far as the Verdigris, the entire stock range has been destroyed, except a narrow margin on the north

of Snow Creek and here and there a small patch where the settlers have fought back the destroyer. The same is true of all the west and north-west portions of the county.[39]

The changeable nature of the weather alternatively confused, irritated, and frustrated the plans and activities of the settlers. Rain was a constant problem. When it rained, it often poured, causing rivers, streams and creeks to overflow their banks. As the *Osage Mission Journal* reported, "The Neosho is on the rampage and has been on it for several days, to the great disgust of the lumber men. The rain was unexpected."[40] The *Journal* noted in another edition, "It rained in great volume and uninterruptedly all night. The water in Neosho River raised 20 feet in 9 hours time. Every creek and rivulet assumed the dimensions of a good-sized river." In addition to threatening crops and livestock, sudden downpours created transportation nightmares. The *Journal* continued, "During Wednesday Capt. Gillmore's new ferry which he had just put into operation a short distance below Buck & Hutchings' Mill, was torn loose and swept down stream. The same befell the upper ferry owned by Neighbors & Johnsons. Owing to this great rain fall the Stages on the various routes centering here failed to arrive on time for several days."[41] At times, unfamiliarity with the rushing rivers could prove fatal. The *Tioga Herald* reported the tragic death of "Mrs. Nichols with her daughter" who drowned while attempting to ford the Neosho River when their wagon became uncoupled.[42]

Unaware of the ferocity of southeastern Kansas rains, settlers were often unprepared for the destruction they wrought. As the *Oswego Register* reported,

> The walls of what was designed for a two story stone dwelling on the north end of Commercial Street, built by Mr. Houghey, fell down during the storms last Saturday. The walls were completely ready for the roof, including the gables, but owing to the great weight, a defective foundation and the wash of the rains, fell in ruins, leaving only a small portion of the front wall standing. The loss is considerable and to be regretted.[43]

Even when the destruction was not so extreme, new settlers frequently complained that the rain made life almost unbearable. The *Neosho Valley Eagle* noted, "Everything is Mud. Every paper in Southern Kansas lets off a few sentences about the Mud."[44] John Horner was more poetic in his lament:

> For some weeks we have had the old Indian's sign of rain: 'black all around and pouring down in the middle.' ... The earth is like a saturated sponge. It is wet — wetter — wettest. Our apprehensions of a Noahic deluge have been aroused.... We are water bound and then the mud! Boundless, ubiquitous, measureless, fathomless oceans of mud! Mud, as a gas, and mud as a fluid;

ink-like, gruel-like, paste-like, pudding-like, tar-like, mortar-like mud; mud in the streets and mud in our sanctum; mud on our boots, mud in our bedroom; mud on our trousers, and mud in our tea; mud on our coat, and mud in our coffee. We have drinked muddy water till we are troubled with the sand bars on the stomach.[45]

In 1869, the rains completely overwhelmed the entire region. A fierce rain dropped eighteen to twenty inches of rain in five hours; the Neosho River spilled over its banks and engulfed the surrounding communities in water. The *Osage Mission Journal* reported the amazing results, "When the morning dawned and here in town a glance to the West showed the Neosho out of its bed thus early, and rushing along over a stretch of a mile in width between its ordinary bank and the western limits of town and Rowland's and Clark's farms with a good deal of the latter already submerged. To the eastward the waters of the usually quiet little Flat Rock Creek could be seen seemingly spread to the extent of a wide river."[46] The damage was immense; entire houses and barns were ripped from their moorings and washed away downstream. Both people and livestock were drowned; the *Journal* reported that one farmer lost over 400 head of sheep. The *Neosho Valley Dispatch* drew attention to the many horses that were unable to escape the confines of their pickets.[47] Both papers reported that entire crops of wheat were destroyed.

The most dangerous event for which the community was unprepared, however, was fire. The *Chetopa Advance* reported that a fire destroyed the dry house of a newly erected Planning Mill. The prompt response of the citizenry was able to stop the fire from spreading, but not before a third of the lumber in the kiln was burned on the ends. To Horner, this was a strong warning: "This fire satisfied us of one thing, *viz*: Chetopa needs a set of fire hooks and an organized fire company."[48] A few weeks later, the *Osage Mission Journal* informed its readers that "the house of Mr. N.B. Clark, some five miles southeast of this place was consumed with all its contents on Monday night of this week." The parents had been away; the three children left at home had only barely escaped.[49] The first fire was started by a defective flue; the second because the children had been inattentive to the stove. In August 1870, the *Journal* reported that another fire had occurred — this time in the stables of the S.K. Stage Company. Although no one had been hurt, "two valuable horses and other property were burned." Observing that the fire had been caused by "the carelessness of a cigar smoker," the editor forcefully pronounced, "It seems to us that a man must be slightly demented, or recklessly foolhardy, who will take a lighted cigar into such a place, where so much combustible material abounds, which a spark may ignite."[50] Unfortunately, as the editor acknowledged, southeast Kansas was not without its fools!

Furthermore, the steady influx of people taxed to the breaking point the limited resources of the emerging communities in the valley.[51] The *Neosho Valley Eagle* explained, "Within the past four weeks we have had accessions to our town to the number of fifty families. They are living in all imaginable kind of structures, not being able to procure lumber to build at this time."[52] The *Osage Mission Journal* lamented, "Our city is without ice. Owing to our rapid increase in population the supply put up last winter was several thousand pounds too small, but we are fortunate in having the coolest and best water to be found in Southern Kansas."[53]

Accidents occurred at an alarming rate; given the lack of adequately trained medical personnel, even minor injuries could prove fatal. This was especially true of cases that dealt with minors. Of special note were the disasters involving children. Given the undeveloped nature of roads and the rugged state of many vehicles, children were routinely thrown out of coaches or wagons. They were run over by errant animals. Given the confined quarters in which many lived, children were scalded by boiling water or coffee. In such cases, the newspaper editors could not refrain from chiding the parents or guardians. After the *Osage Mission Journal* had described the tragic case of "a babe of William Rhodes, living on Flat Rock" who "was badly scalded by upsetting a kettle of hot lye over itself," the editor remarked, "Parents cannot be too careful in placing such dangerous means beyond the reach of young children."[54] Several months later, after describing the sad case of a six-year-old girl who burned herself severely by knocking over a hot pot of coffee, the editor observed, "Too much care cannot be observed in such matters."[55] The editor of the *Labette Sentinel* likewise exhorted parents, "Let us remember that they are ours to learn and protect, to teach and to warn and cherish; ours to love wisely, to deal with firmly and reverently — mirrors of our example, gleaners of the harvest of our home life — not ours to pet and rebuff, and sacrifice to our hundred weaknesses."[56] The necessity of survival combined with the fluctuating vicissitudes of frontier life forced settlers to work together and to depend on each other. Thus, after reporting that "the dwelling house of Mr. A. Johnson accidentally caught fire on Wednesday last during the temporary absence of the family," the *Neosho Valley Eagle* added that the house "would have been entirely consumed had it not been discovered by a neighbor."[57]

Reliance on others is noted in many early settlers' reminiscences. F.M. Abbot, who came to Neosho county in 1867, lived in Canville township and taught school in both Thayer and Chanute, remembered that although "the people were all poor in purse ... they were helpful and accommodating to the last degree."[58] In another letter to the *News*, Abbot expanded this comment by explaining:

Although people were poor, they were good neighbors. They would share their last meal with a neighbor who was needier than they. They would loan anything they had and, if anybody was sick they would make almost any sacrifice to help or assist their suffering neighbor. Their hearts were in the right place. These pioneers loved to visit one another. They were friendly, hospitable. Their visitor was sure to get the best they had.[59]

Undoubtedly, these memories, colored by time and tinted by nostalgia, tended to over-emphasize cooperation and downplay conflict; nevertheless they give voice to a fundamental reality in the settlement of southeast Kansas. As the historian W.H. Hutchinson has noted, because early settlers confronted an uncertain future, their fundament concern "was survival.... Each segment had a common moral code: the primordial ethic of survival."[60] Living on the frontier, settlers were acutely conscious of their vulnerability and turned to each other for sustenance, support and strength. Thus, when Francis Wall discovered that a yoke of his oxen had been stolen, he turned to his neighbors for help. After investigating the situation, they discovered that a nearby neighbor, James Moss, had begun selling meat "on the side" about the same time that the oxen had turned up "missing." Deducing that Moss was guilty, they also decided it was time for him to leave — immediately. When Moss protested his innocence and refused to go, Wall's neighbors insisted. They forcibly entered his residence, gathered his belongings, threw them onto his hitched wagon and watched as he rode out of town.[61]

As this story illustrates, in seeking security through collective action, settlers were confronted by a dilemma: not everyone could be trusted. Cory remembered his own fear, "If I had a good farm and my neighbor Tom Johnson had none, he could come to my cabin and put me off, and if he could whip me or scare me, the place was his.... Cases of this kind were frequent."[62] Furthermore, as settlers quickly learned, people were not always who they said they were! Sometimes the deception could be quite elaborate. The *Osage Mission Journal* reported the story of "A.D. Cunning," who was arrested and taken back to his home state of Indiana in the late summer of 1869. This arrest was of great surprise to the local residents, especially because Cunning had ingratiated himself to his neighbors by serving the community in the "capacities of lawyer, judge pro tem, preacher, Sabbath school teacher and raftsman down the great Neosho."[63]

Another tale of deception was recorded in the *Neosho Valley Eagle*. The story began in Indiana in the fall of 1867 when a married tenant farmer by the last name of Brenner became involved in an adulterous relationship with a younger woman. As the news spread and community disapproval of his actions became apparent, he left his wife and struck out for southeast Kansas with his lover, where he staked a claim about three miles outside of Osage Mission. Establishing himself as a newly married man, Brenner endeared himself to his neighbors and became an active member of the local community. However, when his wife, who had been left behind in Indiana, discovered where he had gone, she decided to follow him. When she arrived in southeast Kansas, she staked a claim less than a mile away from that of her errant husband. Not content to sit quietly by and allow another woman to pass herself off as his lawful wife, Mrs. Brenner proceeded to tell anyone and everyone the true story — much to her husband's annoyance. The *Eagle* related the conclusion of the sordid affair: "The husband, maddened, and full of revenge, is said to have poisoned the one he swore to honor and protect."[64]

That this was not an isolated occurrence is seen in another story that appeared in the *Journal* in the spring of 1870.[65] According to this report, the local constable, R.A. Davies, had failed to return after borrowing a horse and buggy to serve papers in the northeastern part of the county. It was initially believed that the newly married Davies had been killed. However, when no body turned up and no evidence could be found of foul play, an investigation was initiated. To the surprise of everyone — especially his new bride — it was discovered that Davies (whom the *Journal* described as "rather genteel in appearance" with "an oily tongue ... apt to deceive the unwary") had three other wives — "one in Rushville, Illinois who has three children by him; one in Knob Nostur, Mo., who has one child by the wretch; he has also a wife somewhere in Arkansas whom he married about two years ago and it is supposed that he has more wives in other parts of the West and South."[66]

I also note the following notice printed in the *Osage Mission Journal* in August of 1870 as evidence of the attraction Kansas held for many who were seeking to flee from obligations and responsibilities incurred elsewhere: "WANTED — Information is wanted of Loren B. Holbrook, who is thought to be in Kansas. Any information regarding his whereabouts will be thankfully received by his wife at Fort Dodge, Iowa."[67]

Another example can be found in the letters of the Jesuit priest, Fr. Paul Ponziglione. Fr. Ponziglione complained of an "imposter" who was traveling from house to house in the remote areas of Neosho and Labette Counties claiming to be his nephew and offering to baptize children for a small fee. Fr. Ponziglione advised the duped families to have their children conditionally baptized, telling them: "I do not believe in the sincerity of that man who went about calling himself a priest and imposing on the credulity of poor simple Catholics."[68]

The uncertainty these kinds of experiences wrought in the hearts and

2. Vigilance Committees and Settlers' Clubs (1868–1870)   71

minds of the settlers is clearly manifested in the following poem. Written for the *Neosho Valley Eagle,* the anonymous author advised settlers not to take people at their words, but instead to prove their friendship before pledging their trust.

> Many to serve their selfish ends
> Warmly declare that they are friends
> But soon as serving self is over
> Behold they are your friends no more.
>
> Others will act a part more base,
> Always be friendly to your face,
> You turn your back then they your name
> Expose to obloquy and shame.
>
> Apparent friends others show,
> That you may confidence bestow,
> Your secrets thus they oft obtain
> And use to injure your good name
>
> Those who of others tell you much,
> My counsel is beware of such
> They bring your neighbors' faults to view,
> And in absence speak the same of you.
>
> A faithful friend I highly value,
> But mere pretence I do despise,
> When you're disposed a friend to trust
> Always be sure to prove them first.[69]

In many respects, the truths contained in this poem transcend geography and time. Yet, in southeast Kansas in the late 1860s and early '70s, the warning was especially pertinent. Settlers were caught on the horns of a dilemma. They could not survive by themselves; yet they did not know whom they could trust.

The solution towards which these settlers moved was a variation of the old saying, "there is safety in numbers." They created cooperative clubs, committees and assemblies by which groups of "law-abiding" settlers could help and defend each other against those who were intent on circumventing the law. One of the earliest of these cooperative Clubs to be formed in Labette County was organized on January 5, 1867, in Labette City. They began their meeting officially by nominating Enos Reed to be secretary and appointed him to record the details of their inaugural meeting.[70] It is striking to note how this small group of neighbors who met on a Saturday afternoon in the dead of winter paid strict attention to parliamentary detail. Living at the edge of what they considered to be civilization, in the vicinity of men they considered to be savage, subject to the vicissitudes of weather they did not understand and certainly could not control, they were intent on doing everything "decently and in order."

They stipulated when the meetings would be held ("the last Saturday in each month at one o'clock"), the procedure by which a special meeting could be called ("it shall be the duty of the President to call special meetings of the club whenever he may deem it necessary so to do), and the number of settlers required to form an official meeting ("ten men shall constitute a quorum at all club meetings; any number of men less than quorum shall be considered insufficient to transact business"). They then continued to lay out clear procedures to be used in regulating the settlement of the land adjacent to their farms: "Each member of the club shall have his or her name and the numbers of his claim recorded by the Secretary and any person not having such record with the Secretary shall not be considered a member of the Club nor be entitled to any protection from the Club."

In creating a judicial procedure for protecting the property rights of its members, the bylaws established a method by which claims to property ownership could be tested. At the very least, to even be considered as a possible owner, the would-be settler had to build a foundation at least 14 feet square on the property. Then, within 30 days the house must be completed — with a full roof and an entry door. Those unable to complete a house were required to show consistent progress, by placing a new round of logs upon the structure at least once every 7 days. But even this was not enough to establish a permanent claim; to fully secure ownership the land itself had to be put under the plow. Only settlers who had registered their claim with the club and then proceeded to build a house and plow the fields would be recognized as owners and thus entitled to protection by their fellow settlers. The fact that the settlers' progress was reported regularly to the members of the Settlers' Club ensured a paper trail that would stand up against the pretensions of claim jumpers; the fact that the settlers had to consistently maintain improvements upon the property, "as often as one day a week," protected the area from the machinations of land speculators who would stake out a property, hastily throw up a "log cabin" (usually composed of a few logs leaning against each other) and then wait for the value of the land to rise before selling it at a handsome profit to new settlers.[71]

Although what is meant by the term "protection" is not clearly explained in these documents, the following story illustrates the kind of security these clubs provided to their members. In Neosho County, in the late 1860s, a young, unmarried man by the name of Bob Campbell established a quarter-section claim. One winter, in need of the ready cash farmers in southeast Kansas seldom possessed, Campbell traveled to Missouri to find work to earn a few dollars. He left his small cabin locked up, with some furniture and a few cooking utensils in it, intending to return in a few months. When he returned in the early spring, however, he discovered that, during his absence, a man had moved into his cabin and begun to plow his fields. Instead of confronting him directly, Campbell went to his local Settlers' Club, where he registered a complaint. The claim jumper shortly thereafter was visited by three men, each with lariat ropes and guns. According to Cory, the claim jumper later revealed what transpired when the three men appeared:

> "I was out north of the house one mornin' breakin' prairie," said he, "with a pair of Texas steers. Along came a feller on horseback an' asked me whose claim that was. 'Whose claim is this you're plowin' on?' sez he, jest like thet. An' I told him 't was mine. An' he wanted to know my name, an' I told him. An' then sez he, 'I come to tell you to git off this claim; this claim belongs to Bob Campbell.' An' then, sez I, 'Who the devil are you?' An' he sez, 't was none o' my business who he wuz, but he wuz ordered to come an' tell me to git off. An' I told 'im I guessed I wouldn't, an' I didn't think he wuz big enough to put me off. Then he said he didn't want to have no trouble with me, but I hed better go. So we fussed and cussed each other for a while. An' I told him I guessed I would go on plowin.' An' he sez, 'All right; you go on plowin.' You might break one or two more furrows, but you'll have to go jest the same. Yer time has come.' An' then along come, over the ridge, two other fellers, horseback, an' both on'em had lariat ropes hangin' to the horn of their saddles. They wuz all three strangers to me, an' I don't know wher they come from ner wher they went to; but these two other fellers said I'd better get off; and I said I wouldn't do it. An' then one feller went to untyin' his lariat rope and puttin' a slip-knot into it, an' the other two fellers pulled out guns from sumers about ther close, an' they looked like mountain howitzers. I'll be damned if they didn't — to me, anyway. They didn't say nothin' more. But thet feller kept foolin' with his lariat rope and started to git off his horse. An' then, by gunny, I made up my mind I'd go. An' I went. An' you bet, I hain't ben on thet claim sence."[72]

In the absence of legal authorities, local clubs mediated various categories of disputes. Neosho County was established in 1864 by an act of the state legislature; Labette County was formed out of the southern portion of Neosho in 1867. In the early years, both counties had a rudimentary system of justice; although they elected a full set of officers, including a probate judge, coroner and sheriff, these men were not trained in any way for the exercise of their office. As the large number of "business card advertisements" (typically found in the first column of the newspapers) indicates, southeast Kansas did not lack attorneys (or, at least those who called themselves attorneys). In fact, lawyers flocked to southeast Kansas in anticipation of the looming legal battle they could see would be waged. The following advertisement indicates the potential role many attorneys wished to play: "Settlers upon the Osage Lands are hereby notified that the undersigned are now prepared to receive filings of settlement upon such lands to be presented at the Land Office in Humboldt by W.P. Bishop, who will attend in person and thus save the trouble and expense of each settler going to Humboldt. We will also attend at the Land Office at the time of proving and tender our services to those desiring assistance. Bishop and Perkins, Attorneys."[73] However, many settlers were unwilling to trust their property to such men.[74] And, even those who were, found it difficult to pay the fees lawyers charged.

District courts met twice a year (in the fall and spring), but there was no set place for these meetings. Neosho County rotated the court between several buildings. In October 1867, the first term was held at the store of Roe & Denison about two miles northwest of Erie. The second term, in April 1868, met in a small, one-story frame building which was also used as a school building. The next term, in October 1869, was held in the upper story of the Gilbert building in Erie. The court continued to meet in the Gilbert building until the spring of 1871 when it was transferred to Osage Mission. There, the court met in a hall over the Blue Wing Saloon, where, as Judge Leander Stillwell commented in his remarks on the occasion of the inauguration of the first permanent court house in Neosho County in 1904, "this close proximity of the seat of justice to a place where liquid refreshments could be obtained was quite a convenience to many members of the bar of that period, and probably, in a mild way, it was also appreciated by the Court."[75] Labette County's district court was established in 1867, but according to the county records did not hear any cases in 1867; cases only began to be heard on a semi-annual basis in 1868. Needless to say, for many settlers the court was, at best, an unreliable means of obtaining justice.

Another difficulty for settlers lay in the undependability of officials. Since their establishment in 1866–67, both counties were able to elect a full complement of officers (i.e., probate judge, county clerk, register of deeds, treasurer, coroner and sheriff), but they were unable to support them; most were thus compelled to maintain their own farms in addition to fulfilling their public duties. The size of the county, the lack of adequate roads and bridges (which made rapid travel impossible many times of the year) and the "part-time" status of county officials made "official justice" difficult to find, let alone obtain. As Nelson Case explained, "they were so far away and the organization ... was at the time so crude and imperfect, that little reliance could be placed by the settlers in this part of the county receiving any aid from the officers up there."[76]

2. Vigilance Committees and Settlers' Clubs (1868–1870)

The reminiscences of Judge Leander Stillwell offered on the occasion of the opening of the Neosho County Court-house in 1904 confirm Case's analysis:

> For some years in the early '70s and prior thereto you could seldom find to exceed two county officers under the same roof. The county clerk was at one place, the register of deeds at another, the treasurer at another, and so on. At one time I remember distinctly the county attorney held forth in New Chicago (now Chanute), the County Superintendent of Public Instruction could be found on his farm in East Lincoln, the probate Judge on his farm on the upper waters of Big Creek and such small fry as the surveyor and coroner at any old place in general, but no where in particular. The Probate Judge would attend to his alleged office only on one day in the week, to-wit, Saturday. If he was wanted in the mean time, you had to hire a livery rig and hunt him up."[77]

To underscore the difficulty this posed to the settlement of disputes, the judge reminisced about his attempt while still a lawyer to obtain justice for a group of men accused of horse-thievery:

> The only remedy in sight was a writ of Habeas Corpus, which was the great king cure all in those days. I wanted that writ then, and wanted it bad, but on inquiry, I found that Judge Fletcher was on his farm in Big Creek township, ten miles away, and 'hit a snowin'. Mike Barnes was sheriff of the county at the time and had my clients in his custody. He was a kind hearted man and good to us young lawyers, and at my earnest request he agreed simply to hold my people till I could get the desired writ. I went to Rube Lake's livery stable here in this town, got a rig consisting of an old, open buckboard drawn by a span of Indian ponies, and started to interview Jones, as we boys used to call him. I got off a little after dinner, the ground being covered with a soft, heavy snow which made the traveling difficult and laborious. Reaching Judge Fletcher's late in the afternoon, I found him not at home, and was told by the family that he had gone to New Chicago that morning, that maybe he would return that evening and maybe not till the next day. But my case would tolerate no delay, so I turned the heads of my tired ponies to the west and started for New Chicago. As the wintry sun, gleaming through the clouds angry and red, was just sinking below the prairie swells west of New Chicago, on the summit of that high divide east of the Neosho River and which overlooks the river bottom, there I met Judge Fletcher in his farm wagon on his way home. The place of our meeting was near a little log school house situated on the south side of the road. School had been dismissed, but there was no lock to the school house door, so we tied our teams to some saplings, went in and found a comfortable fire still burning in the stove. After warming our numbed hands, I produced my papers all prepared for the judge's signature, we made a raid on the children's pens and ink, the judge signed the writ, and verbally authorized me to go to his office at Osage Mission and attach to the document the seal of the Probate Court. Then we

started, he for his home and I for Erie, which place I reached about midnight. But I kept busy until the writ was duly served, and in the end my men were finally discharged.[78]

Most settlers did not have the time or the wherewithal to pursue judges throughout the countryside. The multiplicity of creeks and the lack of free ferries compounded transportation difficulties. Settlers also seldom had the patience to wait for the slow and (what often seemed to them) tedious wheels of justice. And, even when the settlers were willing and able to utilize the officials of the courts, they were frequently stymied by the rudimentary nature of justice as local Justices of the Peace vied with each other for "business" and issued contradictory rulings. Under the heading "Treason, Strategems and Spoils," the *Neosho Valley Dispatch* reported the story of a court in Labette County that was "arrested and charged with the very tall crime of conspiring to resist and obstruct the execution of the sovereign laws of the land in the county of Montgomery" in the middle of a trial! When the Labette judge refused to recognize the authority of his Montgomery County counterpart, "the authorities of Montgomery declared Labette County in a state of blockade" and initiated the early stages of "having the militia called out."[79]

Confronted by these difficulties, settlers looked to local committees and clubs who took upon themselves the responsibility of protecting the innocent and punishing the guilty. As Austin Thomas Dickerman, the author of the constitution and bylaws of an early Vigilant Committee and the first county clerk of Labette County, explained: "It was the policy of the committee to give every person taken in charge a fair trial and mete out punishment according to the merits of the case. Banishment was a common penalty. It also the policy of the committee to hang persons found guilty of grand larceny. There were no appeals from the verdicts of this pioneer court and no sharp lawyers to bring up technical points. Those who know say that the brand of justice they meted out, while stern was attended by fairness and a sincere desire to promote the public good."[80]

This was a pattern repeated in many frontier communities throughout the west. As historian Everett Dick noted in his classic work on frontier settlement, "These first settlers, running ahead of the government and its paternal protections, protected their own needs. Extralegal organizations were formed to protect the settler in his possession of the land and to act as an arbiter in the case of disputes."[81] Richard Brown agrees, arguing that Settler Clubs and Vigilance Committees "arose as a response to a typical American problem: the absence of effective law and order in a frontier town.... The regular (and by regular, I mean legal) system of law enforcement frequently proved to be woefully inadequate for the needs of the settlers."[82] In southeast Kansas, these extralegal associations were given various names (i.e., "Settlers' Clubs," "Vigilance Committees," "Solders' Clubs," "Claim Clubs," etc.) and were scattered throughout the counties. Created as a response to the initial atmosphere of legal confusion and judicial chaos southeast Kansas presented, the geographical boundaries of these clubs were undefined and often overlapped (although in time they would solidify and ultimately unite to become a single Settlers Protective Association). Some were semi-permanent and lasted for several years before disbanding; others were occasional and episodic, created in response to specific crises that confronted the communities. In each case, however, the fundamental purpose remained the same: to protect the claims of legitimate settlers and to (re-)establish social order. The historian Thomas Clark points out, "These settler organizations had an even broader implication than their function in protecting land claims; they helped to maintain law and order in the frontier community."[83] In Cory's words, "if laws were not made for them in the regular way, they would make them for themselves."[84] As Francis M. Dinsmore, a Union veteran who settled on a claim in East Lincoln (Neosho Country) in 1865, recollected in an oral interview with newspaper editor W.W. Graves: "Our first government was the vigilant committee organized for protection and to prevent claim jumping. This committee kept records of the claims of each man, etc and likewise served as a court of justice. It gave an offender a trial and if found guilty usually banished him. The mandates were always respected. It never used violence in enforcing equity."[85]

Living on the "frontier," on land until recently inhabited by the Osage native peoples (a fact they were frequently reminded of by the presence of native peoples from the nearby Indian Territory), settlers were convinced that they were living at the edge of "civilization." A comment, imbedded within a description of a church social, clearly illustrates the kind of psychological pressure many settlers experienced. As he described the overflowing tables of "cakes, pies, fruits, jellies, ice cream, lemonade and candies," John Horner remarked "It occurred to me that if I had been brought blindfolded from my native 'Hoosier State' and placed suddenly within the midst of that large, well-dressed, well-behaved, and intelligent company, ... it would have been banished forever even the very idea that this is a land of doubtful civilization and the verge of savage dominions."[86] The identity that the settlers had constructed for themselves and the internal justifications they offered for their struggles and sacrifices, required consistent and continual social reinforcement. Within this context, any behavior that threatened the social peace of the "well-dressed, well-behaved and intelligent company" of settlers could not be tolerated. As the *Neosho County Dispatch* reminded its readers, "The protection to the property and lives of individuals is imperatively required of society."[87]

It was undoubtedly true, as the editor of the *Neosho Valley Eagle* discovered, that men (and some women) of dubious past and character made their way to southeast Kansas. But, and this is where the historical story diverges from that of the popular version of the "wild, wild west" myth, these people were not welcomed by the majority of settlers who had come to southeast Kansas with a deep desire for order and a commitment to work as a community to build supporting interpersonal attachments and social networks. As the *Neosho Valley Eagle* explained, "The rough pioneers so common in the early settlement of some of the western States are few here. The 'backwoodsman' has but little show in a country like ours."[88]

Richard White has commented in his description of the settling of the West, "Communities aspired to create order, predictability, security, mutuality, and familiarity. They promised a known, bounded world."[89] Phillip Paludan confirms this analysis: "In regions lacking controlled settlement strong respect for the necessity of an ordered way of doing things tended to prevail. Settlers created their own law and enforced it."[90] This was the reality that the settlers struggled to create for themselves. As veterans brought their wives and children with them to take up claims, build towns and establish communities, they were thus acutely conscious of their civic responsibilities. For settlers, as Paludan explains, "Government ... was not them; it was us."[91] Historian Earl Hess argues that "self-government was a system ... in which the average citizen had a very real and personal stake."[92]

This commitment could be framed as a negative rejection of centralized government and corporate monopolies but also a positive engagement in community building. Hess continues, "No laws, social organizations or governmental interference were called for as long as the citizen respected the rights of all, while he enjoyed his own."[93] The bedrock of their political philosophy was the notion of individualism — a strong belief in the autonomy of the individual. Historian Melinda Lawson explains, "Americans believed that a national state was formed by a contract that guaranteed them a body of rights and bound their country to an ideal. If the state violated those rights, or failed in its continuing representation of that ideal, the contract could be broken."[94] The comments of the best-selling antebellum author George Sidney Camp expressed this perspective clearly; Camp had argued in 1841 that "laws are merely the resolutions of a community to abide by and enforce the principles of justice."[95] As Professor Bigger of the Johnson County (Mo.) Normal School explained to his students in 1867: "The right of the people to take care of themselves, if the law does not, is an indisputable right."[96] That this was the attitude of the early settlers in southeast Kansas is clearly revealed by the statements of the *Neosho Valley Dispatch* which argued "Society has a right to protect itself and the property of its individuals from danger, emanate from what source it will, and when the ordinary rules of action fall short of accomplishing the desired end, extraordinary ones must be invoked.... We hope that hereafter the people of Neosho County will see to it that the law shall be something more than a dead letter, an artificial scarecrow that can be thrown down and trod over at the will of him who may."[97]

Settler society was governed by a set of (often) unwritten rules and assumptions. These assumptions governed the interactions of people within the nascent communities and were based on preconceived notions of race, gender and class as well fundamental convictions about the inherent differences between men, women and children. To the early settlers, these convictions were at the heart of their notions of "civilization" and thus, their defense was absolutely essential to the existence of the communities they were seeking to build. As the editor of the *Kansas Democrat* noted, "Onward and upward and outward shall be the watchword of every true man. The coward only wavers and trembles and falters and turns back, such would better remain back. The churches of the east, with all their pomp and pride and paganism and good, send up no better record than does the stern pioneer, in his manly efforts to extend the boundaries of civilization, to care for himself, his wife and little ones, a threshold and hearth stone that will perpetuate and stand as a monument to his memory after he and they shall cease to enjoy them. Effort, hardships, hard work, beating back and over coming obstacles, strong men glory in. They take hold and lift themselves out of all difficulties and become master of every situation. They aid others too by examples to stronger pulls and final success."[98]

In southeast Kansas there was no place for "weak men"; the *Kansas Democrat* suggested that every "cowardly man" should return to "his wife's people." There was also no room for those who were unwilling (or unable) to live by commonly accepted norms. Anyone who violated them could no longer remain as a member of the community; the penalty was either banishment or capital punishment. Justice demanded the removal of the criminal; not his rehabilitation. The geographic boundaries of the settlers' land were mirrored by behavioral boundaries; by failing to observe the latter the transgressor lost the privilege of inhabiting the former.

In the worldview of 19th-century immigrants to southeast Kansas, certain crimes threatened the essential structure of society. To allow those who committed these heinous acts to go unpunished would initiate a process that would quickly destroy all that they were sacrificing so much to build. Thus, even when they were forced, because of the absence of strong legal structures, to create their own, this did not imply disrespect for those structures or an unwillingness to be governed by law. In fact, the opposite was true. As the historian William Culberson has noted, "When civil government was not sufficiently organized or established to control or punish violators of public peace, community leaders of the Old West often took matters into their own hands, and met violence with violence. Vigilantism arose from practical needs in the absence of foundations regulating social order."[99] The creation of Settlers' Clubs and Vigilance Committees allowed settlers in southeast Kansas to establish and maintain the institutions that made the community function.

Historian Michael Pfeifer has used the term "rough justice" to describe the mentality of 19th-century Americans. After making the observation that "historians have not noticed that extralegal violence also flourished in the Midwest into the late nineteenth century," Pfeifer roots this violence in the particular social context of the postbellum West. "Real justice was lodged in the community. It was administered face-to-face with a measure of retribution that matched the offense, and it sought to 'preserve order,' ... Law only had value as far as it served this understanding of justice." An interesting comment in the *Chetopa Advance* demonstrates the deeply held notions of justice. After describing the horrific torture and murder of a local settler, John Horner commented: "Justice cries out from the lonely grave and mercy will hide her face until the mercy they gave to poor 'Milt' is meted out tenfold to them."[100] Justice was defined by "a cultural context that demanded the harsh, personal, informal and communally supervised punishment of what was perceived as serious criminal behavior."[101]

The legal scholar Herbert Packer has described this approach to confronting criminal behavior as the "Crime Control Model" of social justice. Based on the belief that the failure to bring criminal conduct under tight control will inevitably lead to the breakdown of public order and thence to the disappearance of an important condition of human freedom, the Crime Control Model assumes that "if the laws go unenforced ... a general disregard for legal controls tends to develop. The law abiding citizen then becomes the victim of all sorts of unjustifiable invasions of his interest. His security of person and property is sharply diminished and therefore, so is his liberty to function as a member of society." Instead of emphasizing the importance of due process, "the Crime Control Model requires that primary attention be paid to the efficiency with which the criminal process operates to screen suspects, determine guilt and secure appropriate dispositions of persons convicted of crime."[102] Within this perspective, partic-

2. Vigilance Committees and Settlers' Clubs (1868–1870)

ipants in extralegal associations did not see their behavior as being outside or above the law; they were serving the law by punishing those who broke it.

This point was made explicit by an editorial that appeared in the *Parsons Eclipse*. Commenting on the recent hanging of a murderer by the citizens of the city of Jacksonville, the editor wrote:

> A feeble administration of the law the effect to cause the taking of his execution into their own hands, and do speedily and cheaply what might have been sought in vain at great public expense. They naturally reason with themselves, it is a poor satisfaction for the life of a fellow-citizen, and the injured peace and dignity of the community, to be dragged around from post to pillar for a year or two to make three or four thousand dollars expense for the county, and succeed in getting a culprit into the penitentiary at last, only to be pardoned out by the Governor in order to give still another influence for some future political race. Such trifling has the effect to bring the law into contempt; the balance and the rod should be held with a firm hand and when people feel they can trust the regularly prescribed process of law to deal with these high offences with a strong hand, that their lives and the peace of community are safe under its protection, then and not till then, mob violence will cease.[103]

This helps to explain why the leaders of the "Vigilance Committees" and "Settlers' Clubs" were primarily the elite of southeast Kansas. In defending the existing social order, they were both protecting their own places in society and upholding their vision for the future of southeast Kansas. As the editor of the *Neosho Valley Eagle* urged his readers on the occasion of Jacksonville's first official celebration of the 4th of July: "Let us fondly hope that our own bright Ark of Liberty may successfully breast every billow and breaker of discord or anarchy, and that each returning anniversary of our nation's birthday may find our people more firmly united, happy and prosperous, and the world may say of us and our institutions: they are 'Like Nature's bulwarks built by Time, Against eternity to stand.'"[104]

The historian Richard Maxwell Brown has pointed to the existence of two important cultural characteristics (localism and instrumentalism) to explain the existence of vigilantism in the nineteenth century. Basing his interpretation on the work of the legal historian James Willard Hurst and the legal scholar Herbert L. Packer, Brown concludes: "Americans did not feel any less public spirited when they participated in lynch law. Instead they saw vigilante participation as an act of public spirit in its own way as the election of upright officials. Americans felt that there were certain functions in preserving public order that the legal authorities would not, could not or should not be expected to perform. These functions the people themselves assumed as vigilantes."[105]

Although the Settlers' Clubs in southeast Kansas were originally organized for the protection of private property, it is a mistake to understand their concerns to be solely economic. In point of fact, the protection of private property was an essential building block to the establishment of an ordered and structured society. As Brown explains, "The American community of the 18th and 19th centuries was primarily a property-holder's community and property was viewed as the very basis of life itself."[106] Protecting private property therefore was one way of ensuring the achievement of the much larger goal of the "preservation of the hierarchical prerogatives of the dominant residents of the locality" through the imposition of "communally based solutions to the dilemmas of social order ostensibly provoked by serious criminal acts."[107]

Horse thieves were a menace because they imperiled not only the settler's ability to improve his land, but also his standing in and engagement with the local community. The early newspapers are replete with notices about lost horses and with warnings similar to that of the *Neosho Valley Eagle* which cautioned its readers, "Horse thieves are plenty in this and surrounding counties. Watch your horses."[108] For settlers, horses were absolutely essential to survival. Horses were the sole means of transportation; as F.M. Dinsmore remembered: "a riding pony was usually kept lariated near the house to be used in times of emergency."[109] Horses also provided entertainment, as evidenced by the following notice in the *Neosho Valley Eagle*, "A little horse race took place in our town on Saturday the 13th in which a pony from Labette County took the stakes. Jacksonville holds some fast stock, and we've money that says so. Fetch along your rusty nags."[110] More importantly, in this early community, horses were an important symbol of status. As Cory explained, "For instance, Uncle David Fowler on Flat Rock Creek, lived in a five room house with a roof of sawed shingles; he actually had a team of good American horses. He was a bloated plutocrat. But then he was so kind and genial that we didn't hate him. Then there was a somewhat larger class of aristocrats who had mustangs and Indian ponies. It must be admitted that they were a little inclined to be patronizing to us fellows who had to drive oxen to church."[111]

The theft of a horse was a direct assault on the ordered community the settlers were seeking to establish. Thus, as Judge Stillwell explained, "People were most particular and 'tetchy' about their horses in those days."[112] Settlers worked together to recover lost horses and to dissuade those so inclined from future thievery. As the *Osage Mission Journal* reported, "During the summer several horses were stolen from the good people along Big Creek. And they thinking the Kansas law slow to punish horse thieves have organized themselves into a vigilance committee. We

2. Vigilance Committees and Settlers' Clubs (1868–1870)   83

learn that about sixty of our best citizens belong to the organization and horse thieves visiting the neighbors in the future will doubtless have the pleasure of looking up a limb. Suspicious characters are taking the hint and leaving the neighborhood."[113] As a brief note in a later edition of the *Journal* made perfectly clear, this was not an idle threat. The *Journal* reported, under the heading "Man Hung," that "a man named Coleman, living on Flat Rock, has been hung by a party of citizens on the supposition that he was a horse thief."[114]

Another threat to property which the Settlers' Clubs confronted was that of the Texas Cattle Trade. In the 1860s, it was common practice for ranchers to drive their cattle through Labette and Neosho Counties to northern markets. Like many Kansans in this period, settlers in southeast Kansas were convinced that Texas Cattle spread disease to their own flocks. Thus, as the counties began to fill with people, one of the earliest concerns was how to stop the Drive. As the *Osage Mission Journal* informed its readers, "We understand that meetings have been held in many parts of southern Kansas and that the people have resolved to stop this cattle importation at all hazards." Interestingly, the *Journal* also proceeded to utter a warning: "Owners of good stock are alarmed and have taken precautions to prevent further introduction of southern cattle into our midst. We are not at liberty to state what these precautions are, suffice it to say, that we advise all owners and drivers of southern cattle, if they value their property and their own lives, to avoid Neosho County."[115]

One of the meetings mentioned in the newspaper was held on September 9, 1868, in Osage Mission. At this meeting, the settlers unanimously passed the following resolutions:

> Resolved, that we the people of Neosho County, in mass meeting, assembled in order to protect ourselves and our property from the ravages of disease introduced by such cattle do enter our solemn protest against the driving of the same into or through our county.
>
> Resolved, that we as a law abiding community are in favor of submitting to the laws enacted for our government; but when such laws are not enforced we are in favor of protecting ourselves and property by force if necessary.
>
> Resolved, furthermore, that we hereby invite every man in Neosho County to cooperate with us in our endeavors to protect our stock from diseases introduced by Texas and Indian cattle.[116]

The structure of this set of resolutions is striking; the settlers list their grievances and then logically state their own response. They were very concerned not to appear "out of control" or to behave as lawless vigilantes. The settlers wanted their actions to appear rational and orderly; they have been forced to defend their property against those who flaunt the law. The wording is official; they speak of their actions as a "solemn protest" against the "ravages of disease." They emphasize that they are a "law-abiding community" who are only responding to the unlawful activities of others; they are only acting because the existing laws have not been "enforced." From the vantage point of 21st-century social norms, these settlers were taking the law into their own hands; they, however, did not believe that they were.

Settlers did not see their clubs and committees as being in conflict with legal authorities but instead understood themselves to be cooperating with official personnel in order to enforce existing statutes. Another example of this attitude is revealed in the manner in which settlers responded to the disappearance of two of its prominent citizens in 1870. After noting that there "can be but little doubt that either one or both parties have fallen victims to a murderous conspiracy," the *Osage Mission Journal* applauded the people of Elston for their proactive response and urged the officials to coordinate their efforts to support the community: "We understand that the citizens of Elston are doing all they can to clear up the mystery and it is proper that the representatives of law and order all over the country should use their authority in aiding them. When innocent and unoffending citizens become the victims of foul strategy at our very doors it is high time that the people woke up to self-protection."[117]

Veteran settlers prided themselves on their commitment to law and order; they were certainly willing to stand by and allow the legal authorities to enforce it. But when the political situation was unresolved and the presence of the law periodic and irregular, the settlers would not sit by and allow lawbreakers to destroy their lives and steal their property. As the *Neosho Valley Dispatch* reported, "We learn that a number of farmers adjoining Erie, who have heretofore suffered a loss of stock by reason of the introduction of deceased cattle, propose undertaking such means as will prove a preventative to any further loss." The next statement clearly explained their reasoning: "They have become satisfied that the laws upon the statute book are of but little value and that a more summary dispensation of justice is necessary."[118] In the minds of these farmers, taking extra-legal action against lawbreakers was justified by the demands of justice. They would uphold the law by enforcing it themselves![119]

An example of their determination and joint action took place in the spring of 1869. A man by the name Dunn drove a large number of Texas cattle into Richland Township. According to the citizens, the cattle were badly diseased and posed a serious threat to their own stock. They therefore took possession of the cattle and arrested the owners; however, when they brought Dunn and his workers before the local Justice of the Peace, the cattle traders were acquitted. After being cleared of the charge of driving diseased stock into the State, the cowboys left Richland Township and headed towards Missouri. Before leaving, however, they boasted that they would bring a large number of cattle back into the Township at a later date. The *Neosho Valley Dispatch* recorded the settlers' reaction to this threat: "The citizens of Richland Township have unanimously resolved that if the law will not protect them, they will take the matter in their own hands, and are determined that Texas stock and they diseased, shall neither be driven through the Township nor herded in it, and ask the cooperation of all the citizens of other Townships in this matter. They claim that it is done for self-protection and propose to fight it out on this line if it takes all summer."[120]

In Osage Mission on January 18, 1869, in a meeting to declare their intentions to form a Settlers' Club in defense of their property rights, the settlers asked a series of rhetorical questions that highlighted their perspective clearly:

> What has capital, in the shape of railroad monopolies, done for the development of the resources of Kansas compared with the arduous trials, sacrifices and sufferings of the hardy pioneers in opening up and improving this soil?
>
> Was it the capitalist or laboring man that bared his breast and stood a living wall of adamant between our late domestic foes and the threatened disruption of our country, and which prevented the realization of that disastrous fate?

The answer to the first was clearly "Nothing" and to the second "the laborer." They had earned the right to be heard; they had proven their ability to fight for a just cause. They had saved the Union. They were bringing civilization to the West. It was inconceivable, therefore, for them to allow their fellow-soldiers to be swindled out of their farms, their cattle to be diseased, and their horses to be stolen.

Three basic types of crimes necessitated swift and severe justice in the late 1860s and early 1870s. The first was any violation of the community's hospitality or disrespect for its hierarchy; the second was the theft of private property; and the third was the abuse of weaker, defenseless members of the community. To these early settlers, each one of these crimes struck at the very heart of the society they were seeking to build and could not be tolerated. Settlers were forced to depend upon the goodwill and trust of fellow settlers. Thrust into a situation in which they were struggling for their very survival, they depended upon each other. Any violation of that trust threatened the community and necessitated swift and forceful rebuttal. An interesting comment in the *Osage Mission Journal* helps to elucidate the attitudes of the settlers towards their own responsibility for upholding and enforcing the law. After describing the activities of a "mob" in "cleaning out" a house of prostitution, the editor then explained that the "mob then paid their respects to a house in the eastern part of the city, warning the inmates to leave or they would be dealt with according to the law."[121] Quite clearly, the people involved in this "mob action" did not think that they were acting in opposition to the law — they were upholding it by enforcing it.

Perhaps no story illustrates this better than the brutal tale of murder, abduction and gang rape that occurred in the summer of 1870. On May 10, a group of seven men entered the small town of Ladore and, after a few hours of drinking in the local saloon, proceeded to terrorize the citizens. After screaming obscenities at those whom they found on the streets and firing pistol shots repeatedly in the air, the drunken seven advanced to the largest house which was built just outside the town; it was owned by the city's founder, I.N. Roach. Forcing their way into the house where they were met by Roach, they beat him with their pistols and clubs, leaving him unconscious and covered in blood on the floor of the front room. Stationing a man outside to guard against any outside interference, the remaining men savagely tortured and raped Roach's two young female servants throughout the night. As reported in the *Osage Mission Journal*, the crime was especially abhorrent given their young ages — "the two girls were sisters, and one of them was not twelve years old." In the morning, the men attempted to slip out of town. However, since one of the perpetrators had been shot by his comrades in the night, his dead body was discovered by the townsmen wrapped in a blanket next to an insensible girl. Immediately, as the *Journal* explained, "the alarm was given — an organization effected and pursuit commenced." A posse of almost three hundred men set out in pursuit and quickly caught the six men. A hasty trial followed in which it was decided that five of the men deserved to die. Since the sixth man had remained outside the house and thus had not participated in either the beating or the rape, it was decided to turn him over to the local authorities. Justice demanded, however, that the five die for their crimes. Thus, rope was brought and the men were immediately suspended from the limbs of a large hackberry tree that grew near the town along the banks of the Labette River. It was their lifeless bodies that first greeted the sheriff and coroner as they made their way to Ladore. Upon entering the town, the coroner summoned a jury and initiated an inquest while the sheriff arrested the lone living perpetrator. The *Journal* summarized what happened next: "In the case of the man who was shot, the jury returned a verdict that the deceased came to his death by reason of a pistol shot discharged by a person unknown, and inflicted while the deceased was attempting to commit a rape. The verdict in the case of the five men who were hung was that "they came to their death by reason of strangulation inflected and caused by persons to the jury unknown."

Since the men who served on the jury were residents of Ladore and eye-witnesses to the events that had transpired, it defies logic to believe that they were unaware of who had been involved. Yet, as the *Journal* informed its readers, "The most rigid questioning of witnesses by the Coroner failed to elicit any information as to who were concerned in the lynching, although it is said that more than three hundred of the most respectable men of the community witnessed the affair." Quite clearly, therefore, the men of Ladore believed that their actions had been justified; the crime had been so abhorrent that immediate action was required to restore integrity to the community whose social order had been so violated. The editor of the *Journal* was forced to concur — "We exceedingly regret that any persons should deem it necessary to take lives of human beings 'without due process of law'— heretofore, we have borne the reputation of being a law abiding people. If the people of Ladore and vicinity have forfeited it, they certainly had grave reason for their proceedings. If justification is possible, they are *justified*."[122] The editor of the *Kansas Democrat* agreed by noting: "We are opposed to mob law under general principles, but under the circumstances which surrounded this shocking crime, the sooner an outraged community suspends the scoundrels between the heavens and the earth, the better."[123] The men who came to southeast Kansas brought with them fundamental assumptions about their role as protectors of women and children; when forced, of necessity, to leave their wives and children alone and defenseless for long stretches of time as they labored in the fields from dawn to dusk or traveled to distant towns for winter work and supplies, they depended on the moral decency of their neighbors and incoming settlers. Thus, any assault on a woman or child was a direct attack on the masculine structure of society and could not be tolerated — as Charles Dash discovered. Dash killed his wife on Tuesday night, December 20, and the next morning his neighbors "collected and hung him."[124]

At times, the settlers cooperated with the existing authorities in responding to this crime. On February 27, 1868, a settler by the name of Clay Livingston, who had staked a claim with his wife and two boys near Big Creek stream in Neosho County, strangled his wife to death. It was a very strange tale. A Civil War veteran, Livingston was 50 years old, his wife 24 and the boys aged eight and 13. On the evening of February 27, Livingston began to act strangely (according to the report of the 13-year-old boy). He locked all of the doors and then took the unusual precaution to completely nail up the front door so that it could not be opened from the inside. He then confined the boys to the loft, instructing them to sleep on the floor, by locking the trap door so that they could not descend. Sometime in the middle of the night, the older boy was awakened by the cries of the woman, who was begging someone not to kill her. Although he had been trapped in the loft, he managed to escape and, once freed, he ran to the neighbors to tell them what he had heard. The neighbors contacted the legal authorities as well as members of the local Vigilance Committee. Upon the arrival of T.F. Rager, the local justice of the peace, a number of citizens joined him in proceeding to the house. When they entered, they found the woman lying upon the bed dead. An examination showed that she had been strangled. Since there was no sign of forced entry, the evidence clearly pointed to Livingston as the murderer. The justice agreed and in further discussions with the settlers decided that the crime merited death. Thus, as Rager later recalled, "late in the evening a group of citizens gathered Livingston from his home and hung him in a nearby tree."[125]

Cooperation between the legal authorities and extra-legal committees was surprisingly (by modern standards) frequent. Sometimes the authorities looked to local citizens for support; other times the local citizens could overwhelm local authorities and bend them to their will. A case of the former occurred in the summer of 1870. The body of a young boy who had been reported missing by his mother was found in a well. His stepfather, E.G. Dalson, was known to his neighbors as possessing a violent temper and so suspicion immediately pointed to him. The local sheriff therefore interrogated Dalson, and after obtaining a confession, arrested him and lodged him in the county jail to await the arrival of the justice. However, towards evening as news of the arrest and confession circulated through the town of Oswego, a large crowd gathered outside the home of the sheriff and demanded that the prisoner be released to their custody. The sheriff complied with their request and delivered Dalson to them bound and gagged. Taking him to a barn, the crowd strung him up and hanged him. As the *Oswego Register* reported the story, it defended the actions of the mob by revealing the nature of Dalson's confession: "that he had been punishing the boy with a switch; that he was impudent when Dalson placed his foot on the boy's neck to hold him down and, when released was found to be nearly dead and soon expired. He then threw the body into the well to conceal his crime."[126]

At other times, settlers acted on their own either to repair what was (in their estimation) a miscarriage of justice or to deal with a situation that the authorities were either unwilling or unable to manage. In November 1868, a man by the name of Thomas Oden moved with his family from

2. Vigilance Committees and Settlers' Clubs (1868–1870)   89

Missouri, into the western portion of Labette County near the Verdigris River. Shortly thereafter he attempted to "jump" one of the oldest claims in the county, owned by William Parker. Parker appealed to the local Settlers' Club to verify his claim, and for a while it looked as if Oden had accepted their decision. However, early in the morning of January 25, Oden returned to Parker's cabin with his brother William, where they brutally beat him to death. They then loaded Parker into their wagon and took him to the house of William Phelps, one of the leaders of the local Settlers' Club, and unceremoniously deposited him, announcing: "Here is your man, dead." As they departed, Phelps immediately alerted his fellow settlers to what had happened. A Settlers' Court was hastily called, the evidence was presented and the verdict reached that Parker had come to this death at the hands of William and Thomas Oden. When word reached the Odens of what had transpired, they sent word that they would not accept the deliberations of the Settlers' Court but would only give themselves up only to a justice of the peace so that the matter could be settled by the legitimate authorities.

When they finally were taken to the justice of the peace in Labette County, a trial was held which the settlers considered to be a "sham." According to the account published in the *Chetopa Advance*, "it was a trial in which one of them appeared as his own accuser ... a trial in which it was reported that no evidence for the prosecution had been adduced — a sham trial in which six men sat as jurors, instead of an examination as the law provides." The Odens were thus acquitted and returned to take up residence in what had been the Parker house. As the news of the events circulated, citizens throughout Labette County were outraged. Several Vigilance Committees and Settlers' Clubs sprang into action and dispersed members to investigate the scene of the crime, try the case (if necessary) and administer justice. Twenty-five men set out from the Chetopa region; when they arrived, they discovered the evidence of a shoot-out and the dead bodies of both Thomas and William Oden. Apparently, another committee's men had arrived earlier and had already administered the justice that the community had demanded. As the editor of the *Chetopa Advance*, who had accompanied the posse of 25 men, explained, "It was a plain case of unprovoked, cold blooded murder, which could not go unavenged with safety to the community."[127]

A similar situation erupted in the late summer of 1870 in the Ladore and Chetopa townships of Labette County. A man by the name of James Barrett was arrested on the charge of bringing Texas Cattle into the county illegally. There was confusion over which court had jurisdiction — he was first brought before the Ladore justice of the peace, but after some delay, was transferred to the court of Thomas Burns, the justice of the peace in Chetopa Township. However, as the court waited for Burns, Barrett escaped and immediately fled north into Neosho County. He was arrested in Osage Mission and brought before Rager, the local justice. The court immediately heard the case and, after finding that Barrett was guilty, commissioned the local sheriff to drive the cattle out of the state. By this point, the local citizenry had lost patience, and (as the *Neosho Valley Dispatch* later reported) "a number of the citizens of the county, variously estimated at from one to two hundred, surrounded the drove and shot and killed the entire number."[128]

The citizens of Oswego responded in a similar fashion to the presence of a house of prostitution that was established on the outskirts of town in 1870. As reported in the *Kansas Democrat*, "A house not suspected of being overly virtuous was cleaned out Tuesday night. The windows were smashed in and the house otherwise injured, and the gay Sore-o-Sis gals [prostitutes] left on the first train." As the editor explained, "While we are opposed to taking the law out of the hands of those who are its custodians, yet when you cannot reach this class of houses and sinks of iniquity any other way, we say go in and wipe them out. Bully for the unknown hands that sent these nymphs afloat."[129]

Those who violated the community's trust were especially unwelcome and posed a direct threat to the longevity of the pioneer experiment. A clear example of this is found in the case of "one McGreggor." McGreggor had lived in Tioga (Neosho County) for several months in 1870. A boisterous and violent man, he arrested for threatening the lives of citizens and was transferred out of the county to the jail in Allen County. In jail, however, he became sick. Finding hope in the relationships he had established in Tioga, he then sent a pleading letter to Samuel Wickard (described in the paper as a "prominent citizen of Tioga") asking for money so that he could pay the fines associated with his crimes and be released from prison (which he blamed for his illness). Wickard responded positively and raised the needed money by asking for donations from other "prominent citizens." In sending the money, however, he laid down the stipulation that McGreggor was never to return, stating that "if he did he would have to suffer the consequences." When, McGreggor ignored this warning and returned to Tioga upon his release, the people were alarmed and took action to defend their collective honor. As the paper reported, "the vigilance of our citizens being on the alert watched his movements until a favorable opportunity offered, when he was given ten minutes to make good his exit from the town, which he did *instanter*. This McGreggor is a desperate character and always goes well armed. The next breach of his contract here, he won't be allotted ten minutes."¹³⁰ The charity of the community, so graciously expressed in monetary donations, did not change the essential requirement that the person who transgressed the behavioral boundaries of the community must leave the community. McGreggor had demonstrated his unwillingness to abide by community standards both by threatening his neighbors and by not heeding the "advice" of its prominent citizens; this violation of social order (notably described in the paper as a "breach of his contract") could not be tolerated without serious damage to the social arrangement (i.e., the "contract") by which the community survived.

3

THE TRANSFORMATION OF SETTLER SOCIETY (1870)

On April 17, 1869, the *Humboldt Union* (the "Official Paper of the Land Office") published encouraging news for settlers on the Osage Ceded Lands. According to dispatches just received, the paper announced, a resolution had been passed by Congress and approved by the president guaranteeing that their land, "a strip 30 miles wide across the east end and a strip 20 miles wide on the north side of the Osage lands, ... can now be sold to actual settlers in the same manner and at the same price as other public lands."[1] As the news spread throughout Labette and Neosho Counties, excitement grew. The settlers were ecstatic. Newspaper editors joined the fray, assuring them that the resolution and its accompanying instructions to the Land Office "fully settle the Osage Land Question in favor of the actual settler."[2] As the editor of the *Osage Mission Journal* announced, "In common with our entire community and the great body of settlers on the Osage Lands we rejoice that this vexed questions of title has at length been adjusted.... A great feeling of relief is experienced by all."[3]

The settlers believed that right had prevailed and that they had won. Thus, throughout the summer of 1869, in anticipation of the opening of the Land Office in September, they met throughout the counties, in various locations, to celebrate and to declare their commitment to support each other. Meetings were held in Neola (June 17), Erie (June 30) and in many locations on July 4. The largest and most jubilant assemblage was held in Jacksonville on July 28. As reported by the *Chetopa Advance*: "The largest assemblage ever gathered in southern Kansas convened to listen to the distinguished speakers who had been announced to be present. Men, women and children, in wagons and on horseback, on foot, by every conceivable mode of conveyance flocked to the grove adjacent to town at an early hour of the morning. The Oswego Band came in on time as they always do with music hard to be matched."[4]

39TH CONGRESS, } HOUSE OF REPRESENTATIVES. { MIS. DOC.
2d Session. } { No. 32.

SETTLERS ON OSAGE LANDS.

RESOLUTION

OF

THE LEGISLATURE OF KANSAS,

PRAYING

The passage of a bill extending the benefit of the Homestead Law to the settlers on the lands recently purchased from the Osage Indians.

JANUARY 25, 1867.—Referred to the Committee on the Public Lands and ordered to be printed.

Be it resolved by the senate, (the house of representatives concurring therein,) That the Congress of the United States be, and they are hereby, memorialized to extend, if consistent with the public interest, the benefit of the homestead law to the settlers on the lands recently purchased from the Osage Indians, and known as the east treaty.

Be it further resolved, That the secretary of state be instructed to forward a certified copy of these resolutions to each of our senators and our representative in Congress, and a copy to the Secretary of the Interior, who are hereby requested to bring the subject to the attention of that body at as early a day as practicable.

Adopted by the senate, January 16, 1867.

ALEX. R. BANKS,
Secretary of the Senate.

Concurred in by the house of representatives, January 17, 1867.

JOHN S. MORTON,
Chief Clerk.

I, R. A. Barker, secretary of state, do hereby certify that the foregoing is a true and correct copy of the original on file.

In testimony whereof, I have subscribed my name and affixed the great seal of the State, January 17, 1867.

[SEAL.]

R. A. BARKER,
Secretary of State.

This resolution from the House of Representatives mandates that the requirements for settlement under the Homestead Act of 1862 be extended to lands in Kansas recently purchased from the Osage Indians. Copied from *The Miscellaneous Documents of the House of Representatives*, 2nd session, 39th Congress.

After listening to speeches during the day, the crowd celebrated late into the evening. As many as two thousand people gathered in the public square to participate in what was billed as "Pomeroy's Funeral." An effigy of Senator Pomeroy, long suspected by the settlers to be on the payroll of monopolists and speculators, was suspended above the ground and, as the settlers screamed and yelled, set on fire. The revelers then set in for a long night of music and dancing, followed by another day of speeches. All in all, as reported by the *Osage Mission Journal*, "great enthusiasm prevails[ed]."[5]

The settlers were soon to discover, however, their enthusiasm to be short-lived. The Land Office officially opened its doors to settlers on the Osage Ceded Lands on September 2. Many settlers traveled across the northern Neosho County line to Humboldt to register their claims; when they arrived, however, to their dismay, they found railroad lawyers waiting for them. As the *Osage Mission Journal* explained: "The great majority of settlers on the Osage Lands affected by the joint resolution had made arrangements to attend to perfect their claims and expected to do so with but little delay or trouble where they came within the beneficial provisions of the act in question. But at the outset they were doomed to disappointment and found that the railroad companies claiming a large portion of these lands under grants of Congress withdrawing them from sale for the benefit of such roads were intending to contest every claim made and if possible keep it from the settler."[6]

The *Neosho County Dispatch* reported a similar sense of disappointment: "Upon passage of the joint resolution, a large majority of the settlers felt quite jubilant over the prospect of soon realizing this long desire but are now again doomed to disappointment by the construction put upon it by the wise men who passed and the long-headed officials who are to carry out its humane and magnanimous provisions."[7]

According to the reports that circulated, several obstacles were put in the way of the settlers. Buried within the resolution passed by Congress (and thus not emphasized by the local papers) had been an agreement that the railroads could lay claim to the odd numbered sections that lay within 10 miles of either side of the road. Many settlers thus found that their claims could not be entered because they had already been claimed. In addition, under heavy pressure by railroad lawyers, the land agents chose to interpret the resolution's mention of "bona fide settlers" very strictly. As one settler (who signed his name as *C.*) bitterly complained, "Young men who have made improvements on odd sections or even sections outside of the ten mile limits but boarded with a neighbor and cultivated and improved their claims cannot enter under the present rulings." Each settler

3. The Transformation of Settler Society (1870)

who came forward to present his claim found himself grilled by an attorney from the railroads; as noted by C., "The Railroad Attorney, Dr. Torbert, subjects all parties applying to enter odd numbered sections and the even numbered sections outside of the first ten mile limits to a very rigid cross examination."[8] The *Neosho County Dispatch* reported that out of the two thousand petitions initially received by the Land Office, only sixty were approved.[9]

The response of the settlers was frustration and anger; as settler C. dryly noted, "Considerable feeling among the settlers here toward the Railroad agents."[10] The *Dispatch* explained, "The hard-fisted yeomanry do not understand why it is they are prevented from securing homes by the officers of the local office.... Four-fifths of the settlers in this

Pomeroy served as United States Senator from April 4, 1861, to March 3, 1873.

and Labette counties are honorably discharged soldiers who, upon the termination of the war, came to Southern Kansas with the view of making it their future home and having led four years of degraded camp life in the army are not so fascinated with the manner thereof as to continue therein now that the mantle of the civilian rests upon them."[11] In similar fashion, the *Osage Mission Journal* made the settlers' displeasure very clear as it declaimed "the spirit of Shylock avarice thus shown has already caused a bitter feeling of opposition to spring up among the settlers who will not submit to any injustice or chicanery in this matter so vital to them all."[12]

Within days of the opening of the Land Office, as news of the difficulties circulated, a renewed sense of "republican anxiety" gripped the settlers. Convinced that their rights were being violated by a conspiracy of greedy monopolists and corrupt politicians, a large number of concerned settlers gathered to discuss their options on September 15 in Jacksonville. After several fiery speeches in which the perceived collusion between the Land Office and the railroads was roundly denounced, the assembled men agreed to hold a series of meetings throughout the Ceded Lands — in Erie on the first Saturday in October, Osage Mission on October 4, Ladore on October 5, Jacksonville on October 6, Oswego on October 7, Elston on October 8 and McCormick's Big Hill on October 9. The purpose of these meetings, as noted in the *Dispatch*, was "to take into consideration the status of affairs in regard to the entry of the Osage Lands under the joint resolution of April 10th, 1869.... Let the people turn out and unite on some method of securing their rights."[13]

The question faced by the settlers was what they should do next. Their options were limited; with their backs against the proverbial wall, and their homesteads threatened, they could easily have resorted to violence. But they did not — instead choosing to pursue a legal battle by fighting both the Land Office and the railroads in court. As a correspondent of the *Lawrence Tribune* who visited Jacksonville in the summer of 1870 explained, "The feeling against the railroad is as bitter as ever, but the threats of violence have given way to an earnest determination to test the validity of its title in the courts and in the halls of Congress to the last."[14]

This choice, not to use guerrilla-style violence but instead to use the available legal means, is all the more important to note because of the violence that was pursued by their neighbors, the settlers living to their east (present-day Cherokee and Crawford counties). Settlers in the Osage Ceded Lands were deeply interested in the ongoing struggle being waged on these lands, called at the time, the Cherokee Neutral Lands. In many respects, the situation of settlers on the Osage Ceded Lands and the Cherokee Neutral Lands was similar. Both groups had come as squatters upon receiving the news of pending treaties with Native peoples. Both faced the rival claims of railroads and, within a context of legal uncertainty, were forced to form extralegal clubs and committees to record claims and establish social order. In fact, from the beginning, settlers from both regions had joined together in political rallies and community festivals. It was common for local clubs and committees through Labette and Neosho counties to end their meetings with statements of support similar to the following resolution: "RESOLVED: that to the settlers on the Cherokee Neutral Lands who are sought to be divested of their homes by the nefarious schemes of a corrupt speculator, one James F. Joy, we extend our earnest sympathy and assure them of all the assistance and co-operation in our power."[15] Passed by settlers who had gathered in Erie on March 20, 1869, to urge Representative Sidney Clarke to defend their interests in Congress, it illustrates the solidarity settlers on the Osage Ceded Lands felt with the settlers on the Cherokee Neutral Lands.

But there were significant differences as well. Specifically, the neutral lands had been sold *in toto* to the railroad magnate and land speculator James Joy. Unlike the Osage lands, where the railroad claims were based on disputed interpretations of treaties, Joy's claim was based in contractual law and thus on more solid legal ground. Furthermore, the controversy on the Cherokee Neutral Lands exploded several years before the crisis came to a head on the Osage Ceded Lands. On the Cherokee lands, as settlers were forced to choose between purchasing their lands from the railroads and waiting to purchase their lands under the Homestead Act, violence erupted between settlers. This violence threatened not only the order and stability of the existing communities in Cherokee and Crawford counties, but also seriously slowed the influx of new settlers.[16]

The lesson of extralegal clubs and vigilance committees gone wild was not lost on the

A poster distributed by the Kansas City, Ft. Scott & Gulf and the Kansas City, Lawrence & Southern Railroads promoting 500,000 acres of land in southeastern Kansas open for settlement. The posts lists numerous reasons for selecting the southeastern portion of Kansas for settlement rather than the western area.

veteran settlers in Labette and Neosho counties. Commenting on recent attempts by Cherokee county agitators to enlist support among the settlers on the Osage Ceded Land, the editor of the *Neosho County Dispatch* pointedly rejected any similarity between the two groups: "The question comes up right here, why are these speeches made in Neosho County where the interests and troubles of our people are not at all identified with those on the Neutral Lands? Are we in any way responsible for the acts that have been committed by Mr. Laughlin or his followers? Most certainly not. It seems very much as though Mr. L. has gotten his people into a serious difficulty and, as misery loves company, seeks now to involve us."[17]

The *Dispatch* was not alone in decrying the violence in which Cherokee County was engulfed. Looking eastward and reacting in horror to the stories emanating there from, John Horner of the *Chetopa Advance* urged his readers in bold letters: "LET US HAVE PEACE." He explained, "The condition of anarchy which now exists upon what is known as the 'neutral lands' and the deleterious and disastrous effects it has exercised in retarding the development of the country and in turning aside the tide of immigration from the counties of Crawford and Cherokee is an irresistible argument against a resort, by any people, to violent or irregular measures to secure their rights." Horner was walking a tight-rope here, and it is clear that he knew it. Not wanting to appear to be taking the side of a land monopolist in the conflict, he hurriedly continued, "We condemn the policy and deplore the effects of such legislation as that by which Mr. Joy became possessed of the 800,000 acres of lands over which the iron scepter of monopoly has been extended. The settlers upon these lands had been led to expect pre-emption and homestead rights." Horner wanted his readers to understand: he was on their side. However, he also was eager for them to recognize the important lesson to be learned from the way in which the settlers had mismanaged their opposition to Joy. "However great the disgrace which this legislation has inflicted upon the nation, and however hostile it may have been to the genius and spirit of our republican government, we have always opposed and shall forever oppose an appeal to any other than the legally constituted authorities, for the redress of these grievances."

Why? According to Horner, the key point was that "any organization which interferes with freedom of speech and opinion, which uses or threatens violence or resorts to unwarranted and overt acts, can only jeopardize the interest of the settlers." To Horner, there was an additional reason to avoid the debacle of the Neutral Lands; as he stated, "Hundreds of settlers are leaving the neutral lands on account of the chaotic condition of things, only too glad to get to Labette and Neosho Counties where peace and quiet prevail. Their towns have ceased to grow, improvement has stopped, uncertainty prevails and the evils of anarchy exist."[18] A few months later, as violence continued unabated on the Neutral Lands, the *Neosho County Dispatch* drew a similar conclusion: "Violence and mob law will only have a tendency to alienate the sympathies of the law-abiding people and react to the detriment of the parties interested."[19]

What is most interesting about this development is that an older cultural idea of "local sovereignty" is pulled into and reconciled with a new emphasis on "due process" and "law." Consider the following announcement: "The settlers on the Cherokee Strip and on the Osage Ceded Lands are notified that a meeting will be held at the house of Mr. John Davidson, situated on Lake Creek at 10 o'clock Monday morning, Feb. 21st, to consider the steps necessary to be taken for the establishment of a Herd Law, either for the whole county of Labette or for local districts, as the meeting may consider best."[20] Much about this is familiar; local settlers are concerned about roaming cattle. They call a meeting to discuss the issue and to take action. This is recognizable behavior; it is the proposed action that has changed. The solution which they put forward is to take "steps necessary ... for the establishment of a Herd Law." Instead of drafting their own "resolutions" and creating their own "laws," they are now working together to influence the political process for a county-wide law.

A similar change of focus can be discerned in an interesting editorial in the *Kansas Democrat*. Under the heading, "Gambling Hall," the editor wrote disapproving, "Oswego is cursed with a first-class gambling hell." He then chided his readers, "Really, we are a city. Let us reflect a moment. We claim to be civilized and Christianized; we boast of our churches, Sabbath schools and free schools and two live newspapers, one of which has been running nearly two years, a good Republican paper at that, and yet Oswego in some shape or manner has not been without her gambling holes." He was clearly advocating for change: "Let us say to the good people of this town and city; for we are a city with a Mayor and city Fathers, that a gambling hall ... is a shame and disgrace to a city of such enterprise as Oswego." It was now time for the authorities to properly interpret and enforce the laws: "It is a pitfall in the pathway of our youth and older men that should not be permitted to exist under the laws of our city."[21]

According to these community leaders, the time had come for the extralegal settlers clubs and vigilance committees to be disbanded. They were, they argued, a short-gap measure necessitated by the primitive infrastructure of the Counties. The long-term goal was to develop judicial and legal institutions that would be responsive to local concerns and needs.

Horner stressed this in an editorial printed in early February of 1870; reflecting on the changes that would occur when the railroads came to Chetopa, he warned the citizens, "An immense immigration will be thrown in upon us, our town will be crowded to an overflowing, an army of adventurers will swarm in upon us, thieves, gamblers, pickpockets, will blossom out on every corner." The only solution, according to Horner, was to organize Chetopa as a city "at the earliest practicable moment" so that "for self-protection" the city could "have an efficient city organization and a rigid police force."[22]

As the organizational structure within the counties evolved, the structure of the original Settlers' Clubs and Vigilant Committees changed as well. This was not a consecutive process of cause and effect; it is not as if the changes in the administrative structure of the courts forced the hands of the clubs and committees. Both were happening at the same time; each influenced the changes experienced by the other. In fact, many leaders of local clubs and committees took up roles in the official institutional structures.[23] An early indication that the structure of the various clubs and committees was beginning to change can be found in the large gathering of settlers that had met in Jacksonville on July 28, 1869, to celebrate the resolutions of Congress and their victory over the monopolists.

During the day, the crowd was harangued by political speeches stressing the importance of coming together to defend their lands. After the raucous night of dancing and celebrating, on the following day, July 29, the crowd reassembled for more speeches. The keynote speaker was Representative Sidney Clarke, who, according to the *Advance*, "deplored the growing influence of monopolies and denied the right of the Senate of the United States to alienate the public domain." Clarke then called upon all who were present to band together and work as a community in the defense of their rights. As we have noted, this was not a new concept for the settlers; it is exactly what they had been doing since they had emigrated. But Clarke's call was new in one respect; instead of calling them to take control of the situation locally, "he counseled them to seek redress in the courts through the forms of law, in a determined effort to maintain their rights."[24]

In the early 1870s, legal authorities struggled to establish themselves as the defenders of justice and upholders of community order. The following story, reported in the *Osage Mission Journal*, discussed one aspect of this change. After reporting the arrest of a "couple of rural gents" who had come to town and drunk themselves into noisy pests, the *Journal* noted, "This is the first arrest ever made in our city for the offense of being 'drunk and disorderly' but we are glad to learn that Mayor O'Grady intends to have peace and good order prevail if the citizens will cooperate with him. Under *the new order of things* it will cost from $10 to $25 to have 'an old fashioned drunk' in Osage Mission."25

By the early 1870s, both Labette and Neosho Counties had established courts of law that were beginning to assert themselves in legal cases. It is at this time as well that the attorneys practicing law within the 7th judicial district met to officially form an "Attorney's Association" out of perceived necessity to "reduce the practice of the law to a system of uniformity for the government of all." In an obvious attempt to distance themselves from the extralegal system that had been active in regulating legal questions in southeast Kansas in the early chaotic years of the counties' settlement, the attorneys proposed the formation of a "permanent organization" so that they would be able to "to maintain the dignity and character of each individual member of the Bar."26

Transportation had dramatically improved with the building of bridges and roads throughout the Counties. In addition, as settlers continued to immigrate, the open space between claims was shrinking; it was thus more difficult for strangers to "jump" the claims of "old-time settlers" unnoticed. This was observed by Captain W.J. Haughawout, a member of the land appraising party of the Union Pacific Southern Branch Railroad, in a diary entry entitled: "Camp on Labette, January 3, 1870." Haughawout, who had passed through southeast Kansas as a Union soldier in 1865, noted, "I find great change in the counties of Neosho and Labette, since I traversed them in the time of the war; then a vast wilderness, now densely populated by an intelligent, energetic and wide-awake class of people, principally from the states of Illinois, Ohio and Iowa."27 These settlers had taken up claims and established themselves as active members of the developing communities. As the *Chetopa Advance* reported, this new wave of settlers would render the activities of claim-jumpers and land speculators ineffective. Editor Horner was pleased to announce "the arrival of a number of claim hunters from Missouri and other parts, who have taken claims and have come to stay as actual settlers, and who do not belong to the four pole and thirty days class, who have claimed and cursed the country like a swarm of locusts from time immemorial; but who have come with their wives and babies to make permanent homes among us. This is the class of settlers we need and not those who take a claim for the romance and name, and then go back to settle up some business and wait until the country settles up without their aid."28

The early 1870s was thus a time of great organization growth and solidification in southeast Kansas. From the initial days of immigration, settlers had understood the importance of churches to the establishment of order on the plains and they thus worked accordingly to build up religious communities. As an early correspondent announced in the *Neosho Valley Eagle*, "With the banner of Jesus Christ flung out to the breeze and putting our whole trust in God our Creator, and the deep interest manifested by Christians everywhere we expect to spread gospel holiness all over this new Country in an unusual length of time. Ministers of the gospel of Christ have been sent among us, Sabbath schools and Churches have been organized everywhere. Prayer meetings, male and female, are kept up weekly in many communities."[29] This perspective is also evident in an early editorial in the *Chetopa Advance*, "It is a matter of gratification to observe how generally our religious meetings are attended. It is a cheering promise of that high cultivation which is soon to crowd the magnificent valleys of Southern Kansas with an energetic, teeming population and make our fertile prairies 'to bud and blossom as the rose.' The light house perched upon the ocean headland, does not give comfort and assurance to more thousands of storm tossed mariners than does the glittering church spire to the thousands of dwellers within the circle of its cheering light."[30]

Few among the settlers disagreed with this notion; as the *Osage Mission Journal* noted in its report that the Baptist Church was about to be completed, "We hope our citizens generally will each give to the accomplishment of this public enterprise, irrespective of denominational bias or character. Every one in town is more or less benefited by building up churches, of whatever kind, and we hope will give their mite toward the erection of every such structure which shall be projected in Osage Mission."[31] In fact the vitality of the developing religious communities was something upon which many visitors to southeast Kansas remarked. As a reporter from the *Fort Scott Monitor* explained after a visit to Chetopa in February 1870, "In a moral point of view, Chetopa is certainly an exception among Western towns. No people in the State patronize the church more liberally or are more zealous in the cause of Christianity, then the citizens of Chetopa."[32] Had this reporter visited other southeast Kansas towns, he would have witnessed similar patronage. The *Osage Mission Journal* observed, "The number of people who regularly attend the House of God is usually a fair index to their intelligence and enterprise. This place in this respect will compare favorably with many older towns. Our places of worship are crowded every Sabbath by appreciative and attentive congregations."[33]

Significantly, by 1870 religious communities had been established in every community in both Neosho and Labette counties and many were in the process of building houses of worship.[34] As reported by the *Advance*, "If the ranks of wickedness have been filled so have the ranks of those whose duty it is to persuade them into better ways. Major McCreery of the Presbyterian fold has had a year of success — has added largely to his flock — and bettered his facilities for further additions. The Rev. Evan Jones, long years a laborer in the vineyard of his Master, has sought a home among us to enjoy in good old age a grateful respite from the labors of a noble life of usefulness. The Reverend Bateman, the genial kind hearted fisher of men, is doing a good work. We like the ring of his sickle in the fields white for harvest. There is yet much hard evangelical work to be done before the Devil relinquishes his determination to lay his head right on this community."[35]

Church communities thus became a focal point for a network of social relationships that sought to reinforce the moral values that the settlers had brought with them to the West. Through membership in social clubs and religious communities important social networks were created; these networks would prove crucial in the looming struggle against the railroads. As reported in the *Oswego Register*, ministers took upon themselves the responsibility of leading their communities. "Rev. H.W. Conley, pastor of the M.E. Church, preached a practical sermon last Sunday morning. He admonished the hearers to take a more active part in matters pertaining to their temporal welfare: to discountenance under all circumstances everything having a tendency to corrupt the morals of the community and take a bold stand against intemperance and political corruption. He handled the subject without gloves." The paper then added an important comment, which reveals the expectations and attitudes of many early settlers: "To cry against the sins of our day and generation is most becoming the high calling of the ministry."[36]

The resulting personal attachments created within the context of religious communities helped to reinforce societal norms by creating the social infrastructure of a consistent moral order. Editor Horner explained it clearly in an article entitled "Railroads and Religion"—"It pays to favor godliness, for godliness invites people to the towns on their road; godliness builds meeting houses, school edifices, and makes society desirable and pleasant; godliness makes is safe to invest in county bonds. It raises their value, and never repudiates an honest debt.... Religion always and everywhere carries intelligence among the people; and who ever knew of a railroad that depended upon local support to be a success where the people lacked intelligence. Christianity always disseminates a spirit of benevolence and liberality."[37] It was the existence of these social networks that led the *Oswego Register* to assert: "A significant characteristic of this state and more especially of this county is the hearty manner in which people stand out for their friends. We attribute the success of so many undertakings to the unity of feelings among our citizens. Attachment for one's surroundings is not remarkable in old and established communities, in which its inhabitants have been born and bred; but here in this new country there seems be strife in one direction alone, the general good."[38]

As people became familiar with one another, the hazy atmosphere of newness and uncertainty that the speculators and claim-jumpers had used to their advantage evaporated; in its place set patterns of social intercourse emerged.[39] It became possible, as the *Osage Mission Journal* advised its readers, for citizens to "be on their guard against certain suspicious characters loafing about saloons, &c, with no visible means of support."[40] More importantly, as these new settlers arrived and as the communities they established began to form themselves, a change in mentality began to evidence itself as cities began to incorporate and thus to abandon the earlier structure provided by "for-profit" town companies. In an editorial arguing for the establishing of the city of Chetopa (i.e., "The *Town* of Chetopa should become a *city* at the earliest practicable moment."), Horner articulated this mentality: "An immense immigration will be thrown in upon us, our town will be crowded to an overflowing, an army of adventurers will swarm in upon us, thieves, gamblers, pickpockets, will blossom out on every corner, and we must for self-protection have an efficient city organization and a rigid police force."[41] This is a striking argument; whereas in the not-so-distant past citizens throughout Neosho and Labette counties had relied on each other and the various extralegal committees and clubs they had formed for "self-protection," in the newly evolving cultural climate of the 1870s Horner urged them to begin to look to elected officials and a duly appointed (notice the use of the word "rigid") police force.

A similar development occurred in Labette City. On the last Saturday of December, 1870, several burglaries took place. After reporting these, the editor commented: "We hope soon to be incorporated as a city of the third class, until which time we shall have to suffer such inconveniences."[42] March 2, 1871, the *Labette Sentinel* announced: "The time has come for Labette to be incorporated." The paper then proceeded to list the "advantages" of incorporation: "the trustees elected have power to pass bylaws and ordinances to prevent and remove nuisance, restrain and prohibit gambling, to provide for licensing and regulating dramshops, to establish and regulate markets, to open, grade, pave or improve the streets and alleys of such town, to have side walks and footways made at the expense of the owners or occupiers of adjacent lots, to impose and appropriate fines, forfeitures and penalties for breaches of their ordinances, to levy and collect taxes, and all other powers not repugnant and contradictory to the laws of the land."[43]

In July 1870, three men became involved in a quarrel on a Saturday

3. The Transformation of Settler Society (1870)   105

morning near Elm Creek. The quarrel, which began rather serenely, gradually grew violent. Finally, one of the men, Joseph Barker, after he was knocked off his feet by another man (Harrison Seward), pulled out his revolver and began to shoot. The other men responded in kind and, in the ensuing gun fight, all three were seriously wounded. This was certainly not the first time men had been involved in a violent quarrel; nor was it the first time that men had been shot. What made this event significant was the way it was reported. After detailing what had transpired, the editor of the *Kansas Democrat* added this explanation: "The parties are under arrest and will be dealt with according to Kansas law, by a Kansas justice, in regular Kansas style."[44] What is striking about these words is that by the summer of 1870, for the editor of the *Democrat* and his readers, "regular Kansas style" was no longer quasi-legal settler institutions administering their own form of community justice but rather "Kansas" judges adjudicating according to "Kansas law." By 1870, a significant switch in community attitudes and standards had begun to occur. Southeast Kansas was changing.

This does not mean that the Vigilance Committees and Settlers' Clubs disbanded at once; nor does it imply that local citizens no longer acted to impose order and to administer justice. The transition took place over several years and in varying speeds in different locations. An interesting story of a custody dispute in the summer of 1869 helps to identify the shifting attitudes of southeast Kansans to the law and their own responsibility for it. On June 1, Sarah Disbro filed a petition for divorce in the District Court. On the face of it, the existence of this petition was not unusual. Court records reveal a consistent pattern of divorce petitions initiated by women. Examples include *Phebe M. Lynch vs. John W.* on the grounds "that the said defendant had for more than one year abandoned and deserted her," *C.C. Gallaway vs. James* on the grounds of "gross neglect of duty and extreme cruelty," and *Julia Hayes vs. E.T.* "on the ground of adultery."[45] As illustrated in these three cases, divorce petitions were usually based on (at least) on of three charges: desertion, neglect and/or abuse, and adultery. Sarah's petition was unique in that she also filed a petition asking that sole "custody and control" of their one-month-old daughter "be decreed to her." In looking to the courts to adjudicate her situation, Sarah illustrates the growing reliance on the courts; her husband's response, however, points to the existence of the earlier perspective.

As the *Neosho County Dispatch* explained, "To this petition her husband filed an answer." The answer came in the form of a confrontation and the violent seizure of the child. "On Thursday last, Mrs. Disbro and her mother were returning from Erie, having the child in their possession, they were met by the defendant who requested to see and finally succeeded in obtaining and walking off with the child."[46] Sarah and John represent different attitudes towards the law and its role in the lives of citizens that continued to coexist in southeast Kansas during the 1870s. It is significant to note, however, that Sarah's attitude increasingly prevailed.

This view is confirmed by a letter to the editor of the newly renamed *Southern Kansas Advance* written on January 5, 1870 from a "correspondent" living in the small town of Montana who opined: "Southern Kansas is settling up very fast.... Where only six months ago nothing but the boundless expanse of prairie could be seen, you will now see the cabins of the settlers thickly spread about, and the cattle quietly grazing on the rich grass which the country affords. And here and there are enterprising villages that have sprung up as if by magic, but looking really like old established towns of the East."[47]

Another interesting example of this developing cultural shift occurred in January 1870. A Danish immigrant, Soren Neilson, was accused of jumping the claim of Jane Mosher in the Snow Creek region of Labette County. Jane asked the local Settlers' Club to investigate and to remove the claim jumper if their findings supported her assertions. Since she had lived at the claim for over a year, it was not difficult for the local citizens to substantiate the fact that she was the lawful owner and that Neilson was a jumper. When the settlers met, as the *Advance* reports, "to adjudicate the rights of the parties," they decided "that said Dane and his effects should be removed, which was done in a quiet and friendly, although decided manner."

Although apparently Neilson did not resist his removal, he was discomforted with the manner in which it had occurred. He proceeded to make an appeal to the court and accused the settlers of bodily assault. As a result, all of those who had been involved in his removal were arrested and placed into the custody of the local sheriff. In response, the citizens of Snow Creek, "indignant at the meddlesome disposition on the part of the prosecution," decided to take action. They hired defense attorneys! These attorneys demanded a jury trial and when the case was brought before a jury, Jane Mosher and her brother Nicholas were acquitted of all charges. The rest of the citizens who had been involved were found guilty but only fined "one dollar each as minimal damages."[48]

This case is fascinating in what it reveals about the changing attitudes of settlers. In those places where the land title was still not resolved, settlers continued to register claims with their neighbors, expecting them to adjudicate any disputes that might arise. However, when the authorities became involved and settlers were arrested, local citizens looked to the courts for redress. On April 14, 1870, a "Notice of Contest" appeared in the *Osage Mission Journal.* Although these notices were common in newspapers in other regions of Kansas throughout this period, this is the first time an official "Notice of Contest" was printed in a paper published in southeast Kansas. This, then, is the first public record of a debate over landownership being fought in the Land Office rather than local extralegal courts. It is also significant, for it is a dispute involving a woman's claim.

> An application having been made by Mary Branson to purchase the West half of North-east quarter and East half of North-west quarter of Section 24, Township No. 30 S, Range 21 E, under the joint resolution of Congress approved April 10, 1869 for the disposal of the lands ceded by the Osage Indians, under the 1st and 2nd articles of the Treaty of September 29, 1865.
>
> John H. Holt, being an adverse claimant to the same land, is hereby notified that the said Mary Branson will be permitted to offer proof in support of her claim to said land, at this Office on the 8th day of June, 1870, at 9 o'clock a.m. The said John H. Holt, will have an opportunity at said time to offer counter proof and also proof in support of his claim.
>
> Watson Stewart, Register
> D.M. Emmert, Receiver[49]

As this case illustrates, settlers continued to emphasize local control and believed that they were the ones who both made and enforced social behavior, but now instead of performing this function in "extra judicial" or "quasi-judicial" courts, they use this authority within more accepted social institutions by serving as members of juries in civil and criminal court cases. While it is true that local Vigilance Committees continued to appear periodically in Labette and Neosho Counties throughout the 1870s, two differences from their role in the 1860s can be noted. First, whenever they appear, there is significant resistance to their activities by leading members of the community. Second, their activity can be directly linked to the perception that the courts have failed to provide justice. In other words, they come into existence *after* the normal legal procedures have been completed to correct perceived injustices rather than (as in the 1860s) coming into existence to act in the role of non-existent established courts.

In December of 1870, the struggle over the legitimate role of the local community in adjudicating criminal cases reached a climax in Neosho County. On Thursday, December 15, a popular resident of Osage Mission, James Kerns, was arrested for drunkenness and disorderly conduct by Sheriff Taylor Horne. On the way to the jail, an altercation between Kerns and Horne erupted with the tragic result that Horne shot and killed Kerns. The *Osage Mission Journal* summarized the response of "nineteen-twentieths" of the local population by describing the event as "the shooting down in cold-blood of an unarmed blood," truly "deserving the severest condemnation of every citizen who while having respect to law and order yet demands that human life shall not be wantonly sacrificed by anyone 'clothed with a little brief authority.'" As the news of the killing spread, a mob of angry townspeople gathered and rushed the second floor of the store in which Horne was confined; grabbing Horne, they proceeded to drag him outside of the town intending to hang him immediately. As the *Journal* reported, "This they were so near carrying out that they had a rope around his neck and were ready to suspend him to the limb of a tree selected for the purpose." What is striking about this report, however, is what happened next—"At this critical juncture John Ryan appeared on the scene and being permitted to speak, made so moving and effective an appeal that the party consented to return Horne to the custody of the law."[50] Although willing to allow Horne to be tried, the people who had responded to the situation by threatening to hang him did not believe that the situation was out of their hands. Convinced that Horne was guilty and that justice demanded his punishment, they raised funds to hire their own prosecuting attorney and when the case came to trial in April of 1871, they packed the courtroom and actively agitated for his conviction. When the jury returned the guilty verdict, the local community was jubilant; however, some wondered whether justice had been served. As the editor of the *Erie Ishmaelite* explained, "The trial throughout was considered by the most intelligent and impartial class of the people who heard it, a solemn mockery of justice, and a gross outrage on the rights of the prisoner and many unite in the believe that the Judge who presided prostituted the high functions of his office, and pandered to the people who desired Horne's conviction for the purpose of making political capital. The utmost partiality was manifested throughout the trial, he being a poor man without money or political influence.... It is pitiful to think that a man's rights, in a court of justice are to be measured by the number of sheckles and his personal influence."[51] Although the *People's Advocate*, a paper published in Osage Mission, disagreed strongly with the *Ishmaelite* over the nature of the trial by arguing that it was a fair proceeding, it is most important to note is that both agreed on the importance of fair trials and the importance of due process in administering justice.

Thus, when the settlers were faced with a recalcitrant Land Office, they decided to fight the railroads in the courts rather than resorting to violence on the ground. An important event occurred in the city of Ladore on July 4, 1870, to solidify this decision. Celebrations of the 4th were held each year throughout Labette and Neosho counties and attracted large crowds of settlers. The celebration in 1870 was, however, significant. In each village, town and city, as the members of the community processed to the central square, as lengthy toasts were offered with their accompanying "responses" and as the requisite fireworks were set off, settlers were informed that a new bi-county Settlers' Protective Association was being formed. This Association would coordinate the legal efforts of the settlers and focus their energies on defeating the claims of the railroads. The following day, July 5, 1870, thousands of settlers joined the association and passed the following preliminary bylaws:

> *Whereas,* We, the settlers on the Osage Ceded Lands, in the State of Kansas, believe that under the treaty by which the said lands were ceded to the United States, and under the joint resolutions of Congress, April 10, 1869, actual settlers were entitled to purchase any part of said lands in tracts not to exceed 160 acres, at $1.25 per acre, and that no corporation has acquired any vested rights therein; and whereas, certain railroad corporations are claiming certain portions of said lands; now, therefore,
>
> *Resolved,* 1. That we will proceed at once to test the validity of, said claims, by instituting legal proceedings in the proper courts.
>
> 2. That we respectfully request the Governor of our State to withhold all patents from said corporations for said lands until the termination of said proceedings.
>
> 3. That we will support no candidate for county and legislative offices who is not thoroughly identified with the settlers and in sympathy with their cause.[52]

It is striking to note the difference between this set of resolutions and the earlier bylaws of local Settlers' Clubs and Vigilance Committees. There is no discussion of registering claims or of protecting settlers from claim jumpers; the situation on the ground had changed. The threat to their liberty had shifted as the settlers began to understand the political power of their collective strength.

4

CHALLENGES TO PUBLIC ORDER (1871–1874)

Even as settlers were becoming aware of their collective political strength in the early 1870s, however, they were discovering that the foundation for that unity was beginning to disintegrate. Although many had come to southeast Kansas as individuals or small solitary family units, they shared a common political perspective. As Union veterans who had migrated west after the Civil War had come to an end, they were Republicans who voted for Republican candidates.[1] Undoubtedly, this identification with the Republican Party was passive and did not imply active political engagement. The settlers were more concerned with local issues and were dedicated almost exclusively in the early years to building lawful ordered societies even as they labored to feed their families and improve their claims. As Milton Reynolds of the *Parsons Sun* reflected, this left little time or energy for politics. "The people of Parsons," he noted in 1871, "are not yet aroused on political matters. They are not strong partisans."[2] This would change dramatically in the 1870s.

The veterans who immigrated to southeast Kansas in the late 1860s came with a deep and abiding commitment to republican principles that had energized their dedication to the Union cause.[3] Priding themselves on their service in the war as Lincoln's soldiers, they self-identified (both publicly and privately) as valiant defenders of freedom against tyranny. As the *Neosho Valley Eagle*, the first newspaper published in Neosho County, explained: "The secret is, Kansas started right. Peopled by colonies from the New England States they brought with them their ideas of, and their high regard for free institutions, and intellectual and moral culture.... Loving freedom and hating tyranny in all its forms, they stood like a wall of adamant against the encroachments of slavery and saved Kansas forever to freedom and freemen. Their example and influence are not lost, and Kansas is today and will always remain, radical on the right."[4]

In this short paragraph, we encounter the fundamental political ideology that framed both politics and culture in southeast Kansas. Clifford Gertz has argued that ideology is imbedded in every culture, where it provides "maps of problematic social reality."[5] By accepting his axiom that ideology is to be located in those ideas people take so for granted that they assume no definition is needed, we can uncover the fundamental presuppositions that structured the political thought and cultural activity of these veteran settlers by paying attention to the frequent use of the terms "freedom" and "tyranny." Some scholars have argued that the republican ideology of the founders, emphasizing self-disciplined virtue and equality of opportunity, was replaced in the antebellum period by an encroaching liberalism emphasizing competition and individual freedom. However, the political rhetoric used by settlers in southeast Kansas indicates instead, as J.H. Hexter has written, that there were in fact "two languages of politics ... that had liberty as the key word in their vocabulary."[6] Linda Kerber explains, "The first stressed participation as the foundation of civic virtue; its key words were participation, virtue and corruption. The other language was defensive, a freedom against intrusion, whose key words were limited government, due process, and fundamental law."[7] Both of these languages were spoken by southeast Kansans and are clearly evident in this paragraph.

In all of this, it is quite clear that the defining event remained the War and that the political allegiance of these settlers was filtered through the prism of Civil War politics. To them it was self-evident: those on the side of freedom (i.e., the Union) were Republicans; those who supported tyranny (i.e., the Rebellion) were Democrats. As the *Eagle* explained in announcing its support for Grant in the 1868 election, the upcoming political campaign was "a fight of Loyalty against Rebellion."[8] A few weeks later, as it commented on the nomination of the Democratic candidate for president, the *Eagle* remonstrated: "What of the War? Is it possible that all the treasure and sacred blood have been expended in vain? God forbid."[9] To the editor of the *Eagle*, there was no question about the issue — as he declared, "It seems incomprehensible how a returned Federal soldier could vote the Democratic ticket. Vote with men who cursed you for going, cursed you when gone and expressed the wish that a bullet ought to have laid you low? Vote with the rebels you fought, with the ones who called you 'hell-hounds, mud-sills, &c'?"[10] In similar fashion, the *Oswego Register* informed its readers that "it is a fact we dare not dispute that the strength of the so-called Democracy rests where nests of rebels and traitors hold sway."[11] Commenting on the attempts of Democratic candidates to be elected throughout the South, the editor described it as a "plot" by which "men who glory that their hands were once stained with the blood of Union soldiers ... lend a helping hand to place the Democracy in the ascendancy." Let there be no doubt, he asserted, "The principles of the so-called democratic party are adverse to freedom, justice and reform."[12]

The *Labette Sentinel* concurred — in urging local citizens to vote in the 1870 election, the paper reminded them that "we have an opposition. The same opposition that we have met before; the same opposition that we met on the tented field; the same opposition that took the heart's blood of our children, our fathers, our brothers, and our loyal friends and neighbors; the same opposition that after failing to dismember the glorious Union, took revenge on the nation by directing the assassin's bullet at our President, who had been re-elected to the office of President as an endorsement of his past Administration. Yes, we have met the same opposition, and put them to flight by the bullet and now we can, must and will put them to flight by the ballot."

Pushing still further, under a bold heading entitled "Read This Before You Vote," he then went on to enumerate the "sins" of the Democrats that should be remembered by every citizen who approached the polling place:

Who kept four million slaves bound down in chains? The Democrats.
Who kept as many whites in ignorance and degradation? The Democrats.
Who used their power and means to sever the Union? The Democrats.
Who turned the money and arms of the United States over to the rebels? The Democrats.
Who caused the murder of President Lincoln? The Democrats.
Who made our homes desolate? The Democrats.
Who caused our country to be filled with widows and orphans? The Democrats.
Who brought desolation and weeping into every household? The Democrats.
Who shot down our fathers and brothers, or starved them in loathsome prisons? The Democrats.[13]

The earliest voting records corroborate the assertion that the majority of settlers were stalwart Republicans. In 1867, the first year for which voting records are complete, out of the 949 votes cast, Grant electors received 783 and Seymour's 166. And, as Nelson Case, an early local historian noted, "The candidates for the several State offices received substantially the same proportion of the votes."[14] It is also clear that these settlers voted the way they did because they believed the Republican Party best upheld the principles that had inspired their dedication to the Union in the Civil War. As the *Oswego Register* explained, "the principles of the Republican Party embody equal rights, protection and progression.[15]

In fact, it was not until 1870 that the first edition of a Democratic newspaper appeared on the street corners and newspaper shops of Neosho and Labette counties. Published by William Bennett, a recent immigrant to southern Kansas from Iowa, the paper announced its intentions: "We shall advocate the time-honored principles of the Democratic party which have ever been in favor of cheap land and free homesteads, and opposed to handing the broad and fertile prairies of this nation over into the hands of a few land sharks and capitalists."[16] In this bold salvo, Bennett publicly asserted a new identity for the Democratic Party. Instead of arguing, as the other newspapers had done, that the Democratic Party was the organization of Southern slaveholders and rebellious traitors, he presented the party as the friend of Western settlers and the enemy of Eastern capitalists. In so doing, Bennett skillfully redrew both the geographical map of the Civil War and the political map of his readers by presenting the war not as a battle between Northern freemen and Southern slave-holding aristocrats, but rather as a clash between Eastern capitalists and Western settlers: "We are opposed to a high protective tariff, because it robs the western man to enrich the eastern manufacturer, and compels the consumer and laboring man to pay a tax to support capital that pays no taxes."

Using the same vivid imagery of war sacrifices as the Republican papers, Bennett drew radically different political conclusions. The real divide, he asserted, was between those who had suffered and those who had profited from the war. For the man who had trudged through fields of mud and blood in dedication to the cause, the war had brought great sacrifice and personal loss; but, for the northern capitalist, who had avoided the duty of soldiering, the war was a time of great financial gain. In a series of powerfully emotive comparisons, Bennett asked his readers to consider which party pursued policies that truly represented their interests:

> If the bondholder who bought his bonds with currency is to have gold for them, the soldier who with his blood enhanced the value of the bonds should have the same.
> If the shoddy contractor who speculated upon the blood of the brave men and enriched himself through the havoc of war by selling one dollar of gold for two dollars and ninety cents in currency, and then bought two dollars and ninety cents worth of bonds must now after six years of interest have been paid in gold, then in the name of justice we demand for the widow and orphan, who gave the blood of a husband and father to protect these same bonds, gold for their bounties and pensions....

If any should be exempt from taxation, let it be the little house and lot of the widow who sent to the army in the ranks a husband that she loved and who laid down his life for the country and its flag.

Let the maimed and crippled of our land who for a paltry sum shouldered their musket to support the "best Government the world ever saw" and lost a limb to protect capital be exempt and compel the bondocrat and rich man to shell out the necessary taxes to support the Government that has so suddenly enriched him.

This theme — of Northeastern wealthy capitalists reaping benefits denied to Western-bound veterans and those who suffered with them — was a powerful weapon in Bennett's hands as he sought to create a new identity for the Democratic Party: "We claim that the policy of the Democratic party has always been to protect the laboring man from the encroachments of the capitalist who in every age and country have invariably robbed the poorer classes to enrich themselves."[17]

Bennett's message was received with interest — 1,000 copies of the first edition of the Kansas *Democrat* were distributed within a week. Further indications of the changing political environment are the establishment of Democratic Central Committees in both Neosho and Labette counties in 1870 followed by successful nominating conventions in the 1871 which were then followed by the election of several Democratic candidates in November of 1871. The Republican paper the *Erie Ishmaelite* publicly acknowledged that the situation had been greatly altered in March of 1871 when it noted: "It must be confessed that the signs of the times are not as favorable to the future success of the Republican Party as it has been in the ten years past."[18]

Undoubtedly, the factors that influenced this political shift were part of national developments — the papers that began to endorse "the Democracy" often referred to the corruption of the Grant administration as a prime example of what had gone wrong with the Republican Party. But these national issues paled in comparison with the importance of the intensifying struggle between settlers and the railroad companies over land title. For it was in this emotionally charged environment that the identity suggested by Bennett of the Democratic Party as the friend of the settlers and of the Republican Party as the ally of the monopolist began to resonate in a new way. As the prism through which politics was envisioned shifted from the past to the present and as the focus of debate shifted from the events that led to the Civil War to those that occurred after it, political terms began to be understood in a new context and to take on new meanings.

A new paper appeared in Labette County on January 12, 1871. Called

The Anti-Monopolist and published in the city of Parsons, the most important railroad town in southeastern Kansas, the paper declared itself to be "the voice of the settlers" in their struggle with the railroads. Its prospectus, boldly presented, represented an important development in southeast Kansas politics. Utilizing the basic themes and political rhetoric of the Civil War, it did so in a decidedly new way and with a new focus:

> Two thousand and five hundred settlers upon these lands, whose humble homes we have visited within the last three months will bear us witness that they experienced a regeneration of life when assured that an advocate of their rights should be exclusively and sacredly devoted to the promulgation and defense of their rights as American citizens. Being such, they felt with more or less intensity, that no apology could be accepted for making them slaves. Yet they saw the chains forged, and they saw the base men who forged them. They knew also that the men who welded the links were their servants — servants whose services they had secured for two years to represent their interest in the Congress of the United States....
>
> Thousands of the readers of the Anti-Monopolist put in life honor and fortune to save the republic — in the terrible ordeal a race of four million slaves were incidentally enfranchised. It would be a terrible comment upon the power of that Great Instrument if while our servants were creating citizens of the United State out of four million colored slaves, it was engaged in enslaving twenty million free white citizens of the United States.... We were not born to be slaves, and there is no power on the face of the earth able to enslave us.[19]

The rhetoric employed in this editorial was familiar to the readers — it mentioned "slaves" (six times), chains, base men and oppressive tyrants. It utilized the classic imagery employed in the 1850s by abolitionists; but this was a new form of abolitionism. The slaves of whom he was speaking were not black but white; the oppressors were not Southern plantation owners but Northern politicians supported by Northern capitalists. It was a call to war — but this was a new war and in this new war, new political identities would be constructed.

The *Anti-Monopolist* was the first paper to articulate a new orientation for southeast Kansas politics, but it was by no means the last. The *Southern Kansas Advance*, published in Chetopa, explained the change in this fashion: "The republican party sprang into existence at the bidding of a great exigency, beginning its life in the interest of the oppressed. Of that illustrious party we have now chiefly the name left. Republicanism — popular and sweeping in its past successes — has become simply a boat with which to carry whoever can pay his passage to the Washington greenback mines. Theoretically the principles of the party are vital enough, but practically, the Dead Sea presents more animation. A wealth aristocracy ... is still the foe of the true and rightful freedom of Americans. The Republican party has failed in its functions, and lost its legitimate track. The South is no longer the enemy of the North."[20]

The *Osage Mission Transcript* published a poem from a local author that gave voice to a similar perspective. Entitled "The Plowmen," the poem linked together three dates in American history: 1775, 1861 and 1873. The dates are significant; as the poet explained, in 1775, a band of loyal yeoman farmers fought tyranny in the name of freedom; in 1861 their grandsons again fought tyranny in the name of freedom; in 1873, these same loyal Americans must unite again in the name of freedom to wage war against another oppressive foe. As the poem explained:

> In this dark hour, when Honor is cast in the dust,
> And Corruption sits high in the places of trust;
> In this dark hour of Peace, Freedom turns to the hand
> For relief, that in war ever guarded her land.
>
> To you, honest Yeoman, she calls at this hour,
> When Dishonor and Greed hold the scepter of Power;
> When derision and scorn at the nation are hurled,
> And Freedom is mocked by the jeers of the world.
>
> "Will the sons of the bold sires who braved tyrants of old,
> Bow the knee to the power of the briber's base gold?
> For Gold will ye barter Faith, Freedom and Fame,
> And then plow the green graves of your martyrs in shame?"
>
> At her call, lo! the Plowmen are rising again,
> And the shackles of Party are bursting in twain;
> On the broad Susquehanna their shout rises high,
> And the peaks of the Sierras re-echo the cry:
>
> "Rise, Plowmen! United, arise in your ire,
> And to victory sweep, as the broad Prairie Fire,
> When blown by the breath of the Autumn, that chill
> Sweeps down from the crest of the cold Northern hill;
>
> "And as soon as the path of the Prairie Fire's seen
> The young blade arraying the black earth in green,
> So let there be seen in the path we pursue,
> The green growth of Conscience upspringing anew."[21]

Loyal Republicans used several tactics to respond to this challenge. Milton Reynolds, editor of the influential Republican paper the *Parsons Sun*, at first tried to dodge the challenge by arguing that the struggle over land title was not political: "The settlers do not consider the land question a political question. It should not be made a political question.... Those who are Republican and soldiered with Grant will certainly vote as they fought."²² As it became increasingly obvious that the settlers did in fact consider the struggle in political terms, he changed his tune and began to argue that the Democrats were the ones who supported the capitalists. The Democrats were only, he argued, pretending to be on the side of the settlers — "The Democratic dodge of sympathy for the Democratic candidate on account of the land question is 'too thin.' It won't hold water."²³ Most emphatically, however, he sought to return the focus onto the events of the past by warning his readers not to be fooled into complacency: "They who "seek peace and composure," who are content with the perfect reign of justice and equality, and desire to maintain the supremacy of the law, cannot afford to give their influence to the elevation of men who will be obliged to yield concessions to the devilish spirit that actuated the rebellion.... The spirit of the rebellion has been kept smothered. And gradually the old fires have died out. Shall they be re-kindled anew?"²⁴

The editor of the *Thayer Headlight* agreed: "Never before did it seem so necessary for the friends of universal freedom to stand firm as to-day.... Thousands of good men in the south look to the Republican party for protection and encouragement. Shall they have it or will we return to the good old days of slavery?"²⁵ "It is not a time for experimenting," he asserted a few weeks later. "Let every honest Republican stick to his principles and his party, and if possible avert the calamity of another civil war. Let liberty be proclaimed and the proclamation be enforced till free speech may exist and the anthems of freedom be sung all over the American continent."²⁶

As Republican editors found themselves on the defensive, they increasingly sought to cast the present controversy in the light of the past — "'This glorious record of the past is the party's best pledge for the future.' This simple sentence is more pregnant than a thousand resolutions. It is alone such an assurance to the people's hearts as will enable the party to withstand the onslaughts of a thousand coalitions. What will they care for *words* when the 'glorious record' of such *deeds* as has thus far marked the Republican Party stand out in bold relief. To say nothing of that mightiest of National accomplishments — the subjugation of an organized and armed Treason such as the world had never known, its principles of universal freedom coined into inflexible law and secured forever in our great charter, the National Constitution; the emancipation of a race; human equality as made by God decreed; the great debt gradually reduced; the revenues honestly collected;— these are some of the *deeds* which no *Words* can match; these are the 'party's best pledge for the future.'"²⁷

The struggle to maintain party cohesion was, however, made much more difficult by the news that a national Liberal Republican Party had been formed. This party was an attractive alternative to the settlers who, although distraught over the current land crisis, and convinced that the leadership of the Republican Party had abandoned them by entering into political alliances with the monopolists, still found it difficult to abandon the Republican Party and claim membership in the Democratic Party. Thus, the appeal of a political *via media*: the Liberal Republican Party. In southeast Kansas, the Liberal Republican Party allowed those who were Republican to join with the Democratic Party in promoting the cause of the settlers against monopolies without taking the tainted name of Democrat.[28]

The first mention of this new political movement appeared in the *Parsons Sun* on March 9, 1872: "An attempt has been made at Topeka to organize the so-called 'liberal' Republican party in Kansas."[29] In May, settlers from southeast Kansas were informed that a National Convention of the Liberal Republican Party had been held in Cincinnati on May 3, 1872. Most papers carried the press release that emanated from the Convention, and printed the party platform in full. On August 17, 1872, the first grand mass meeting of the Liberal Republican Party was held in Labette County; two weeks later, on August 31, the Liberal Republican Convention of Neosho County was held in Osage Mission. On the same days, and in the same cities, the Democrats held their county conventions. According to published reports, members from the conference committees of both conventions met to coordinate the process by which the two organizations would be cooperate as one political entity.[30] This occurred in both 1872 and 1874 as the two parties worked in unison to put together a slate of candidates for local, state and federal offices. Significantly, in both elections, the candidates chose to run under the label "Liberal Republican" rather than "Democratic." And, significantly, both elections revealed a shift in voting patterns indicating widespread support for the newly emergent Liberal Republican/Democratic Party. Things had changed; as the *Neosho County Journal* explained:

> Four years ago Grant received a large majority in this State. No one was surprised at the result; it was expected, and was received as a "matter of course." Since that time the republicans have at each election been successful, but it has been a matter of no surprise.... Amid all, however, the people have been not meek, but submissive. Their efforts have been defeated, their interests ignored, their wishes frustrated, but still they clung to the party, and voted for and elected its candidates by the usual majorities.... This was the condition in Kansas two months ago. The revolution in public sentiment in this country had just begun, and the tide was turning in favor of the Liberal causes.... Liberalism is progressing. New accessions are constantly being made of those who have been prominent republicans in the days of that party's honesty and usefulness. They are still republicans, but not "loyalists;" and

rather than unite with the truckling thousands in shouting "Long live the King," they are leaving that party to its disintegration, and ranging themselves on the side of progress and reform, and supporting the candidates of the party whose watchword is "Long live the Republic."[31]

In this editorial, we witness firsthand the transformation that had occurred. The rhetoric retains its classical republican themes — it is the context that has changed and along with it, the referents. Undeniably, this change did not lead to the Democratic Party's emergence as the dominant party in southeast Kansas politics; nevertheless its ability to emerge in the post-war period as the party of reform rather than the party of rebellion and its remarkable success in political reidentification as the champion of settlers' rights rather than the defender of the slave aristocracy was a significant political achievement. From the vantage point of the 21st century, two realities are most striking vis-à-vis this transformation. First, we witness the pervasive and compelling power of republican political ideas — "freedom," "slavery," and so on — in Kansas politics in the post–Civil War era. But, secondly, we are reminded of the elastic nature of these terms. Context is everything — thus, in southeast Kansas by using these terms in reference to the past (i.e., the Civil War), the Republican Party was able to effectively marshal its followers and demand their allegiance; its power, however, was in the past. Thus, by switching attention from the past to the present and by emphasizing the contemporary struggle against monopolies, the Democratic Party was able to redefine itself and to create a new, more level political playing field, in which it could compete for votes and power in southeast Kansas.

The founding fathers of Labette and Neosho counties also saw their vision for a unified and ordered society contested along gender lines. The *Labette Sentinel*, a newspaper published in the small city of Labette, Kansas, in the early 1870s, gave voice to the cultural expectations of the white settlers who were flooding into southeast Kansas: "Ever since the Pilgrim Fathers landed at Plymouth Rock, the settler, bold and defiant, has pushed his course westward. State after state has been developed, rivers and plains have been crossed, mountains and valleys reconnoitered and the broad domain from the Atlantic to the Pacific placed within the grasp of civilization through the indomitable energy, severe toil, and hard earnings of the laboring community."[32]

This is the myth of the frontier painted in broad and vivid colors.[33] The pioneer settler, characterized by the traditionally constructed masculine qualities of aggression and power, forces his way west, energetically conquering every obstacle that confronts him, refusing to quit until he establishes his own dominance over the wild and previously untamed wilderness. It is the phallic mentality of force, control, and boundaries — the forceful grasp of civilization bears the unmistakable scent of men as it seizes rivers, plains, mountains and valleys through severe toil and labor.[34]

In a response to a letter which inquired, "Is the frontier life really as hard as people imagine?" John Horner, of the *Chetopa Advance,* echoed the masculine perspective of the *Sentinel.* In an early edition of the "real men don't eat quiche" mentality, Horner insisted that real pioneers don't feel pain, get tired, count the costs, or complain: "The hardships of frontier life are greatly overrated. Indeed the hardships are rather the experience of those who march with the real columns of the advancing army of civilization. The sick, gouty, and decrepit fall to the rear. The bold, stalwart, enterprising, young, and energetic are in the van."[35]

In similar fashion, the editor of the *Osage Mission Journal* assured his readers that the struggle to conquer the prairies was "part of God's providential instrumentality" to distinguish genuine men from those who were only pretending: "The wind you know blows away the chaff and leaves the sound wheat."[36] That this triumph was conceived of in a gendered context is made clear by the comments of several other editors. For example, the editor of the *Thayer Headlight,* in announcing the remarkable achievements of farmer F. Sharp, who had raised 1,000 bushels of corn for a net profit of $750, stated with obvious delight: "His wife's people can come to him."[37] Likewise, the editor of the *Kansas Democrat* argued that men never quit—"Onward and upward and outward shall be the watchword of every true man. The coward only wavers and trembles and falters and turns back, such would better remain back.... Efforts, hardships, hard work, beating back and overcoming obstacles strong men glory in. They take hold and lift themselves out of all difficulties and become master of every situation." Thus, according to the *Democrat,* men do not fall short of attaining their objectives. Any sign of failure or even of hesitancy in achieving the goal was an indication of a serious defect in gender identity—weak and/or cowardly men were not welcome (nor, one can reasonably assume, were strong and assertive women); in fact, the editor went on to suggest that a cowardly man was no more than a "child" who should leave the work of prairie settling to real men by returning to the place where his kind would be more welcome — namely "to his wife's people to curse a country whose soil would be no better had he been buried in it."[38]

This image of a barren soil made productive by the presence of a man's body is laden with rich sexual imagery. To 19th-century settlers, southeast Kansas was "virgin" land previously inhabited by sterile men who did not possess the requisite virility to reap its bounty. The Euro-American settlers had come as "real men" to civilize the land — to subdue the wild prairies, to subjugate the forces of nature, and to impregnate the soil with their blood and sweat — in the words of the *Democrat*, "to convert a raw piece of prairie into a producing farm."³⁹

At the very same time, however, as these men were assuring themselves of the potency of their manhood, they were possessed by a deep anxiety. The editor of the *Western Enterprise* gave voice to this repressed angst in a published "Ode to the Prairie." Using feminine imagery, the author lamented the destruction of the pristine purity of the native prairie by the onslaught of civilizing settlers: "The prairie, God's foot-stool, with its beautiful green carpet of waving grass, and the sweet perfume of a thousand flowers, its gurgling springs and rippling brooks in whose waters sport myriads of the merriest of the finny tribes. Who! Who can be fanned by the gentle breeze and drink in the pure atmosphere of the broad and beautiful prairie and not feel himself a better and happier man and worthier citizen?"

Once again, the author uses sexual imagery — like a young virgin, the prairie tantalizes the male who watches her "waving grasses," "sweet perfume," and "rippling brooks." But, as the editor goes on to mourn, men, thus stimulated, could not restrain themselves — "We look upon the prairie and the scene is changed.... Civilization has robbed dame nature of her savage wilderness."⁴⁰ This author thus asks the question that pressed in upon many settlers: In subjugating the expansive prairies, did the phallic desire to confine and border destroy the openness and limitlessness of its original purity?

Furthermore, as the settlers quickly learned, neither the virgin prairies nor frontier women seemed ready to roll over and let the men have their way. For all of their masculine bravado and bluster, the prairie seemed remarkably unimpressed. As reported in the *Osage Mission Journal*, "The Neosho [River] is on the rampage and has been on it for several days, to the great disgust of the lumber men."⁴¹ In the winter of 1869, the editor of the *Chetopa Advance* complained: "The Neosho is brim and booming.... The earth is like a saturated sponge. It is wet — wetter — wettest.... We are water bound and then the mud. Boundless, ubiquitous, measureless, fathomless oceans of mud!"⁴² The *Labette Sentinel* joined the chorus of complaint and concern in October of 1870: "We can see from our office window the prairie fires raging to the north of town. They look beautiful, fanned by the calm night breeze, but these fires are as destructive as they are beautiful."⁴³

As surely as the beauty of a prairie fire could beguile the unsuspecting naïve settler, so too could the feminine beauty that awakened the fires of desire and passion within him. In December of 1869, the *Osage Mission*

Journal published the proceedings of a "convention of the bachelors of Osage Mission" that had met to warn its younger members against the "captivating influence of Eve's daughters." Noting that "many of our veteran bachelors, who have enjoyed the luxury of single blessedness during a series of years and who have resisted the devil, the world and the woman ... have recently fell victim to that terrible destroyer and have been taken from our midst in the prime of life to be offered in bloody sacrifice on the altar of Hymen," the convention passed the following resolutions:

> RESOLVED, that we the bachelors of Osage Mission hereby enter our solemn protest against any more of our brotherhood uniting themselves to the daughters of Eve;
> RESOLVED, that we pledge ourselves to take immediate steps to check the progress of the destroyer of our peace and happiness.[44]

Although it is highly likely that this article was meant to be tongue-in-cheek, its underlying themes reappeared regularly in the reflections and editorials of early newspaper editors in Labette and Neosho counties. Certainly, these missives were part of a larger 19th-century genre of popular literature in which, as the historian Laura Edwards has noted, "domestic writers bombarded their audiences with practical advice, heavy-handed prescriptions on appropriate womanly conduct and syrupy sentimental fiction." However, as Edwards makes clear, we should not overlook their significance by "mistak[ing] the genre's melodramatic superficialities for historical insignificance"; instead it is important to understand that these "domestic writers were involved in a profound ideological project."[45]

In his study of nineteenth century agricultural newspapers, Richard Farrell found that editors overtly solicited farm women in their papers, allotting an ever increasing amount of space to topics that appealed to female readers.[46] Indeed, as Lisa Bunkowski has noted in her study of emerging communities in Butler County, "newspapers in the West actively disseminated the more conventional paradigms of separate spheres and 'True Womanhood.' By defining the appropriate roles and behavior of women, purveyors of social norms clearly delineated the appropriate roles and behavior of men."[47] This is also noted by Bennett who argues that "Newspaper editors knew they had access to women and therefore catered to this female reading audience to encourage their interest in newspapers and by extension, purchasing newspapers."[48]

This was particularly true in southeast Kansas in the late 1860s and early '70s in the early days of settlement when the lack of available labor forced men to depend upon their wives in new ways even as it opened up new opportunities for them to expand their role in public society. In a

4. Challenges to Public Order (1871–1874) 123

candid observation, the *Osage Mission Journal* noted the manifold roles played by Kansan women: "It is the wife's occupation to winnow all manner of corn, to make malt, to wash and wring, to make hay, to shear corn, and in time of need to help her husband fill the muck-wain [or manure carts], to drive the plow, to load corn, hay and such other; and to go or ride to the market to sell butter, cheese, milk, eggs, chickens, capons, hens, pigs, geese, turkey, and all manner of corn ... and to bear and rear children."[49] Although arduous (the list of duties is exhausting to read, let alone perform), many of these new duties expanded the boundaries of the domestic sphere in which white women in 19th-century America had been confined; they also adjusted the level of control that the husband had over his wife by lessening her dependency upon him for survival.[50]

The *Oswego Independent* noted one aspect of the change in an article entitled "Female Hunter." After relating the exploits of "a Mrs. W. M. Bowen" who had successfully shot three prairie chickens who had alighted in the cornfield next to her house, the paper asserted: "We mention this to show what the women of Kansas can do, when they try. In the East it would be considered a good shot for a man who was an experienced sportsman."[51]

As is evident by the number of men filing for divorce on the basis of "abandonment" in the late 1860s and early '70s in southeast Kansas, many women understood all too well the freedom these new found responsibilities and opportunities afforded them. As the *Osage Mission Journal* noted in reporting George Rich's petition for a divorce from his wife Amanda (whom he had married less than two years earlier in June of 1868), even though "he has ever since conducted himself toward you as a faithful and affectionate husband ... you disregarding your duties as wife have been willfully absent from him for more than one year last past without any cause or justification on your part."[52] Wives were not the only women to explore the contours of the evolving reconstitution of gender relations. In 1870, a warning appeared in the Southern Kansas Advance. Paid for by Jacob Ebert, the notice read: "FOREWARNED: All parties are herby [*sic*] forewarned not to trust or harbor my daughter, Barberry Ebert on my account, as I will not be responsible for debts contracted by her, as she has left my home without cause or provocation."[53] Daughters were not the ones to help their mothers escape the domination of their fathers; the *Oswego Register* recorded the following story: "Lowe and his wife were in dispute and from words went to blows. It is alleged that the woman's husband was choking her when she called to her boy, a lad thirteen years of age, to shoot him. The boy did as he was directed."[54]

An interesting poem in the *Oswego Register* pointedly warned men of the collusion that was occurring between their wives and daughters. Entitled "Fowl Rebellion; Or, Women's Rights in a Poultry Yard," the poem dramatized a conflict between a hen and her chick over the hen's acceptance of abuse from the rooster. After exposing the manifold faults of the rooster, the chick finally persuades her mother to leave him. She then expresses her great joy in these words:

> Well, mother, I'm glad you've waked up at last
> I feared you'd sleep on till the good time was past
> That forever you'd run at his nod and his beck
> But now you're my free, darling, blessedest mother
> Well rid of one rooster — don't get another;
> You and I are both able to care for ourselves;
> I'll bet you, dear ma, we'll live on the top shelves.
> ...
> For my part, I've seen so much trouble and strife,
> I vow and declare I'll never be a wife
> I hate — yes, I hate all tyrannical men
> Independent I'll live, a single old hen![55]

Thoughts like these accentuated a deeply rooted anxiety felt by many southeast Kansan men about their own masculinity. Their identity as "men" was constructed around the ideal of a passive "woman"— as editor John Horner reminded his readers: "He is not a man that hath not a woman."[56] Historian Bruce Dorsey has noted, "Gender has functioned so that 'man' is constituted as the binary opposite of 'woman,' and 'woman' as the opposite of 'man.' In other words, what proves that a man is definitely a man is that he is not a woman."[57] As Simone de Beauvoir explained, in classic patriarchal thought "humanity is male and man defines woman as relative to him; she is not regarded as an autonomous being.... She is defined and differentiated with reference to man and not he with reference to her, she is the incidental, the inessential as opposed to the essential. He is the Subject, he is the Absolute — she is the Other."[58] De Beauvoir's comments apply with amazing exactitude to the perspective of men in southeast Kansas in the late 1860s and 70s. Women were the "other" against which they constructed their own notions of masculinity and maleness. It was vitally important that women remain static and unchanging in order for men to feel secure in their own sense of maleness. Thus, the presence of strong, assertive women in their homes and communities not only threatened the patriarchal structure of the community they were seeking to build — it also called into question the very nature of their own masculinity.

An article entitled, "Ask the Old Woman," which appeared in the

Oswego Register in 1872, highlighted the ultimate fear engendered by these questions. The account told the tale of a traveler "out west" who happened upon an isolated log house in a clearing. Noticing that the owner of the house was sitting in the open door of the "shanty," the traveler asks him for a drink of milk. The man responds, "Well, I don't know. Ask the old woman." As the subsequent dialogue reveals, this is the man's response to every question. Noting the changing weather, the traveler inquires, "Think we are going to have a storm?" To which the man replies, "Well, I really don't know. Ask the old woman — she can tell." The traveler queries, "How much land have you got cleared here?" The man again responds, "Well, I really don't know. Ask the old woman — she knows." Finally, as a group of children appear, the traveler asks, "Are these your children?" The response remains the same, "Don't know. Ask the old woman."[59]

Upon arriving in southeast Kansas, men quickly discovered that the nature they were seeking to subdue was not passive; neither were many of the women upon whom they depended for survival. In fact, many of the "women" were not wearing faces of pure contentment — as an early female correspondent, calling herself "Lady Labette," explained in a series of letters to the editor of the *Neosho Valley Eagle*, "They call us the weaker sex — good for nothing but to dress and flirt, have no mind of our own, and not capable of reasoning and acting for ourselves ... We thought when we emigrated to Kansas that we would find a home in one spot on the globe where a woman was (for the first time since she was banished from Paradise) considered equal to the lords of creation. But in that we were mistaken."[60]

Interestingly, this comment of Lady Labette was actually the result of a casual comment made by the editor of the *Eagle* who had noted that since it was a leap year, it was "year of Jubilee — of repose to all young gentlemen!" This year, he asserted, "the ladies have the 'say so.'"[61] From future remarks, it is clear that the editor intended his words to be a lighthearted attempt at humor. However, he soon found out that his words carried deeper meaning to some of his female subscribers. Lady Labette's words must have stung when she wrote, announcing her pleasure in finding "one man in Kansas frank enough to acknowledge that women are smarter in one calling in life than man, if it is only in courting, for as a general rule, they are very rare who will pronounce her on an equality with man."[62]

Lady Labette then went on to express her own frustration with the state of gender relations in southeast Kansas. The historical background to her anger was clearly the political issue of women's suffrage that emerged in Kansas the previous year. In February 1867, the Kansas legislature passed two amendments (the first gave African-American men the vote; the second granted suffrage to all women). Since both amendments needed a majority vote from the white male electorate to become law, they were placed on the ballot in November of 1867. Male voters in southeast Kansas voted 2–1 (535 votes opposed; 266 votes in favor) to deny African Americans the right to vote and 3–1 (584 votes opposed; 196 votes in favor) to deny suffrage to women.[63] As Lady Labette explained, she had immigrated to Kansas believing that in the settling of a new geographical region, men would be willing to reconsider the traditional strictures placed upon women by giving them new opportunities for both political and social activity. However, upon arriving and settling down, she and her female companions had found themselves thoroughly disappointed.

As the subsequent debate which unfolded on the pages of the *Eagle* over the next few months demonstrated, not all women agreed with "Lady Labette"— in fact, some, like "Mollie" from Erie argued that they found great joy in fulfilling the passive position of "helper" men were eager to assign to them.[64] However, the fact that "Lady Labette" and her supporters were willing to publicly challenge the gendered vision of a patriarchal society indicates the existence of disagreement over gender roles within southeast Kansas families and communities. As "Firmness" explained in response to a letter to the editor in which Mollie had called "Lady Labette" demented and misguided, "I am one of those unfortunate, demented creatures who believes that woman's sphere should be enlarged, that she can and should be more useful and that unless her sphere is enlarged we as a people, and as a nation must sink to nothingness.... With wishes for the improvement of our race, I remain one of the demented, FIRMNESS."[65]

The traditional categories which had defined masculine and feminine behavior were furthered blurred by the emergence of the temperance movement in southeast Kansas. Upon arriving in southeast Kansas, men quickly discovered that many of the women upon whom they depended for survival, illustrated by both "Lady Labette" and "Firmness," were no longer content to remain "passive" and "subservient" to their needs and desires but were demanding to take a more active role in constructing ordered societies. In southeast Kansas, this desire for more direct participation in the structuring of society pushed many women both to embrace the goal of female suffrage and to join the crusades of the early temperance movement.

"Firmness" was the first to publicly connect women's rights with the issue of temperance in her letter of July 11, 1868, when she argued that "men alone, are a selfish set, thinking or caring but little for anything, unless for their own selfish ends and enjoyment." It was this inherent pleasure-seeking mentality of men that led them to accept the presence of saloons, gambling halls, houses of prostitution, and the like in their midst.

For, as she insisted, "Would woman's vote or voice be heard in favor of distilleries and dram shops? Of gambling halls? And prostitution? No! The noble nature of woman revolts at all these; but she submits, for she is in chains, and has no other alternative." In fact, she concluded, when a woman was forcibly secluded in her home, "doing no good outside, the four walls that conceal her from God's light," it was inevitable that the community in which she lived would "see the Whiskey Demon with his attendance of prostitutes, casting their cursed, blighting influence over the land, destroying the peace and happiness of thousands."[66]

Some historians have argued that the temperance movement was a conservative movement premised in women's domestic status and designed to advance middle class ideals, not primarily a way to challenge gender roles or boundaries.[67] However, as Nancy G. Garner has written about the temperance movement in Kansas, "central to the crusade was a rethinking of gender roles." Furthermore, she writes, "The Crusades offered a crucial opportunity for rethinking and revisioning gender roles."[68] It should also be noted that the immigration pattern that characterized the settlement of Kansas in the post–Civil War years suggests that, at least in this geographical region, the emergence of the temperance movement must be seen within the context of an ongoing debate over gender roles in the newly established communities.

The idea of temperance as a moral crusade in southeast Kansas first surfaced in Chetopa in 1869, where, according to the *Chetopa Advance*, "a rousing and enthusiastic meeting of the friends of temperance was held at Spaulding's Hall on Tuesday evening last." At this meeting, "the best and most substantial citizens of the place ... evinced, in most decided language and action, a determination that public drunkenness and riotous conduct should not be permitted to disgrace our community."[69] Established before the Civil War as a trading city, the antebellum merchants of Chetopa had attempted to cultivate a trading relationship with the indigenous peoples who lived less than 12 miles away in the newly established Indian territory. As the last stop before the Territory, a lucrative business in "spirits" had developed — it was the rowdiness associated with the flourishing taverns and bars that had motivated the public meeting. By 1869, the founding fathers of Chetopa, intent on creating a new image for themselves, had embarked on a new course emphasizing sobriety. A desire to set themselves apart from the "native peoples" who were stereotypically referred to as "drunks" by the white settlers also drove the city fathers of Chetopa to embrace the movement to curtail drunkenness.[70] Since the drunkenness of Native men was seen as in gendered terms, as I have argued above, the emergence of a women-led temperance movement was certainly likely to produce a negative reaction among those who believed that dependency upon alcohol was a sign of moral weakness and thus de-masculinizing.

The leading men of Chetopa were not the only authorities to be intent on establishing control over the liquor trade. The *Osage Mission Journal* reported that the citizens of Ladore, in response to the tragedy its citizens had endured at the hands of drunken railroad workers, "have determined that the law shall be executed restraining and regulating the sale of intoxicating liquors and that some regard shall be had for the observance of that higher law ... which has declared that good order, sobriety, safety to life, limb and honor are infinitely greater importance to any community than pandering for filthy lucre's sake to the debased tastes and passions of those who, unfortunately for themselves, are slaves to strong drink."[71]

It is interesting to note the use of the words "slaves" in the announcement — for as the temperance movement grew in southeast Kansas, like the abolitionist movement before it, it soon became a movement in which, contrary to the designs of the men of Chetopa and Ladore, women played a dominant role. The first indication that women were taking a strong interest in combating the "evils of liquor" can be found in the *Labette Sentinel*. By 1871, in villages, towns and cities throughout southeast Kansas, literary societies had been formed. Typically meeting one evening a week, people gathered to discuss the important issues of the day. Ordinarily, the debates were a time for the leading men of the village, town or city to show off their oratory skills. However, in the city of Labette, when the decision was made to discuss the question, "Which is the greater evil, war or intemperance?" the ladies took the lead. As the *Sentinel* reported, "Several of the debaters were young and made their 'maiden' speech, receiving applause from the hearers, especially the ladies."[72] In April, noted temperance speaker Fannie Allyn[e] visited Oswego and spoke to a packed audience in the Methodist Episcopal Church "on the subject of temperance." In May, the *Tioga Herald* printed a poem entitled "The Drunkard's Daughter" in which the author argued strongly that because it was women who bore the brunt of alcohol's scourge, it was women who should take the lead in opposing it.

> Go, to my mother's side
>   And her crushed spirit cheer,
> Thine own deep anguish hide
>   Wipe from her check the tear
> Mark her dimm'd eye, her furrowed brow
>   The gray that streaks her dark hair now
> Her toil-worn frame, the trembling limb

4. Challenges to Public Order (1871–1874)

> And trace the ruin back to him
> Whose plighted faith in early youth
>   Promised eternal love and truth
> But who, foresworn, hath yielded up
>   This promise to the deadly cup
> And led down from love and light
>   From all that made her pathway bright
> And chained her there, 'mid want and strife,
>   The lowly thing, a Drunkard's wife
> And stamp'd on childhood's brow so mild
>   That withering blight, the Drunkard's child.
> ...
> Tell me I hate the bowl!
>   Hate is a feeble word
> I loathe, abhor — my very soul
>   With strong disgust is stirr'd
> When e'er I see or hear or tell
> Of that dark beverage of hell.[73]

Events in southeast Kansas paralleled those in the nation. As women throughout the Northeast worked together to close down saloons, women in southeast Kansas began to challenge the men in their community. It seems to have begun mildly — in the winter of 1872, the papers began to report stories of women entering saloons to find their fathers, husbands, and brothers and bring them home. The *Tioga Herald* was the first to report the phenomenon: "It would appear from what we learn of the saloon on the corner of Main and Fifth streets, that the ladies sometimes pay the concern an occasional visit. Not to drink, however, but to entice their male relatives home. This week one of these lady visitors while trying to get her brother out of the place, took umbrage at something and smashed in a window."[74]

This was a bold move — one that challenged the geographical boundaries of patriarchal society. Saloons were no place for married women — only whores and prostitutes frequented saloons. In fact, so strong was the aversion to women in saloons that it had been put forward as a compelling reason for women not to vote by "Mollie" in the 1868 debate over female suffrage in the *Neosho Valley Eagle*. Mollie had written: "Think of a woman, on election day, at the polls, amongst a class of men whom her husband might not associate with, without danger to his character; a woman cannot well be deaf and dumb and blind to all the obscenity and low jokes of such a place and keep her name spotless." For Mollie, the very act of entering a saloon or associating with those who worked there stripped a woman of her purity and imperiled the essence of her feminine virtue — "Could she look up to her husband with the same respect and confidence she now does? No! Verily No!"[75]

However, as women assumed new positions of leadership in their growing communities in the early 1870s, the "Mollies" of southeast Kansas began to redefine their role vis-à-vis the saloon, and by extension vis-à-vis the men of their community. Instead of withdrawing from society to preserve their domestic tranquility, they began to engage society in an attempt to extend the boundaries of that tranquility and to save their men from the corruption of disorder and chaos. Interestingly, Nancy Garner has noted a similar historical phenomenon in her study of northeast Kansas women.[76] By the summer of 1872, Kansan women had come together to assert their demands for an alcohol free society and by extension to express their political power.

The *Transcript* reported that the Jacksonville temperance society appointed a committee of three ladies to request the "Saloon Keeper" to desist from selling "Intoxicating liquors." On Saturday morning, July 6, the three members of the committee, Maia Ammerman, Hiddie Dement, and Kiziah Moaks, walked down the main street to the Saloon and officially presented their "request" in the form of a written letter to the saloon owner:

> Mr. Joseph Pittman, Sir:— In the name of suffering humanity; in the name of violated law; in the name of those husbands and fathers, who, with blasted reputations, wasted fortunes and ruined health, are tottering on the brink of destruction; in the name of those brothers and sons who are fast brutalizing, and transforming into drunkards; in the name of those wives, mothers, and daughters, whose cheeks you have covered with shame, and whose hearts you have filled with anguish, at the degradation of those they love; in the name of those unfortunate families whose means of subsistence you are unlawfully obtaining, or causing to be squandered, from whose hearth-stones you have already banished peace and happiness and are substituting in their stead, want, wretchedness and ruin; yes, in the name and on behalf of all classes of our long-suffering community,— we, the undersigned, a committee appointed for the purpose, at a public meeting of our citizens, do hereby respectfully, yet earnestly request and entreat you to abandon your unlawful traffic, and henceforth to refrain entirely from selling intoxicating liquors to our community.
> Signed: Maia Ammerman, Hiddie Dement, Kiziah Moaks[77]

Not all women were content to "make requests" of their local saloon keepers. The *Southern Kansas Advance* told the story of Justina Bookter who tracked her way-ward husband down in the local saloon and, "upon entering to find him playing cards, "went for those at the card table, giving all of them a severe caning." She then turned to her husband, who had somehow managed to avoid the attack, and upon seeing a drink in his hand, "dashed the cup from his hand and 'went for' the saloon keeper."[78]

The *Osage Mission Journal* reported that members of the local Temperance Society had sent "postcards" to the owners of local saloons warning them that the ladies would be "going for the saloon keepers, if they don't give up the ghost, or in other words, stop disposing of spirits of the ardent variety."[79] The ladies of the Oswego Temperance Society adopted a similar strategy by sending the following letter to each of the saloon keepers in Oswego:

> Sir: You are hereby notified and warned that unless you desist from your present nefarious business of selling whiskey to the ruin of the business and souls of the community, we shall visit your place of crime in a body on Thursday, March 5th, at 10 a.m. and invoke the aid and blessing of Almighty God to so enlighten your minds that you may be enabled to realize the great sin you are committing, and forever abandon your present wretched business. Ladies Temperance Com.[80]

The editor of the *Oswego Independent* was one of the first to publicly acknowledge the challenge these women of the Temperance movement were presenting to the patriarchal underpinnings of southeastern Kansan society. He clearly interpreted the issue along gender lines. After decrying the absence of male leadership in opposition to the liquor trade and praising the role that women were playing, he wrote: "It is a shame to manhood that it is necessary, it is a glory to womanhood that it is possible."[81] As this quote makes clear, many men conceptualized the fight against alcohol along gender lines. This realization helps to explain why many men were not supportive of the women's increased public activities — for example, the editor of the *Parsons Sun*, Milton Reynolds, himself a vocal supportive of the temperance movement, refused to allow his wife to participate in "the crusades" (as the women's activities were called).[82] It is true that not all local leaders responded this way; for example, the pastor of the Parsons Methodist Episcopal Church, the Reverend Mr. Gunn, publicly announced his support for the Crusade by arguing that "he would be proud to see his wife engaged in that war" and thought that involvement in the Crusades had the ability to "elevate and ennoble womanhood and make them feel the tremendous power they possess for good.[83] Many men however disagreed — and did so precisely because of the "tremendous power" that involvement in the Crusades was giving to women in their communities. The *Oswego Independent* reported that a local preacher was publicly protesting "against temperance reform on scriptural grounds."[84]

The editor of the *Parsons Eclipse* publicly called for an end of the "crusades" arguing that "the women's crusade will do inestimable damage."

He was emphatically clear that his purpose was not to endorse the abuse of alcohol, for "habitual drunkenness should not be tolerated by any community." Instead, his opposition to the crusades was rooted in his perception that as a movement led by women it was prone to "excitement" and "enthusiasm." These words were filled with cultural meaning in the 19th century as they were often used to refer to the unreliable character of women who were prone to both characteristics by reason of what 19th-century American men considered to be their unsteady feminine constitution. The issue of drunkenness thus, the editor argued, should be dealt with according to "settled principles" and not by "fanatical propagandist[s]" who, if allowed to continue their work unchecked, would ultimately make the "evil we are seeking to remedy" grow "worse and worse."[85] Since drunkenness was a man's problem, the editor of the *Eclipse* was arguing, it should be dealt with by men.

The image of women banding together, entering saloons and making demands of men while threatening violence if their demands were not heeded, threatened the patriarchal images of society embraced by many male leaders in southeast Kansas. Although united in the desire for good order and social stability and thus concerned about the effects of drunkenness on their local communities, these men did not wish to see the women of their communities abandoning the social boundaries that had been prescribed for them.

As the editor of the *Oswego Independent* explained, he understood the Crusades to be a clear sign that women had lost "all faith in men."[86] As he told the story, after having "long and patiently watched the efforts of their husbands, fathers and brothers in their efforts to rid themselves of this curse upon themselves," women were finally acting to emancipate men, whom they routinely referred to as "the slaves of Bacchus" and "the willing slaves of the whiskey king," from "the chains" that "bound" them and, in setting them free, lead them to recover their "manhood" which they had "gradually surrendered" to the "maddening effects of whiskey guzzling."[87]

The words used in this newspaper story are significant as they mimic the words used by men to both describe their earlier role as defenders of the Union against the Confederacy and their current role as defenders of the independent patriotic farmer against the oppressive capitalist. Veterans of the Civil War in southeast Kansas had created their own identity around the concept of fighting the enslavement of the oppressed. To now hear themselves called "slaves" and to be told that they must be "emancipated" by their wives and daughters was a clear assault on their own self-identity as men and by extension on the communities they had worked to establish.

In other words, even as the leadership exercised by women in the battle against alcohol served to elevate and ennoble them, at the same time it also provoked shame in many men.[88]

Men thus responded to the perceived challenge by aggressively reminding women of their "proper place" in society in a series of editorials, published by several papers throughout southeast Kansas, that asserted (or reasserted) a traditional patriarchal view of male-female relations. Each article asserted (or reasserted) a traditional patriarchal view of male-female relations. Undoubtedly, interpreting these editorials and articles is complex. On the one hand, editors of local newspapers in southeast Kansas were not simply reporters but functioned as official spokesmen for their local communities and as boosters for would-be settlers. Newspaper editors, like Horner of the *Advance*, functioned as "boosters" by attempting to describe their towns as "settled"—that is, as "civilized" in a way many would have "read" as middle-class. Certainly, opposition to public drunkenness expressed this value as did a reiteration of the value and importance of maintaining traditional eastern gender norms.[89] Editors understood that their papers were being read not only by those who already immigrated but also by those who were considering immigration. It was thus important, in order to encourage continued settlement, that the communities of southeast Kansas be presented on their pages as civilized, developed, urbane communities in which the traditional gender boundaries of 19th-century America were both respected and enforced.

However, the editors were also dealing with a growing group of "Lady Labettes" and "Firmnesses" in their midst who insisted on reconstructing and reimagining these boundaries. Publishing articles championing the traditional and thus proper role of women therefore served two purposes. It assured would-be immigrants that all was well on the southeast Kansas frontier when it came to gender and it reminded those who had already come of the "proper" way in which gender roles should be constructed in ordered, lawful societies.

When reading the newspapers published in the 1860s and early 1870s in southeast Kansas, one is immediately struck by how much space is dedicated to the issue of gender. From the initial editions of the *Neosho Valley Eagle*, male-female relations were a frequent theme. On May 9, 1868, in the second edition of the paper, the editor addressed the subject by publishing a short article entitled "Woman." The article expressed the blend of fascination and confusion many men were experiencing by comparing women to a "complicated machine" with "indefinitely delicate" springs that "differ from those of man pretty nearly as the work of a repeating watch does from that of a town clock. Look at her body, how delicately formed. Examine her sense, how exquisite and nice! Observe her understanding, how subtle and acute! But look into her heart: there is the patchwork, composed of parts so wonderfully combined that they must be seen through a microscope to be nearly comprehended."[90]

In the next edition of the paper, the editor returned to this theme — after opining that "of all women she is most to be pitied who has a slow suitor," he related the story with obvious approval and admiration of a "legendary puritan" who rode up to the door of the house where the girl he had chosen to marry resided, and after announcing without delay "Rachel, the Lord hath sent me to marry thee," received the prompt reply: "The Lord's will be done!"[91]

Other editors made similar use of their columns. The *Osage Mission Journal* published an article entitled "The Quiet Woman" in September. In this article, the editor reminded his readers that "quiet women" are "the wine of life." Unlike "nervous, enthusiastic and talkative women," the "quiet woman" does not agitate for her rights or seek her own interests. Instead, "she is wise and thoughtful, but loving and meek.... In sorrow or illness, the quiet woman is nurse, counselor and friend. She soothes, comforts and caresses, and is the unfaltering guide of the weak and erring, through her own noble and unerring instincts.... She moves silently and orderly; even her garments falling in soft harmonious flow. She does not irritate with questions, but surprises and pleases by her unobtrusive anticipations. She rarely speaks."[92]

The picture painted here of the ideal woman stresses her passivity — she does not initiate but responds; she does not seek to fulfill her own desires but exists to fulfill the wants and needs of her husband. The *Neosho Valley Dispatch* was in complete agreement: "Let the wife only understand and have faith in her true position — that of women 'the helper.'"[93]

The *Neosho Valley Eagle* published a short article entitled, "Good counsel from a wife and mother" on the front page of its November 21st edition in 1868. According to this article, allegedly written by a seasoned and experienced "old woman," it was the woman's responsibility to ensure her husband's fidelity:

> It will not do to leave a man to himself till he comes to you, to take no pains to attract him or to appear before him with a long face. It is not so difficult as you think, dear child, to behave to a husband so that he shall remain forever in some measure a husband.... A word from you at the right time will not fail of its effect; what need have you to play the suffering virtue? The tear of a loving girl, says an old book, is like a dew-drop on a rose; but that on the cheek of a wife is a drop of poison to her husband. Try and appear cheerful and contented, and your husband will be so; and when you have made

him happy you will become so, not in appearance, but in reality. The skill required is not so great. Nothing flatters a man so much as the happiness of his wife; he is always proud of himself as the source of it. As soon as you are cheerful you will be lively and alert, and every moment will afford you an opportunity to let fall an agreeable word.[94]

The *Southern Kansas Advance* sought to ground this conception of "passive femininity" in nature itself: "Women are naturally less selfish and more sympathetic than men. They have more affection to bestow, greater need of sympathy, and are therefore more sure, in the absence of love, to seek friendship. The devastating egoism of man is properly foreign to women.... The cardinal contrast holds that women are self-forgetful, men self-asserting; women hide their surplus affection under a feigned indifference; men hide their indifference under a feigned affection."[95]

The editor of the *Oswego Independent* registered his agreement by arguing that "the loveliest adornment of perfect womanhood is unconsciousness of self." In fact, feminine passivity was more important than any other quality that a woman might possess; as he went on to explain, "If the woman possessed of this rare virtue be lacking in physical beauty, nay, even plain, there is a charm in her innocence and simplicity more potent than the smiles of the fairest featured siren that ever deluded the susceptible heart of man.... True beauty lies in the hidden perfection of the soul.... No feminine face is truly beautiful that does not wear, to a certain extent, an expression of contentment and repose."[96]

The *Tioga Herald* added its weight to the ongoing social discourse by asserting that "the husband's interest should be the wife's care, and her greatest ambition carry her no further than his welfare or happiness together with that of her children. This should be her sole aim, and the theater of her exploits in the bosom of her family."[97]

These perspectives were reinforced by a series of poetic celebrations of feminine passivity. Entitled variously as "A Maiden's Psalm of Life," "The Perfect Woman," "A Wife's Song," "The True Woman," "The Young Wife's Prayer," "A Happy Woman," and "The Old Maid's Psalm," these poems advanced the patriarchal assertions contained within the prosaic editorials.[98]

So occupied were the editors with this theme that in announcing the election of Ulysses S. Grant to the presidency in 1868, the *Osage Mission Journal* rejoiced in the fact that this meant Mrs. Grant would be the first lady. For, as the paper explained to its readers, "It is gratifying to know that the position is one which Mrs. Grant will fill with that true simplicity of an American woman." This simplicity assured Americans that "there will be no attempt to ape the grandeur of a regal court, and no vulgar striving after more sensation." Even more importantly, "Mrs. Grant is a lady, who has maintained through every event ... a marked propriety of demeanor. She has been help-meet in days of adversity and has shared his honors without being dazzled by the position."[99]

Although the paper does not explain any further this reference to Mrs. Grant, the comparative structure of the endorsement indicates that the person of Mrs. Grant was embraced as a symbol of true femininity against women of wealth, power, and independent activity. Mrs. Grant was the opposite of the "advanced female," frequently disparaged in newspapers, who refused to accept her role in her marriage and society. As Mr. Grant epitomized the aggressive masculinity of the Civil War veteran, his wife embodied the simplicity of true American femininity. As the editor of the *Transcript* explained, true American women (like Mrs. Grant) delighted in "the devotion, the poetry, and the honor in keeping house." His conclusion was thus set: "If they are not strong enough for the task, all that can be said is that they are not fit to be women."[100] This comment is made even more interesting when it is compared to a similar comment in the *Erie Ishmaelite* who reported that he had been accused in another paper of being a "hermaphrodite"—a genderless being who "hadn't pluck enough to be a man and too little modesty to be a woman."[101]

According to the men who penned these editorials, the concepts of masculinity and femininity were static; any attempts therefore to challenge or change the basic gender order of the family or of the larger community violated their stated aims in choosing to settle in the region in the years immediately following the Civil War. A change in basic social order also threatened the long-term viability of their plans to build lawful communities in the southeast Kansas frontier. Such plans, in their minds, depended on continued immigration which was contingent upon their ability to demonstrate to would-be settlers that the gender standards of the East were fully implemented in their communities. The image of women banding together, entering saloons and making demands of men while threatening violence if their voices were not heeded, threatened the patriarchal images of society embraced by many male leaders in southeast Kansas. Although united in the desire for good order and social stability and thus concerned about the effects of drunkenness on their local communities, these men did not wish to see the women of their communities abandoning the social boundaries that had been prescribed for them.

5

SETTLERS TRIUMPHANT (1875–1876)

On July 11, 1868, as he mused about the inevitable coming of the railroads, the editor of the *Neosho Valley Eagle* could not quite make up his mind as to whether it was a good thing or bad — "We do not oppose railroads, but as a general thing, railroad companies swallow up whole communities in their capacious jaws. They do everything for the dear people, only to gorge their own plethoric purses."[1] Southeast Kansas settlers often found themselves confounded by the railroads. On the one hand, the railroads clearly stood in their way by actively opposing their attempts establish title to their claims — the railroads were thus clearly on the side of the monopolists and speculators intent on taking away the freedom and liberties of ordinary people. Yet, on the other hand, the railroads offered financial prosperity by promising new markets for their crops.

Like a siren's call, this promise could often sway even the most dedicated adversary. As the *Osage Mission Journal* reminded its readers, "That Southern Kansas is soon to be the great Railroad center of the now far west seems to be admitted by every one…. Possessing a rich, productive country the thrifty farmers of Southern Kansas are already demanding an outlet for their produce."[2] The *Neosho Valley Register* was also won over: "Only one thing is lacking to this splendid domain: railroads. In the advocacy of railroads, making this a distinctive feature of our paper as we do, we know we are advocating the true interests of Southern Kansas and the State at large. At the present rate of immigration and settlement of this portion of the State, railroads become something more than a convenience and luxury. They are an indispensable necessity."[3] Even the *Eagle* was forced to agree, "The many railroads that are now making way, both from Missouri and Kansas, to us will open the country and enhance the value of cultivated land and proportionately increase the value of uncultivated as well as city and town property together."[4]

Yet, behind every note of approval lurked the reminder that the railroads were not an unmitigated blessing — as the *Neosho County Dispatch* informed its readers: "We were led to believe — perhaps foolishly — that there would be some way devised by which each actual settler would be allowed to purchase his land from the government at $1.25 per acre. But now it seems to be settled that the railroad has vested rights here, and that those who have gone on those lands subsequent to the withdrawal will have to look to the railroad company for their title."[5] Editor Horner likewise reminded his readers of the true nature of the 'Railroad Question'— "These facts are simply appalling — In the face of such legislation, the homestead and pre-emption laws are a cheat and a delusion. The public schools are robbed to satisfy the greed of the rapacious monopolist. Senators are bought like oxen in the shambles. The homes of the hardy pioneers are relentlessly wrested from them by soulless corporations, and the foundations of perpetual and ruinous monopolies are being laid, to grow into dangerous proportions and overshadow the land with their withering blight."[6] Yet, even Horner could not resist the bemusing pledge of future prosperity — "Our railroad prospects brighten day by day, and probabilities are fast ripening into certainties."[7]

There were no railroads in southeast Kansas when the first veterans arrived in the months following the Civil War. Railroad interest in southeast Kansas was rooted in its geographic position as a place to go through in order to reach Texas. Motivated by a desire to connect markets in Chicago and St. Louis with the lucrative southern cattle trade, the railroads initiated plans to lay tracks in Labette and Neosho counties. As geographer James Shortridge has noted, "the owners had a bigger prize in mind. To reach the Gulf Coast."[8] Southeast Kansas was "in between"; to the railroads its primary asset was its geographic position.

Three railroads competed to control the Texas trade: the Leavenworth, Lawrence Galveston (LLG), the Missouri, Kansas and Texas (the name assumed by the Union Pacific, Southern Branch, in March of 1870) and the Border tier from Kansas City, owned and operated by railroad magnate, James Joy. Since Indian Territory lay south of Kansas, all three railroads negotiated rights to continue laying track after they had passed through southern Kansas with the Cherokee Nation in the 1860s. In 1870, however, the Cherokees decided that only one railroad would be allowed to enter its territory.[9] Thus, the race was on. The first railroad to reach the Kansas-Indian Territory border would be given exclusive rights to build through Indian Territory. Of the three railroads competing, two decided to build through the Osage Ceded Lands: the Katy (as the Missouri, Kansas and Texas came to be called) and the LLG. Joy decided to take a route that

5. Settlers Triumphant (1875–1876)

This black and white photograph shows a rock cut near McAlister, Indian Territory, on the Missouri-Kansas-Texas Railroad.

hugged the Missouri-Kansas border and thus to build through the Cherokee Neutral Lands, east of the Osage Ceded Lands.

As news of the railroad competition reached southeast Kansans, local leaders began to speculate where the tracks would be laid even as local citizens began to dream about their future prosperity. Horner assured his readers that the coming of the railroads would bring a transformation to Chetopa. "Our town," he told them, "will more than double the number of its population and buildings."[10] Anticipating that Chetopa would be the place where the railroads would build their depot, he promised them "a metropolitan city and commercial emporium. Here will be immense machine shops and manufactories."[11] Most importantly, Horner promised his readers that the coming of the railroads would bring an end to their financial struggles: "Hitherto we have been poor in spirit and in pocket. The near approach of railroads is already bringing an influx of capital without which no country can be developed. Claims will give place to farms, cabins to comfortable farm-houses, squatters to farmers, coaches to railroads, shiftlessness to industry."[12]

Throughout the region, newspaper editors joined Horner in instructing their readers in the transformative powers of railroads. Some insisted that the railroads would bring new immigrants whose demand for land would increase the value of properties already owned by settlers. The *Osage Mission Journal* argued, "Building and operating such road will double the value at once of every farm and village lot in the respective townships which would be traversed by the road in question, and this value would be still again doubled within five years of such a time as the road is finished.... Now do our farmer friends want their land to be worth fifty and a hundred dollars per acre, instead of one fourth those prices; with a brisk demand in the one case and 'no sale' in the other?"[13]

Others chose to emphasize the lucrative effect of being connected to eastern markers. The *Advance* argued, "The products of our fertile prairies must seek the Eastern markers. The great mass of immigration is pouring from the East. All our commercial affiliations are with the East. It becomes us, then, to allow no delay in looking well to our Eastern railroad connections."[14] The *Neosho Valley Register* warned its readers that "without railroads, five years hence corn will sell in Allen, Labette and Neosho Counties at 20 cents per bushel."[15] A correspondent to the *Chetopa Advance* agreed, insisting that without railroads the growth being experienced by local businesses would be short-lived—"Our merchants are doing a good business, but are very much troubled consequent the difficulty of getting goods freighted from the end of the railroad. It is hoped this difficulty will be removed ere very long by the appearance of a railroad through the town."[16]

The *Journal* reminded its readers that a railroad was essential to the future because it would connect Osage Mission "with the commercial centers to which we are tributary" and would "open such means of speedy and cheap transit for merchandise and immigration already of vast proportions." Furthermore, without a railroad connection, the paper warned, Osage Mission risked becoming "an isolated town with Railroads running all around us, yet sufficiently near to cut off our trade and shear us of all local importance and thrift." The danger to Osage Mission was real—as the editor reminded his readers, "We are not always to have a home market made by a preponderance of immigration, who are consumers rather than producers, but soon shall raise and export many thousands of bushels of wheat, corn and potatoes and ship fat beeves from our cattle on a thousand hills to supply distant markets and hungry people."[17]

By far, however, the strongest argument advanced on behalf of the railroads was put forward in the *Parsons Sun*. To editor Milton Reynolds, the railroad was the instrument of civilization "that forced the march of our empire westward"—thus, only by being linked to the great centers of civilization in the east could southern Kansas escape the stigma of savagery and barbarity. As Reynolds explained, "The engine is more powerful than the Indian. The one represents progress and civilization; the other, barbarism and the middle ages. The engine carries with it schools, churches, material wealth, state and national development."[18] In fact, in developing this theme, Reynolds asserted that without the railroad, the settler would be no better off than the Indian whose land he had taken. "Railroads and settlement go hand in hand, and our rich lands stimulate them both. Neither of them would be of value without the other. The state of Kansas was hardly worth inhabiting without railroads." It was the presence of the "railcar" that allowed the settler to "feel still that he is in the midst of civilization."[19]

The editor of the *Tioga Herald* was in full agreement, as he reminded the paper's readers: "As a civilized power, as a sure means of developing the resources of a country, they [railroads] cannot be over-estimated. The history of great Western cities ... proves that railroads make cities."[20] The *New Chicago Transcript* made a similar point in 1872: "The vast territory comprising our commonwealth, now dotted with cities, towns, villages and farms in every condition of improvement was, but a decade since, a vast wilderness, inhabited only by the Indian and wild animals. What has produced the change? Why, our railroads, and nothing else."[21] The *Oswego Register* attributed even more to the railroads, claiming that

> of all the agencies set in motion by the genius and the energy of the nineteenth century, the locomotive is entitled to the foremost rank. By the aid of that marvelous machine it is hardly too much to say, that a social, financial and industrial revolution has been accomplished.... It has given to peace a new meaning and a larger prosperity; it changed the science of war by breaking down the barriers of time and space; it has reached and moved all classes of society from highest to lowest, and permanently associated itself with that indomitable enterprise and wonderful progress which are the most prominent features of the age.[22]

The fact that newspaper editors repeatedly asserted the importance of railroads is a clear indication that adoption of these ideas was far from universal. Behind every positive assertion lay the harsh reality encountered by settlers in the Humboldt Land Office. Added to this was the insensitivity and incompetence of the Railroad land agents who had been sent to convince the settlers to purchase their lands from them. The Missouri-Kansas-Texas Railroad had appointed Isaac Goodnow as their land agent. Isaac Goodnow (often referred to in correspondence and articles as "Professor Goodnow" because of his previous occupation as a teacher) was married to Eleanor D. Denison, the sister of the vice-president of the Katy, George Denison. Masterson notes that "his appointment to the powerful (and profitable) post of Katy land commissioner was consequent upon his marrying the boss's sister."[23] Universally despised by settlers, Goodnow did nothing to advance the cause of the railroad. In fact, as the *Parsons Sun* explained, his presence only made a bad situation worse: "Goodnow has outlived his day of usefulness as Land Commissioner. His vascillating [*sic*] course, his unequal, unjust and high appraisements, his treatment of individual applicants for land, have simply made it impossible for settlers on the Osage lands to do business at the land office with Goodnow at the head." Ultimately, even the railroad was forced to agree with Reynolds. As Levi Parsons wrote to Robert Stevens, "Professor [Goodnow] does not understand men and frequently fails to grasp the magnitude of this Land question. He is faithful & earnest, but at times, rather precise."[24]

Since it had reached the border first and thus was the railroad in the greatest need of cash to continue its track-laying southward, the Missouri-Kansas-Texas tried the hardest to reach a settlement with the settlers. The LLG also tried to come to terms with the settlers; like the Katy, however, its refusal to negotiate and its insistence on its legal right to the lands alienated the settlers.

On January 10, 1870, Levi Parsons, the president of the Katy, announced that he would build a second railroad line, reaching east into Missouri, to a junction with the Missouri Pacific. As he explained to the board of directors, "The moment we reach Indian Territory, this line will require such a connection in order to handle effectively the potentially great traffic between that area and the markets of the North and East."[25] To accommodate this new line and to coordinate the transfer of cattle and other cargo, Parsons asked Robert S. Stevens, the general manager, to choose a strategically position site for a central depot. As a result, the Parsons Town Company was formed in October 1870 to choose the land and initiate the process by which the depot would be built. The town site of Parsons was surveyed in February of 1871, and on March 8, individual lots were sold to prospective settlers. Within a few days, two thousand settlers

Opposite: Railroad broadside advertising the Sedalia, Missouri, route of the Missouri, Kansas & Texas Railway Company.

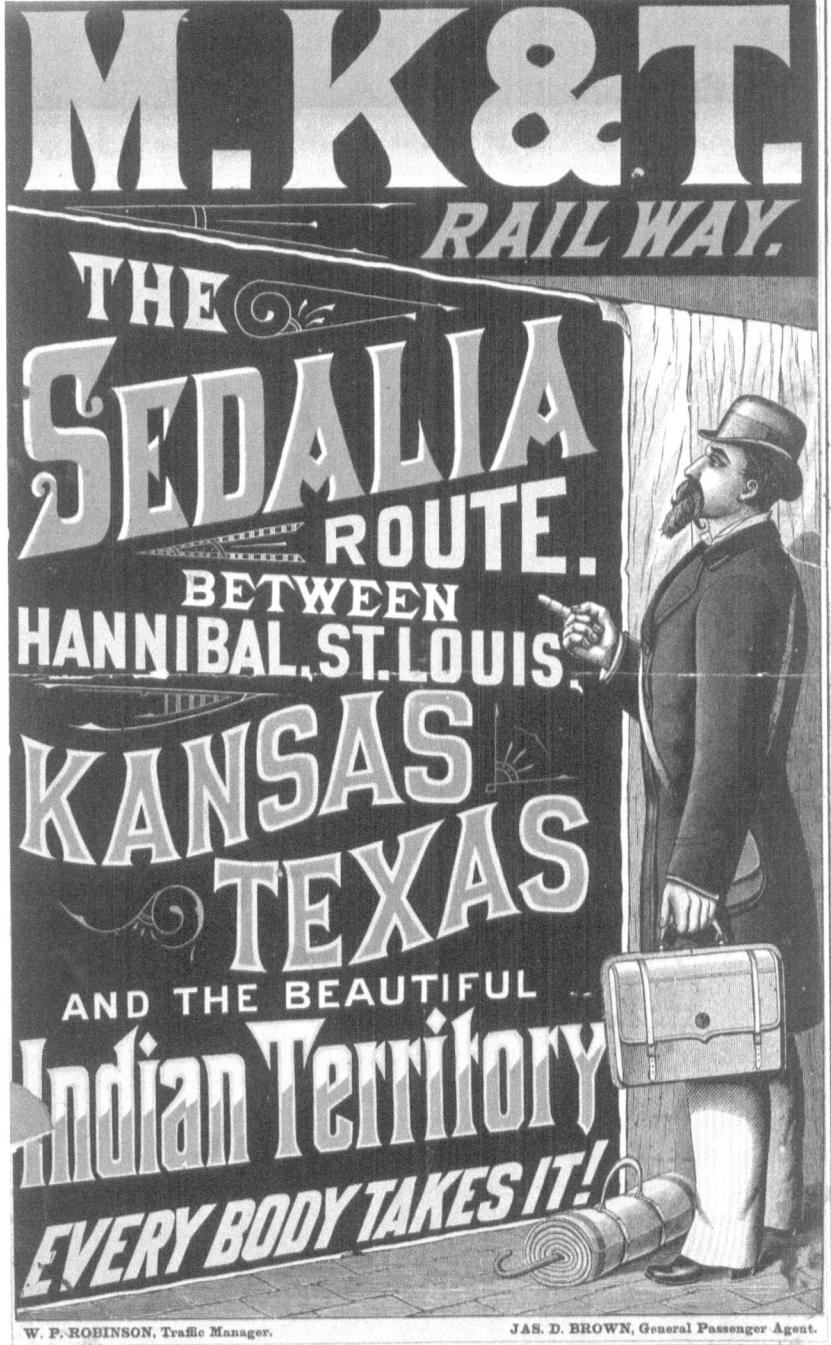

had completed their purchases and were preparing to move to the new town. Meanwhile, Stevens took up residence in the town and, while overseeing the building of the railroad, also spent the first few months working to establish a number of private business enterprises in Parsons. He created the first bank in town (the First National), established the National Mill and Elevator Company, convinced his cousin E.B. Stevens to open the Belmont Hotel, and coordinated the opening of a lumber yard and wholesale grocery operation.

In pursuing his own financial advantage, Stevens, however, did not forget the larger duty incumbent upon him — which was to arrange a profitable settlement with the settlers. Thus, in September, he toured the ceded lands with land agent Isaac Goodnow. The goal of the trip was to convince editors to publicly support the railroad and to see if arrangements could be made with some of the more important settlers to sell the land claimed by the railroad. As Stevens reported to Parsons, the tour met with at least partial success: "While at Chetopa Professor Goodnow and myself had a very long conversation with Horner and I also had a short one. He has been acting under 'Company.'" The meetings with settlers did not however achieve much:

> Coming up to Oswego, we were met by a number of citizens. The land question was immediately taken up. There was great complaint made in regard to the appraisement of lands being excessive.... We however talked plainly to the people. Editors, lawyers, and businessmen together with some bond-holders joined in the conversation and we parted with a very much better state of feeling existing in the minds of the people. Such conversations are productive of great good."

Stevens then went on to propose working to arrange a deal with a few of the more prominent settlers, "a small body of them scattered through the tract," hoping that these settlers would then "become advocates of that being done by all."[26] In May of 1872, Stevens revealed that he had been forced to hire a spy, "a good candid square man," whose charge was "to see them quietly and ascertain the real state of affairs."[27] And, in 1873, as his frustration mounted, Stevens even suggested using violence to influence the settlers: "I have no doubt they would be ready and willing, at any time you desire or think it advisable so to do, to put into operation the 'Ku Klux' law as a means of testing what virtue there is in that method of doing business."[28]

The problem, as Stevens soon discovered, was that settlers were stubborn and editors frequently uncooperative, even though, as he assured Company vice-president George Denison, "efforts are being made to induce all the papers to advise the people in accordance with your views."[29]

His complaints were frequent, and as the years progressed, grew increasingly alarmist.

> Horner of the Advance is a crotchety fellow and to keep him well in line is necessary that frequent interviews should be had.[30]
>
> I also send you a printed letter of Lawrence to the settlers on the Osage Lands which is being quite extensively circulated among the settlers. It is going to be exceedingly difficult to have any compromises or any satisfactory arrangements with them, so long as men occupying the position he does write such letters. Please give it careful analysis.[31]
>
> Great danger is to be apprehended from the settlers on the Osage lands; that they profess to be much dissatisfied with the appraisement and are holding nightly meetings.... I would not be surprised to see the feeling existing in southern Kansas crop out in some unpleasant form at any moment.[32]
>
> The settlers on the Osage Lands are now fully organized, have meetings twice a week in every township, and it is stated that they are determined to resist our claim at all hazards.... The settlers claim that I am responsible for the appraisement and the only way to bring matters to a crisis is by tearing up track, burning the bridge or either seizing upon the person or killing some of the principal men connected with the Company.[33]

The organization of settlers to which Stephens was referring became known as the "Settlers' Protective Association." Formed out of the various extralegal committees and clubs that had functioned in the small communities, towns and cities of the Osage Ceded Lands in the late '60s, this association was the first to unite the settlers into one large integrated force in opposition to the railroads. Although meetings had been held in the fall of 1869 to protest the difficulties settlers were encountering in trying to record their claims, the impetus for the formation of this united Association was provided by an announcement that appeared in local papers in June of 1870. Signed by Isaac Goodnow, the brief statement informed all settlers (both on odd and even sections) that they had 30 days to record their claims or else.

> To Settlers on Osage Lands:
> All persons on EVEN sections of railroad lands will have thirty days from date in which to come up to the principal land offices in Neosho Falls and buy the same at the appraised values, or else give place to others who will buy.
> ISAAC GOODNOW

The response of the settlers was unequivocal — they were incensed. As the *Advance* proclaimed, "We consider the above notice as being an outrage on the settlers, and exceedingly faulty in spirit — Who are the 'High Mightinesses' of the M. K. & T. that speak in such a sharp tone? ...

SETTLERS ON RAILROAD LANDS!

Are notified that the Land Office of the

UNION PACIFIC R. W. CO., SOUTHERN BRANCH,

Is now open for BUSINESS, and all persons on lands belonging to this Company, are requested to come forward AT ONCE and settle for the same, or give place to others.

ISAAC T. GOODNOW,
Junction City, Nov. 16, 1869.   Land Commissioner.

This notice is typical of the statements issued by Isaac Goodnow. Notice that "all persons on lands belonging to that company are to" are instructed to "come forward 'AT ONCE' and settle for the same, or give place to others."

Another notice or two like this would make 'all persons' among such settlers come up in 30 days (or less) and administer a salutation lesson to such haughty toned monopolists as would learn them to treat settlers and others decently in official intercourse."[34] The *Osage Mission Journal* agreed and warned the railroad that such actions could only lead to renewed opposition on the part of the settlers: "We considered this a very extraordinary notice, arrogant in tone, and unaccommodating in spirit, and such a one as would beget ill-will on the part of those affected by it. Such a spirit is already evoked; and there is a probability that 'Leagues' may be formed and an era of opposition to the Railroad and its claims ushered in."[35]

It appears that this notice was the last straw for settlers already on the edge — as the *Osage Mission Journal* announced, the settlers had had enough: "A Monster Mass Meeting will be held at held to commence on the morning of the 4th and last two days."[36] On the morning of the 4th, settlers from Neosho and Labette Counties gathered to deliberate on the appropriate action. As we have seen, the celebration of the 4th of July was an important event in the life of the early communities. The 4th of 1870

5. Settlers Triumphant (1875–1876) 147

proved to be no different; as the *People's Advocate* reflected on the gathering, it explained its significant: "You assembled at Ladore on the 4th of July, the anniversary of the nation's birth and boldly proclaimed your determination to stand up for your birthright as American freemen, cost what it might."[37] After listening to the speeches of the organizers, the settlers voted to organize and appointed an executive committee to arrange meetings in every township in Neosho and Labette counties. The purpose of each "neighborhood" meeting was "to select a good and true man, competent to serve as a member of the permanent Executive Committee" so that each community in the Ceded Lands would be represented at a general meeting to be held in the fall.[38]

One such meeting was held in Mound Valley in the western portion of Labette County on July 23. Gathering in the center of town, the one hundred settlers in attendance voted to call themselves the "Anti-Monopoly League of Mound Valley" and to act in connection to the "grand council of the settlers" that was forming. After organizing themselves into an official organization by voting to approve a Constitution, each settler agreed to donate one dollar and then signed the following pledge:

> I hereby bind myself to buy no lands of the Railroad companies until the question involving title to said lands is settled by legal tribunals of the country, and that I will hold myself in readiness to pay such sum or sums of money into the treasury as may be assessed by the chief executive committee of the grand council of settlers, not to exceed the sum of ten dollars (unless approved by a vote of the members), for prosecution any test case or cases that may be had in this, the settlers behalf; I will also in good faith carry out the orders, rules, requirements of said chief executive committee for the faithful performance of this pledge.[39]

Similar meetings were held throughout Neosho and Labette counties during the months of July and August. On the 6th of September, the men that had been elected in each local meeting met in the city of Ladore to officially form "The Osage Ceded Lands Settlers' Protective Association." Duly formed, the association then voted to elect a small "Executive Committee" of respected men to canvass the counties to raise the necessary funds to fight the railroads in court. Another important task delegated to this committee was keeping the association together. To this end, the decision was made not to endorse political candidates or to align themselves with any political party. Committee members repeatedly insisted that "this society was entirely aloof from politics and intended to remain so."[40]

Throughout the winter of 1870–71, two committee members, D.C. Hutchinson (a Civil War veteran) and G.W. McMillen (a respected doctor), visited each local Association and urged them to cooperate. By February, they had completed their tour, and, as noted by the *Labette Sentinel*, reported a successful mission — "All dissentions, we learn, have been amicably settled, and the township associations are all working in concert."[41]

Most importantly, the association decided to enlist the talents of William Lawrence of Ohio. Usually referred to as "Judge" because of his tenure as judge of the court of common pleas and of the district court in Ohio, Lawrence had represented the 4th Congressional District of Ohio in Congress since his election in 1865. He first came into national prominence as one of the authors of the bill of impeachment against President Andrew Johnson. At the request of the association, Lawrence had visited with settlers on the Osage Ceded Lands in April and May in 1871. Traveling through both counties, he met with groups of settlers to hear their complaints and to assure them of their legal rights. Using familiar imagery he encouraged the settlers in their fight against the railroads; as he explained to an assembled crowd in Chetopa: "The question of land monopoly is not a new one, but as old almost as creation. Nearly 2000 years ago, an old land monopolist proposed to give away all the kingdoms of the earth on terms of worship only. The modern monopolist, less reasonable, demands not only worship, but a price for his lands holds."[42]

Returning to Ohio in late May, Lawrence transcribed a letter to the settlers, which he completed on June 5 and sent to the association for dissemination in local newspapers. After reviewing the legal history of the congressional acts pertaining to the Osage Ceded Lands, Lawrence forcefully argued that the railroads had no legal basis for their claims. As he explained in conclusion, "I believe that the railroad companies have no claim on any of the Osage Ceded Lands.... I have an abiding faith in the legal positions I have taken and in the justice of the cause of the settlers."

Lawrence's legal arguments, presented in this early letter, would prove to be the basis upon which the lawyers would ultimately contest the case before the Supreme Court. He began the story in 1825, when the Osage peoples were assured in a treaty dated June 12 that the land was reserved to them "so long as they may choose to occupy the same." The next development occurred forty years later, in a treaty dated September 29, 1865, when the Osage peoples agreed to cede their lands in Kansas to the United States government. As Lawrence explained, it was this treaty which led to the settlement of the territory: "In accordance with the well known policy of the Government, and the inducements held out by the preemption laws, settlers immediately took possession of the land after the Indian title was extinguished, upon the common understanding that they were entitled to receive from the Government for homes the title to the lands they respectively occupied. An examination of the laws then in force and since passed will show the settlers were by law invited to occupy these lands and granted the privilege of acquiring titles." That the settlers were not misguided, Lawrence argued, can be found in the stipulations of the Kansas-Nebraska Act of 1854 and the Homestead Law of 1862 as well as the joint resolution of April 10, 1869, which guaranteed settlers land at $1.25 per acre so long as they lived on the claim and made improvements.

According to Lawrence, this right of settlement was the legal bedrock upon which the rights of the settlers were based. And, it was the background against which the United States' governmental agreements with railroads should be viewed. The act of Congress on March 3, 1863, had granted to the state of Kansas "every alternate section of land designated by odd numbers for ten sections in width on each side of said road" for the purpose of aiding in the construction of a railroad from Leavenworth by way of Lawrence to the south line of the state. As Lawrence noted, if the law had stopped here, it would be difficult to deny the claims of the railroads. But the act did not end at this point — instead it continued with a significant proviso: "Provided, that any and all lands heretofore reserved to the United States by any act of Congress or in any other manner by competent authority for the purpose of aiding in any object of internal improvement or for any other purpose whatsoever be, and the same are hereby reserved to the United States from the operation of this act." Thus, since the 1825 treaty guaranteeing the Osage Ceded Lands to the Osages "so long as they may choose to occupy the same" was in force when the 1863 act was passed, it followed that, as Lawrence concluded, these lands "by the express terms of the act were reserved from its operation in all respects except only as to a right of way. This is so plain, it seems to me, as to require no argument."

Lawrence was aware that the railroads also claimed privilege under an act of Congress passed on July 26, 1866, that had guaranteed to the railroads in Kansas alternate odd numbered sections to the extent of five alternate sections per mile on each side of the road. But, once again Lawrence reminded his readers, the act did not stop with these words but continued to add another proviso similar to that in the 1863 Act: "excepting from the operations of the act all lands reserved in any manner for any purpose whatever." In 1866, the Osage Ceded Lands were still controlled by the Osage people. Even though they had agreed to the terms of a treaty in 1865, the fact that this treaty had not been approved by Senate or signed by the president meant that the lands were still under their management and thus not privileged to the railroads under the act of 1866. In fact, because the Senate had added amendments to the treaty, the Osages did not sign it until September 21, 1866 — nearly two months after the act of

1866 was passed. Once again, Lawrence insisted: "The reasons already assigned are sufficient to show that no railroad grant was made in these lands."

In conclusion, however, Lawrence insisted that as important as these legal arguments were, they should not be considered the foundation of the settlers' claims. For Lawrence and the settlers, the core issue was one of basic values. To allow railroads to claim land that had been improved and lived upon by ordinary citizens was a betrayal of all that Americans had stood for. As Lawrence argued in conclusion:

> Justice, sound policy, the interests of all, require that the settlers on the Osage Ceded Lands should be secured in the title to, and enjoyment of, the homes which they occupy. To crush them or take from them the earnings of years of industry with which they might beautify and add value to their prairie farms and enable them to share the burdens of taxation and general improvement, is to crush the prosperity of more than fifteen hundred families and farms and homes, in a region as beautiful and fertile as any on the footstool of God.[43]

Inspired by Lawrence's presence and words, the Settlers' Protective Association continued to hold meetings throughout the summer and fall of 1871. Tensions were high as gossip worked its way through communities. Accusations and counteraccusations against the railroads and suspiciously cooperative settlers were spread — the *Tioga Herald* lamented, "Every few days some new rumor is set afloat concerning the land controversy between the railroad company and the settlers."[44]

In the winter of 1872, the LLG and the Katy sent high-level emissaries in an attempt to convince the settlers to agree to purchase their land from the railroads and to stop the pursuit of legal action. However, even the appearance of the president of the LLG failed to move the settlers or to help resolve the situation. The *Tioga Herald* summarized the situation in this way:

> Friday of last week President Walker, of the L. L. & G., came down on the 4 p.m. train, and was met here by Dr. G.W. McMillan and Mr. Greene, a committee on the part of the Settlers' Association, who desired to confer with him in reference to an amicable adjustment of the land question. From what we learn of the meeting very little was accomplished by it. Mr. Walker maintains that the company's title to the lands is absolute and clear, and that the price at which they have been appraised is not above what it should be. He therefore does not consider that the company has any compromise to offer, or any concessions to make. On the other hand, the gentlemen who represent the settlers contend that the price fixed for the lands is much too high and entirely beyond the reach of a majority of them if they were disposed to buy.[45]

The president of the Katy, Levi Parsons, did not come, but he did send his brother. Stevens alerted Parsons to his arrival in May: "Your brother Randolph arrived this morning and is arranging to so South tomorrow morning. Will proceed directly to Neosho Falls, have a consultation with Prof. Goodnow will then go around pretty generally among the settlers, talking with the leaders, ascertaining if possible their sentiments, so as to know how best to act. I hope by this means to get up a better state of feeling, and if possible, to avoid any rupture. Will keep you fully advised."[46]

Although there are no internal records indicating what prompted this full-scale assault on the part of the railroads, a hint can be found in a follow-up letter to Parsons in which Stephens remarked: "Your brother is now down among the settlers and after consultation with him, have decided not to take any application either to the General or Gov. Harvey until he had become better advised in regard to the real status of events."[47] Stephens was well aware that the association had been sending letters to Governor Harvey and agitating its state representative to bring up their case before

This pamphlet, printed in 1874, of the Missouri, Kansas & Texas Railway promotes land sales in the Neosho Valley of Kansas and shows that the railway had no intention of giving up its claim to the land of southeast Kansas easily.

the legislature. Elections were also scheduled for the fall of 1872 and several candidates were running for office on an anti–Railroad plank. The only recourse, as he explained to Randolph Parsons, was to cut them off at the pass — that is, "move among settlers, establish a feeling of good faith and make them understand & realize the Co. is not their enemy. Such is my program. You know how to carry it out, if approved."[48]

As an old political hand, Stephens was not relying solely upon the persuasive power of Randolph Parsons. Before assuming the role of general manager for the Katy, Stevens had served as superintendent for the sale of Indian Trust Lands in Kansas, and in that position, had used his authority to his own financial and political benefits.[49] Thus, behind the scenes, even as he was working to advance his own financial interests, he was also working hard to manipulate the political process to ensure that pro-railroad candidates were elected. As he explained to Levi Parsons, "I have taken measures to secure the nomination of sufficient number of Senators, friendly to the railroads, to checkmate unfriendly legislation on the part of the House, and I hope they may be elected."[50]

Both the Katy and LLG initiated a public relations campaign aimed at discouraging settlers. Utilizing a "carrot and stick" approach, the railroads threatened to sell the land out from under the settlers' feet to new immigrants while at the same promising them leniency should they choose to purchase their land from the railroads. In a pamphlet entitled, *Homes for All, and How to Secure Them. A Guide to the Leavenworth, Lawrence & Galveston Railroad and Its Lands in Southern Kansas*, the Railroad promised "the wealthier and more conservative class of immigrants who follow in the wake of adventurous pioneers" that "no better opportunity can be found" than to "buy land on which a commencement has already been made." That the LLG was warning established settlers on the Osage Ceded Lands was made clear by the explanation that the "commencements" mentioned included "farms well inclosed [sic] and in a good state of cultivation." In the same pamphlet, however, the railroad assured settlers that "although they have no legal rights, the Company is disposed to deal leniently with them."[51] In April of 1872, the *Parsons Sun* reported that the railroad had officially offered a "compromise solution" to the association members:

Propositions to the Settlers on the Osage Ceded Lands
   1st. A reduction of 20 per cent, from the regular appraisal, with usual terms of payment.
   2d. No payment for five years, excepting interest each year in advance; next five years one-fifth payment of principal with annual interest.
   3d. To every purchaser of 160 acres of land who shall plant and systemati-

cally and successfully cultivate five acres of timber within five years shall be given the said land on the final completion of the several payments.

4th. On full payment of purchase money warranty deeds shall be given.

5th. To receive the advantage of the above propositions, each settler shall accept the situation in good faith and contract within sixty (60) days from April 18th, 1872, and shall make affidavits that he is not interfering with the rights of any other person, under penalty of forfeiting all money paid, and every other claimed advantage.[52]

Although the promise of easy credit seems to have induced some settlers to settle with the railroads, the requirement that they cease and desist from supporting other settlers in their struggle against the railroads was too bitter a pill for most to swallow. It is difficult to ascertain the exact numbers of those who took up the railroads' offer for several reasons. The LLG did not distinguish the exact area of its land-sales in reporting them. And there are no early records remaining for the success (or lack thereof) of the Katy's efforts — a fire in the early 20th century destroyed all of the files from the early days of railroad activity in southeast Kansas. Gates estimates that approximately 45,539 acres were sold between June 1871, and April 1872 for an average price of $8.15 an acre. Since the area encompassed by Neosho and Labette counties is roughly 786,000 acres, this number represents only about 5 percent of total acreage bought from the railroads by settlers.[53]

There are several reasons for the failure of the railroads in the Osage Ceded Lands. On the one hand, as the *Tioga Herald* explained, the price being asked for by the railroads was beyond the financial capabilities of most settlers: "the gentlemen who represent the settlers contend that the price fixed for the lands is much too high and entirely beyond the reach of a majority of them if they were disposed to buy; and we are inclined to the belief that this opinion is correct. There is no disguising the fact that very many who are settled upon these lands would never be able with the means they are forced to begin with, to pay for them. They are poor and the fact that they are compelled to make use of everything available to meet present wants absolutely precludes them from making the start necessary to pay for the lands."[54]

Furthermore, as Gates noted, "Kansans were not easily intimidated on land matters, particularly when absentee-owned railroads challenged their rights."[55] Milton Reynolds acknowledged the same in a rueful editorial: "While some of the Settlers have accepted the propositions of Prof. Goodnow, published two weeks ago in the Sun, and contracted for their lands, a large number of them are wholly dissatisfied with them and they are now holding meetings in nearly every township and organizing more thoroughly than ever before with a determination to fight it out to the bitter end. We hoped the matter was settled, but now it seems, if possible, farther from it than ever before. This is much to be regretted by every good citizen."[56]

By far, however, the most important reason for rejecting the offers was the solidarity of the community in opposition to the railroads. In response to the full-scale assault of the railroads, the association successfully rallied most settlers to both ignore the threats and reject the offers made by land agents. T.C. Corey, a prominent local lawyer, argued strongly on behalf of the association in a large gathering in Parsons. From the very beginning, he sounded a clarion call to action: "I am filled with something more than patriotism — a feeling akin to anger, and I feel more like war than compromise." Lest he be misunderstood, Corey then hastened to add his conviction that "reason, and not passion, should control the deliberations of this council." Moving to the heart of his speech, Corey then strongly urged his fellow settlers to unity: "Let no threat or promise divide you; ours is a common cause, a common fate, a common destiny; we are all in the same box, and must all ride on the same gale or sink in the common vortex." He also warned them not to pay attention to the "honied words and promises" of railroad land agents: "If these companies ... could induce large numbers of you to purchase of them, they would have accomplished their object; you would be divided in council, in interest and in sympathy; you would be shorn of your strength, and they would rob you by detail." In conclusion, Corey then called upon them to stand together: "Let your resolution be never to buy of the railroad companies, at least not until after the Supreme Court shall have decided against you."[57]

The settlers remained agitated throughout the summer and fall of 1872 as railroad agents and association surrogates crisscrossed the counties trying to recruit them to their side. Undoubtedly, many settlers found themselves confused by the legal back-and-forth of the lawyers who were representing both sides. On the issue of their rights as citizens, however, they remained certain. An interesting "parable" appeared in the *Parsons Weekly Herald* in the winter of 1873 that summarized the perspective of most settlers. Utilizing themes and interweaving images from both biblical and American history, the parable returned to the themes of "slavery" and "liberty" that were so important in the early years of settlement. Taken from a mythical "First Book of Monopolies," the tale began with "the children of the tribes of Washington and Jefferson and of Adams" debating "the wise men of the East and the scribes and chief men of Ulysses." According to the parable, the "children" stridently proclaim: "We will not become bondsmen and slaves for ten years, as thou desirest and because we are hewers of stone and tillers of the soil, and without great wealth, thou shalt not have any of the lands of the Osage, given as an inheritance to us and our children forever, but we will continue to possess and till the land." Interestingly, after the debate continues, the story concludes on a triumphant note: "And the tribes of Washington and of Jefferson and of Adams did possess the land and prosper, and rose up in their might, and did despoil the powers of the wise men from the East and of the scribes and wise men of Ulysses, even as they had done aforetime with the kingdom of Jeff and again there was great joy and peace throughout the land."[58] Significantly, the reference to the "kingdom of Jeff" is a clear indication that the Civil War remained a powerful image in the settlers' fight against the railroads in southeast Kansas in the 1870s.

Convinced that their only hope for victory was in the courts, in the winter and throughout the spring and summer of 1873, the association coordinated the filing of a series of lawsuits so that by September, as Stevens explained to Parsons, "46 suits [had] been commenced by settlers of Osage lands against the M. K. & T."[59] Ultimately, by August the association had decided to combine these individual suits into two — one filed in Neosho County and one in Labette. Although both local courts decided in favor of the settlers, the railroad declared their intentions to appeal the decisions — as far up the system as the Supreme Court.

Although pleased by the outcome, the association was concerned by the paucity of financial resources at its disposal. Thus, in the summer of 1873, they scheduled another series of high-profile public meetings in an attempt to keep enthusiasm high and to aid in the raising of the funds needed to hire lawyers and coordinate the process of the legal appeals.

One of the largest of these meetings took place in early July in the city of Thayer. The *Osage Independent* reported that over 7,000 people were in attendance — "Seven hundred and fifty wagons were counted in procession. The delegation from Labette county was two miles long."[60] A correspondent to the *Osage Mission Transcript* boasted: "This has been one of the greatest days in the history of southern Kansas, and one long to be remembered."[61] Another large gathering occurred in the town of Erie on July 19. According to the *Osage Mission Transcript*, over 2,500 settlers were in attendance to hear the speech of the Honorable J.K. Hudson of Wyandotte County urge them to "organize — for what? Not to attack but to defend. Not to tear down other interests but to build up our own. Not to rush into a fight to destroy some class or classes who have taken advantage of our want of organization, but to organize as they have."[62]

Kansas Governor Charles Robinson was also present and, in his speech, returned to familiar themes: "The heroes of '76 underwent a seven year's war rather than to submit to an unjust tax on tea and paper, amounting to a few thousand dollars, and we affect to honor their memories for their pluck.... They declared certain truths were self-evident that some rights were inalienable and that governments were for the purpose of securing these rights to the governed. That when a government becomes destructive of these rights it was the right of the people to alter or abolish it." Robinson's purpose in bringing these historical images before the minds of his hearers was to encourage them to remain united in their struggle against the railroads—"The colonies well understood the importance of union in their conflict.... 'Join or die,' was their motto, and it was this point of union that won for them independence."[63]

The last meeting of the year was held in Osage Mission on October 1, 1873. At this meeting, the keynote address was delivered by representative Sidney Clarke. Like the other speakers, Clarke also rallied his hearers by reminding them of the past. But unlike Osborne, who had reached back to review the historic images of the nation's founders, Clarke appealed to the experience of the settlers before him.

> You are not here as the land monopolists assert, either as intruders or criminals. You are not here as enemies of your country or unmindful of its institutions or its laws. With undaunted courage, yet with sufferings and sacrifices such as the first settlers of a new country only know, and with an intelligent understanding of that protection and defense which the laws of your country give to every citizen: you have here made homes more sacred than the palaces of the monopolists, because you have built them by honest labor and money honestly obtained; ... and you would lack that fidelity inspired by the justice of your cause, if you did not defend them by all the legal and constitutional methods in your power.[64]

In February of 1874, the cases which had been appealed by the Railroad attorneys were heard by the federal appeals court. At this hearing, the settlers were represented by Jeremiah Black, who had served as attorney general (1857–60) under president James Buchanan, Judge Lawrence of Ohio, two local attorneys by the names of McKeighan and McComas, and Wilson Shannon, the former territorial governor of Kansas. Buoyed by this news and by the positive reports coming in from the legal team in Washington, the association decided to call one last general bi–county association meeting in late May of 1874. The meeting on May 27 would prove to be the largest gathering of settlers in southeast Kansas in the 1870s and the last public assembly called for by Settlers' Protective Association.

The *Oswego Independent* estimated that over 10,000 settlers were in attendance. As the more than 800 wagons rolled into Parsons in the morning, banners were unfurled. The *Independent* listed some of the more frequently repeated messages prominently displayed:

> Vox populi, vox Dei.
> We mean business. The right shall prevail.
> We will fight it out on the line.
> United we stand.
> We fought for the Union and we will fight for our homes.
> Our homes at all hazards.
> Settlers demand nothing but what is right and will submit to nothing wrong.
> We fight for justice, the battle field is our homes and firesides.
> We only claim justice for our cause is just.
> The public domain for the actual settler only.
> No railroad lands in Shiloh.

Milton Reynolds, of the *Parsons Sun*, was the first speaker. Reminding the crowd of Kansas' role in defending freedom during the Civil War, Reynolds asserted: "The ravines and valleys of this prairie State are vocal and resonant with requiems to the martyred dead who first fell in the cause of the oppressed and that Kansas might be free. Here the revolution was inaugurated, and here has been inaugurated another, and in some respects, a grander revolution against land monopoly and land thieves."

Sidney Clarke was also present and in his speech again cast the settlers' battle against monopolies in the light of their previous struggle to defend the Union against the southern Rebellion: "As the iron heel of monopoly pierces more deeply the vitals of the body politic, and this government becomes more and more the government of the few at the expense of the many, the day of deliverance will come, and we shall all wonder, as in the cause of the emancipation of the slaves, that it was delayed so long."[65]

Many settlers believed that the decision of the circuit court to hear the case would bring about a swift decision in their favor — even though Clarke had sought to disabuse them of this belief by reminding them that "the battle is not yet ended. Your foe is cunning, wiley, unscrupulous."[66] Not understanding the lengthy process by which a case proceeds to the highest court, some papers mistakenly proclaimed final victory when the federal appeals court ruled in October of 1874 in the settlers' favor. The case was heard in circuit court, District of Kansas, in June of 1874. The opinion of the court was written by the Hon. Geo. W. McCrary, circuit judge, and ruled in favor of the settlers against the railroad.[67] The response of the settlers in the Osage Ceded Lands was euphoric. For example, the headline in the *Oswego Independent* in bold letters: "HUZ-Z-Z-AH! GOD IN ISRAEL! GLORY HALLELUJAH! God and Humanity Triumphant! THE

SETTLERS VICTORIOUS! SUPERIOR COURT DECISION IN THEIR FAVOR!"

However, as the settlers had been warned, the decision by the District Court was not the end of the process.[68] As had been anticipated by their lawyers, both the Leavenworth, Lawrence, and Galveston Railroad Company and the Missouri, Kansas, and Texas Railway Company immediately appealed the verdict to the Supreme Court which accepted the case into its October 1875 docket and heard the arguments on October 20–22, 1875. Although each railroad had filed an independent suit, they were represented by the same attorneys: George F. Edmund, Matt H. Carpenter, S.O. Thatcher and P. Phillips. The settlers were represented by Jeremiah Black and William Lawrence. The United States government, which had joined the suit in favor of the settlers, was represented by the attorney general, Edward Pierrepont, and the solicitor-general S.F. Phillips. And the state of Kansas, which also chose to be on the side of the settlers, was represented by the U.S. district attorney for the district of Kansas, G.R. Peck. Although the Supreme Court ruled separately in response to each railroad's appeal, the majority opinion, which was written in response to the appeal of the LLG, appealed equally to the appeal of the MKT.

The final verdict of the court was announced on April 10, 1876. The majority opinion of the Supreme Court upheld the settlers' contention that the railroads had no right to the land in the Osage Ceded Tract. Writing for the majority, justice David Davis declared that the words "nothing adding thereto, nothing diminishing" precluded the railroads from claiming any land in the Osage Ceded Lands. Thus Davis' opinion agreed with that which had been advanced by Lawrence in his original letter to the settlers. As Davis wrote, "In concluding the treaty, neither party thereto supposed that any grant attached to the lands; for, as we have seen, all were to be sold, and the fund invested."

Furthermore, in words that seemed to confirm the interpretation that had been advanced by the settlers, Davis argued that "the policy of removal — a favorite one with the government, and always encouraged by it — looked to the extinguishment of the Indian title for the general good, and not for the special benefit of any particular interest." Thus, "these lands, having been thereby set apart to be surveyed and sold for the benefit

Opposite: This broadside, printed in 1875, of the Missouri, Kansas & Texas Railway promoting the sale of railroad lands in Neosho County shows that the railroad was clearly expecting to win the case before the Supreme Court. The advertisement claims the lands are suitable for agriculture and close to natural resources and established settlements.

5. Settlers Triumphant (1875–1876)

of the Indians, were 'otherwise appropriated,' as much as they had been before the treaty was concluded, and were consequently reserved within the meaning of the excepting clause in the act."[69]

Ironically, as Gates notes, Davis' ownership of many prairie farms in Illinois put him with Richard Scully, among America's richest landlords. Nevertheless, he consistently ruled against land monopolies during his tenure on the Supreme Court. After the Supreme Court decision was revealed, steps were taken to procure congressional legislation whereby the settlers could obtain title. A bill was prepared by Gov. Shannon, approved by the Grand Council of the Settlers' Protective Association, and pushed through Congress. It was signed into law on August 11, 1876.[70]

When the news reached Labette and Neosho counties that the Supreme Court had ruled in their favor, settlers reacted in barely contained exuberance. The *Chanute Times* reported, "Three hundred guns have been fired, bells are ringing, bonfires are burning, and flags are flying."[71] The *Oswego Independent* reported that "the explosion of fire crackers and fire arms exceeded that of the 4th of July. Then the anvils were called into requisition and fired in batteries until their vibration reached a radius of eighteen miles, in the direction of the wind. Processions with fifes and drums, paraded the streets until a late hour, while old and young, great and small, co-mingled in celebrating the event."[72] Similar celebrations were held throughout the counties.

As to the importance of the decision, all were in agreement. The *Parsons Eclipse* declared, "The Osage Ceded Land case is one of the most remarkable instances where truth and equity has triumphed over fraud and wrong."[73] The *Southern Kansas Advance* likewise hailed the decision as forever settling the question of land ownership in the United States: "The long weary days, weeks and months of waiting are passed. The hour of triumph for the settlers has at last come. The decision just rendered in the great Osage Ceded Lands case is by the Supreme Court of our nation and therefore final; and forever settles the question as to where the title to these lands rests."[74] Interestingly, Nelson Case, one of the first to put into writing his recollections of the history of the early years of Labette County, noted that the significance of this legal triumph was not that the settlers could then purchase their lands for $1.25 per acre; in fact, many noted that the cost of the trial which was borne by the settlers actually raised the cost of each acre significantly so that the settlers could probably have paid less for their land by working out a compromise payment schedule with the railroads. But for Case, the battle was just and the triumph justifiably important "because it was a vindication of a right principle, and showed that a body of men, though poor, when banded together and determined may secure their rights, even against great odds."[75]

Epilogue

The story of the settlers who came to southeast Kansas in the late 1860s and their struggles to build communities founded on law and order just told in this dissertation has been largely ignored by historians. Part of this neglect is related to the contemporary insignificance of southeast Kansas in the economic and political life of the state. Part of it is also related to the lack of interest shown by historians in the people and events of the years between the end of the Civil War and the rise of Populism. Another reason has been the influence of the "east to west" paradigm of early historiography. To many earlier historians, the "real" story in the post-bellum period was found in the settling of western Kansas and the struggles of immigrant groups to build communities in the harsh and unyielding climate of the western plains. As social historians of the Civil War have recently begun to note, another complicating factor has been the disregard for the after-war lives of soldiers shown by many historians in early generations. The convergence of these causes (and possibly others unnoticed by me) has led to the eclipse of the civil war veterans who came to Labette and Neosho Counties in the post–Civil War history of Kansas.

Our understanding of the Sunflower State is thus incomplete. Although historians (and thus "history") have passed them by, barely noticing their efforts to both build and defend their homes and communities, the veteran settlers of southeast Kansas have much to teach us. Theirs was the last stand against railroad claims to public land; theirs can also be considered a first battle in the war against monopolies that would be continued in force by the Grangers and then Populists of the 1880s and '90s. They looked to the War of 1776 for abiding political principles even as they struggled to define the meaning of the War of 1861. Struggling against the railroads, they became dependent upon the railroads for their financial survival. Seeking to establish and maintain local control, they found themselves inescapably relying upon the decisions and actions of others. Ironically, their greatest moment of triumph occurred not in Parsons, Chanute or Osage Mission, but in Washington, D.C.

The story of the men and women who settled the farms and built the communities that still mark the maps of southeast Kansas is at its heart quintessentially American. It is the story of people inspired by Republican ideals, of a self-reliant people who look to each other for support and rely on each other in times of struggle, of a people who in seeking to preserve a known past unwittingly create an unknown future.

Their story is also quintessentially Kansan. They bring assumptions with them to Kansas and seek to rebuild their new homes following the cultural and political structure of the old. Yet, the challenges presented by the unique environment and historic situations they encounter in Kansas force them to creatively reassess the past in an effort to create the future. It is this unique mix of conservative idealism and progressive pragmatism that has defined the Kansas spirit and created her unique role in U.S. history. Few areas illustrate this more clearly than that of the Osage Ceded Lands in the 1860s and '70s.

APPENDIX: THE OSAGE IN NEOSHO COUNTY (1825–1865)

When the first Jesuit missionaries to arrive in southeast Kansas alighted from the ox-drawn wagon train that had brought them from St. Louis over the course of fourteen long days, they were enthusiastically greeted by a large group of expectant Osage men, women and children. As Fr. John Bax, one of the priests, remembered: "It would be impossible to paint for you the enthusiasm with which we were received." Interestingly, Fr. Bax was not sure he shared the Osages' joy. As he reminisced in 1850, "At first sight of these savages, I could not suppress the pain I felt.... Half-serious, half-jesting, I thought that a truly savage portion of the Lord's vineyard had been given to me to cultivate."[1]

As this vignette reveals, the relationship that developed between the Osage peoples in southeast Kansas and the Roman Catholic Church was complex.[2] The true story of this interaction reveals that as the Osage and Catholic missionaries met on what Richard White has described as the "middle ground," in spite of cultural misunderstandings, fear, and religious bigotry, they were able to construct a common, mutually comprehensible world.[3]

Like most indigenous peoples, the pre-contact history of the Osages is shrouded and obscured in the darkness of early American pre-history. The Osage creation myth describes the birth of the Osage peoples through the mating of a "Sun-man" with a "Moon-woman." The proto-Osage offspring of this union, looking for a place to dwell, come to earth from the sky but are frustrated in their endeavors because they find only water and no dry land. After vainly appealing to the heavens for help, they ask the noblest of the animals, the elk, for help. The elk calls to the wind and together they provide land and food for the people.[4]

Although scholars have debated the exact meaning of the varied parts of this tale, the basic structure of a wandering people who come to the prairies to find a home is confirmed by the reconstruction efforts of anthropologists and ethnohistorians. What we know about the early history of the Osages can be summarized thus. At some point (scholars disagree over the timing), a large group of Dhegian-Siouan speakers, composed of Quapaw, Osage, Kansas, Omaha, and Ponca peoples, left the eastern forests of the Ohio Valley and migrated across the Mississippi River. Whatever the reason for the move (scholars disagree), once they had crossed the Mississippi, the tribes then separated. The Osages broke away from the larger group and settled along the Great Plains prairies where they established villages near the headwaters of the river that became known as the Osages. Adapting to this location, the Osages merged their older agricultural way of life with elements more in keeping with their new prairie existence. Because the region into which they had moved was a transition zone between eastern forests and western planes, they were able to keep many of their older ways. For example, they continued to live in wood-framed longhouses and to plant the familiar eastern mix of maize, beans, squash, and pumpkins. However, as Stephen Aron has written, "the Osages' move west brought significant changes to their way of life and sense of selves." Most importantly, they modified their seasonal routines. After planting crops along the forest edges in the spring and early summer, they left their villages to hunt buffalo on the short grass plains along the Arkansas, Cimarron and Smoky Hill rivers in the late summer and fall. After a successful hunt, they then returned to their villages to spend the later fall and winter before cultivating the soil in the spring to begin the cycle all over again.

The Osages referred to themselves as "the children of the middle waters" and, from the standpoint of history, this term was fitting—for their way of life was a unique blend of woodland and grassland cultural patterns. As was the case with other indigenous peoples who moved west, the increased importance of hunting (both in terms of time and dietary contributions) greatly influenced gender relations within the family and clan. As each clan became increasingly dependent upon the food provided by the hunt, the stature of men within the community also increased. Women, who continued to be the primary source of food gained by agricultural endeavors, performed secondary roles in the hunt (i.e., that of skinning and butchering). Men led the hunt. The division of labor was therefore stratified according to gender: women cultivated the soil while men executed the hunt.[5]

The Osages were not the only indigenous people to live on the edges of the prairies, nor were they the only ones to seek food by hunting the buffalo on the plains. North of the Arkansas along the Platte, Republican, and Loup rivers were the four bands of Pawnee: Republican, Skidi, Rapage, and Grand. Along the Arkansas Valley and south to the Red River were the Pawnee's Caddoan kin, collectively known as the Wichita. South of the Red River were the Caddoan Hasinai, Caddohadacho, and Natchitoches tribes often referred to collectively as the Caddo. The size and military prowess of these three groups, the Pawnee, Wichita, and Caddo, effectively closed the west to any possible large-scale Osage expansion. They were, however, a potential source of profits. For the Osages, the existence of large villages filled with agricultural products and Spanish horses often proved a temptation too difficult to resist. Thus, from early times, the Osages maintained an uneasy relationship with other Native peoples in which boundaries were frequently tested through controlled violence and limited military conflict.[6]

This uneasy relationship that had evolved over the centuries was significantly changed by the arrival of French traders in the late seventeenth century. Given their strategic location between the Mississippi River to the east and indigenous peoples to the west, the Osages were able to control the lucrative trade routes and, thereby, to limit the access of the Wichita, Pawnee, and Caddo to the valuable metal tools and muskets that the French traders provided. Thus, enjoying a technological superiority over their western neighbors, the Osages were able to expand west throughout the eighteenth century, gradually coming to control the eastern plains (present day Missouri and eastern Kansas).

This newfound hegemony helped to create conditions of prosperity which in turn sustained a population boom. In 1719, when a French soldier-trader, Charles DuTisne, visited, he estimated that there were two hundred Osage warriors living with their families in two hundred lodges along the Osage River. In the 1750s, the Spanish claimed that there were at least 950 Osage warriors, and in the 1770s they reported at least twelve hundred. This rapid population increase led to tensions between leaders and finally to the internal separation of the Osages into three autonomous divisions. The first division occurred about 1713 when a group known as the Little Osages left their villages on the Osage headwaters and moved north to gain better access to the Missouri River trade. Those who remained on the Osage River were called the Big Osages. The Big Osages subdivided in the 1770s when the Arkansas Osages, as they later were called, moved south to the Three Forks Region where the Neosho and Verdigris join the Arkansas River to take advantage of the southern trade.[7]

The cultural and military dominance of the Osages was directly related to their geographical location of *being between* European colonial empires. The Osages carefully and subtly used this position to their advantage. After the Seven Years' War (1756-63) and the subsequent withdrawal of the French, the Osages adapted to the growing presence of British traders and maintained this intermediary position.[8] After the Revolutionary War, the Osages continued to trade (illegally) with the British while establishing trading relations with the newly formed United States. The net impact of these evolving imperial negotiations was that the Osages were able to maintain technological superiority over their indigenous rivals. Their geographic location also helped to protect them from another enemy — the massive population losses of the eighteenth-century epidemics that devastated the Quapaw, Missouri, Kansa, Omaha, Ponca, and other river tribes.[9]

In the nineteenth century, however, their greatest asset — their geographic location — became a heavy liability for the Osage as, to use the poignant phrase of the ethno-historian Willard Hollings, "their eighteenth-century gateway because a nineteenth-century highway for American westward expansion."[10] Although the Louisiana Purchase in 1803 did not immediately affect the Osages, the long-term effects of the Purchase greatly changed their future. For, unlike the French and Spanish who had recognized Osage independence and looked to them as trading partners, the Americans had a different goal in mind.

As has been noted by several historians, official U.S. "Indian Policy" evolved in the 19th century. As originally envisioned by George Washington and his secretary of war, Henry Knox, early Indian policy was based on the supposition that Native peoples would be gradually introduced to Anglo-American cultural ways so as to help them integrate into the mainstream of Anglo-American life. The key to this policy was the abandonment of nomadic traditions and the adoption of the sedentary life-style of small-scale subsistence farmers. As president, Thomas Jefferson adapted this policy by advocating the removal of all Natives peoples to lands west of the Mississippi where they could be detached from direct contact with land-hungry settlers and allowed time to adapt to the changes Americans wanted them to make. Subsequent presidents, especially Andrew Jackson, oversaw the brutal implementation of this course of action as Native peoples throughout the land east of the Mississippi were forced to join the "Trail of Tears."[11]

Given the location of their villages and their proximity to the Mississippi River, the Osage were among the first western tribes to feel the impact of the ensuing aggressive policy of Indian removal. In the 1820s, over six thousands Cherokee moved to settlements along the White and Arkansas Rivers while Creek and Choctaw people moved into the Ouachita Mountains south of the Arkansas River. Threatened by this invasion, the Osages responded aggressively. In fact, throughout the 1820s the entire region from the Missouri to the Red River became a battleground between eastern Native newcomers and the Osage peoples. The additional forced migration of Native peoples in the 1830s exacerbated this situation and increased pressure on the Osages.[12]

The victory of the Mexicans and their ultimate independence from Spanish domination further disturbed the status quo for the Osages as previously closed borders were opened and American traders poured into northern Mexican markets, turning the Arkansas Valley into a busy thoroughfare. These traders brought livestock that overgrazed the valley and disturbed the game, particularly the massive herds of buffalo that grazed along the river valley. This in turn disrupted the buffalo hunts of the Osage and threatened their livelihood. In addition, the flood of American traders, intent on crossing the prairie-plains to Santa Fe, began to trade with the western tribes, thereby reducing the technological superiority of the Osages. Thus, throughout the 1820s and '30s, the Osage experienced severe pressure on their eastern and western boundaries as tribes fleeing American expansion invaded the Osage forests and prairies and as better armed western tribes expanded their territory onto the Osage plains. The strategic position that had once provided the Osages with power and wealth increasingly lost its value as the Osages found themselves caught between expanding Native frontiers.[13]

The Osages met this challenge as they had met every challenge that had confronted them: with pluck, fortitude, and remarkable adaptability. To understand how, it is important to remember the role that religion played in European exploration and colonization. From the earliest stages, Europeans had counted on religious organizations to help subdue and subjugate the Native peoples of the "New World." James Muldoon explains, "In practice, Christianization meant becoming civilized, moving from a semi-nomadic, pastoral, tribally organized way of life into a settled, agriculturally based, urban way of life."[14]

This was as true in the northern hemisphere as the southern, as the "praying towns" of New England clearly reveal. In the immediate post–Revolutionary War period, new energy was poured into this "evangelizing mission" as Moravian, Quaker, Baptist, Episcopal, Methodist, Congregational, Presbyterian, and Dutch Reformed churches launched missionary efforts. Several religious bodies formed special missionary societies, including the Society for Propagating the Gospel among Indians (1787), the Society of the United Brethren for Propagating the Gospel among the Heathen (1787), the Northern Missionary Society (1797), the Connecticut Missionary Society (1798), the Massachusetts Missionary Society (1799), the Western Missionary Society (1802), the American Board of Commissioners for

Foreign Missions (1810), the United Foreign Missionary Society (1817), and the Missionary and Bible Society of the Methodist Episcopal Church in America (1820). As U.S. Indian policy evolved, the government increasingly supported these efforts by including stipulations in Indian Treaties that allowed and subsidized the work of missionaries and teachers. Thus, when in 1808 and then again in 1825 the Osages agreed to relinquish their rights to their ancestral lands in Missouri and promised not to attack settlers passing through their land in the Kansas territory on the Santa Fe Trail, they also agreed that a percentage of the guaranteed government annual annuity would be used to support missionaries and teachers who would come and live among them.

Stephen Aron has suggested that the Osages mastered the art of "being between" and learned to use it effectively to ensure their survival and success.[15] This was clearly the case in the early 19th century. As they realized that it was in their own best interest to adapt to certain aspects of Anglo-American culture, the Osages were proactive in controlling their own destiny by choosing whom they would accept as cultural emissaries and teachers. Thus, in 1820, a group of Osage leaders in St. Louis arranged to meet with the Roman Catholic bishop Louis William Valentine DuBourg (whom they referred to as the "Chief of the Black Robes"). Although they also met with Philip Milledoler, the head of the Protestant United Missionary Society, it was the meeting with DuBourg that impressed the Osages. A highly educated man (with a personal library of over eight thousand volumes), DuBourg was characterized by unflagging zeal for mission work (as well as an unfortunate tendency to over commit the scant resources of Catholics in the North America). DuBourg had opened St. Mary's School in Baltimore, suggested the site for the cathedral in that city and collected $10,000 to build it. He was also influential in the establishment of the Oblate Sisters of Providence, the first Catholic women religious order established by women of African descent. Bishop DuBourg is also credited with inviting St. Elizabeth Seton to come to Baltimore, and he later became the ecclesiastical superior of the order she founded, the Sisters of Charity. The pioneer groups of the Congregation of the Mission (the Vincentians) and the Religious of the Sacred Heart came to the United States through his efforts as well.[16] At the meeting, the Osage invited DuBourg to visit them and promised that if he would come, he "could pour waters on many heads."[17] In return, the Bishop assured them of his eagerness to do so and honored them with gifts by distributing individual crucifixes and a neck ribbon with a medal medallion to each Osage leader.[18]

This was not the first contact between the Osage peoples and Roman

Catholic Church. According to available records, the first meeting occurred on the Osage River in 1673, when several Osage towns were visited by Fr. Jacques Marquette. Fourteen years later (1687), Fr. Anastasius Douay, revisited these villages. Because priests routinely traveled with French traders, the Osages became familiar with the presence of Catholic clergy. In addition, as wandering French traders married Osage women, many had come to accept at least a vestige of Catholic identity. In fact, as Christianson comments, "the contacts between the Osage and the French were more peaceful, harmonious, and lasting than the associations of the Osage with any other people. This was no doubt due partly to intermarriage and some acceptance of Catholicism."[19]

Thus, as it became clear that their future depended on learning the ways of the white men, the Osages initiated a campaign to attract Catholic missionaries and teachers. The Osages had come to trust the French Catholics and to respect the men who walked in their villages in their distinctive ecclesiastical garb; thus, in 1820 the Osage turned to the "Black Robes" for help. For his part, the bishop was eager to fulfill their request but was sorely lacking in both funds and men.[20] In 1822, he sent Father Charles De La Croix who baptized forty of the Osages when he visited. Even though a Presbyterian mission had been established in southeast Kansas by this time, De La Croix found that the Osages were still inclined to receive Roman Catholic missionaries. As he noted in his diary,

> I have had the happiness of speaking to them [the Osages] in the Grand Council where all the chiefs, braves and warriors assembled. I spoke them attired in surplice and stole, and with a crucifix in my hand which seemed to please them very much.... The Osage Nation is disposed to receive the Catholic Missionaries as soon as the Bishop will be able to send them.[21]

Inspired by his own missionary zeal and enthused by the report of De La Croix, DuBourg traveled in 1823 to Washington, D.C., to seek a government subsidy for Catholic missionaries.[22] In his letter to the secretary of war John Calhoun, DuBourg suggested that the Catholic approach of "familiar conversations" and "striking representations" reinforced by "the pious lives" of "men disenthralled from all family cares, abstracted from every earthly enjoyment, inured to fatigue and self-denial, living in the flesh as if strangers to all sensual inclination" would be more likely to "easily subdue the ferocity of their hearts and by degrees assimilate their inclinations to those of fellow Christians" than the Protestant approach DuBourg insisted depended upon "the doubtful and tedious process of books."[23] Anticipating a positive response from the government, DuBourg made arrangements to transfer the Novitiate of the Society of Jesus from

Baltimore to Missouri where they joined the Sisters of the Society of the Sacred Heart on DuBourg's farm in Florissant.[24]

Interestingly, although DuBourg's plan envisioned mission outreach to all of the indigenous peoples in his diocese, the leader of the Jesuits in Missouri, Fr. Charles Quickenborne, concentrated his efforts and concerns on the Osages.[25] Although the Osages had been removed from Missouri, Quickenborne nevertheless devoted himself to ministering to them. In 1827, 1828 and then again in 1830, Quickenborne made the 300 mile trip to southeast Kansas where he visited the Osages in their various villages. In 1827, he baptized eighteen children; in 1828, he returned and baptized seventeen more. At their request of the Osages, he journeyed through their territory, catechizing adults, baptizing children and celebrating Mass in each village. In 1830, Quickenborne made his third (and final) visit in June when he baptized nine and married three Métis couples. Each time he visited, Quickenborne attempted to convince Osage parents to allow their children to return with him to Florissant to attend the Jesuit school for Indian boys, St. Regis Seminary. However, parents were reluctant to send their children so far away, and, although the number of students fluctuated yearly, by 1832 Quickenborne had become convinced that it would be impossible to maintain a school for the Osages outside of their territory. He therefore recommended that the school be moved to the Osage territory in southeast Kansas.

It was not, however, until 1847 that Fr. Quickenborne's recommendation came to fruition. One reason for the delay lay in the unwillingness of the United Mission Society to allow Roman Catholics to take over their Mission even though, as the following makes clear, they were aware of the Osage preference for Catholic mission work. In 1832, one Protestant missionary publicly lamented that, although they had labored for ten years, they were "without being confident that a single Indian had been converted through their instrumentality." In fact, he wrote, "many who had been fostered, and whose intellectual and moral character had been greatly improved" were nonetheless "drawn away by Catholic influence."[26] In 1837, surrounded by controversy and the steadfast refusal of the Osage to participate, the Presbyterian Mission to the Osages closed.

Another cause of the delay lay within the Jesuit community in Missouri. Engaged in a struggle to define their own identify, the Jesuits did not seize the opportunity afforded by the withdrawal of the Presbyterians. Due to internal dissension within the Jesuit community as well as his own advancing age, Quickenborne had stepped down in 1830 as Superior and was replaced by Fr. Theodore De Theux. De Theux did not share Quickenborne's enthusiasm for missionary work to the Osages, nor did he particularly like the older priest.[27] He therefore discontinued the outreach efforts to the Osages and refused to honor Quickenborne's request to be sent as a missionary priest to them. Instead, he redirected Jesuit efforts to support missions among tribes that had already been evangelized.

While the Jesuits were engaged in this debate, the Osage continued their struggles. By all accounts, the 1830s were difficult years. Forced out of Missouri and Arkansas into southeastern Kansas, they settled along the banks of the Neosho and Verdigris Rivers and adapted to the new situation. As they settled themselves, they also continued to wrestle through the implications of their new social environment. In June of 1843, Chief Pawhuska along with three of his fellow Osage leaders wrote a letter to President John Tyler asking for schools and Jesuit missionaries. They wrote:

> We prefer Catholic missionaries & would not wish to have any other — and until we have them to educate our young men and teach them how to use the implements of husbandry, it is not worth while to provide us with ploughs & such articles, not knowing how to use them, they are of no value to us.... For this purpose the missionaries are much needed & from the little acquaintance we have with the missionaries heretofore sent among us as well as among other Indians we think the Catholics would send us the best.[28]

When this appeal went unanswered, the Osage chief George White Hair sent another letter in 1844. Addressed this time to the commissioner of Indian affairs, T. Hartley Crawford, he repeated the request for a school and again suggested that Catholic missionaries be sent to operate it. White Hair wrote:

> Hear what we have to say on this subject: We do not wish any more such missionaries as we have had during several years; for they never did us any good. Send them to the white; perhaps they may succeed better with them. If our Great Father desires that we have missionaries, you will tell him to send us Black-gowns, who will teach us to pray to the Great Spirit in the French manner.[29]

An interesting story related in the correspondence of Fr. Bax confirms the attitude revealed about the "other missionaries" in White Hair's letter. When Bax arrived in southeast Kansas in 1847, he toured the scattered villages of the Osage with an interpreter. Entering one village of the Little Osage on the Verdigris River, called Huzegta, he appeared before the village elder and offered his hand (as he explained) "in token of friendship." The chief refused to take it, asking instead: "Who are you?" When the interpreter announced that he was a missionary, the chief lowered his eyes and refused to acknowledge his presence. After a few moments, the chief uttered under his breath the dismissive words, "The missionaries never did any good to our nation." Hearing this, the interpreter hurried to tell the chief that Bax was different — he was a "French *tapouska*, a Black-gown." Hearing this, Bax reported,

> Serenity reappeared on the visage of the chief, and he cried out, "This is good news." He immediately offered me his hand, called his wife, and ordered buffalo-soup, wishing to feast my arrival.... As soon as he knew us and learned the object of our visit, his prejudices and his apprehensions vanished.[30]

The eagerness of the Osage was not reciprocated however by those in the Commissioner's office, where the letter sat unanswered until the summer of 1846. At that time, the Missouri vice-provincial, Father Van de Velde, traveled to Washington to press the issue with William Medill, the new commissioner of Indian affairs. Velde brought up the Osage request to the commissioner and volunteered to send several Jesuits if the bureau would provide the funds. After haggling over the cost, the government finally agreed to support the initiative and promised the Jesuits one-half of each year's interest on the Osage educational fund (as had been stipulated by the 1825 treaty) — a sum equaling approximately $1000 per annum. It was thus, not until the spring of 1847 that Fr. John Schoenmakers, a forty-year-old Jesuit from Holland, and Fr. John Bax, a Belgian Jesuit, along with Brothers John De Bruyn, Thomas Coghlan, and John Sheehan, arrived in southeast Kansas to begin their work of educating, civilizing and converting the Osage.

Upon their arrival, the Jesuits threw themselves into the work with zeal. The population of the Osage at the time was approximately 5,000, of whom 3,500 resided in small villages along the banks of the Neosho River while the rest lived in similar sized villages on the Verdigris. The fathers built a small log-cabin church building and two small school buildings near the village of the head chief in the central location of Osage Mission (now St. Paul) on the Neosho River. Fr. John Schoenmakers was given the task of administering the school. On May 10, 1847, barely a month after they had arrived, the Osage Manual Laboring School opened. The total enrollment for the first year was twenty-eight. By the beginning of the second year, this had swelled to fifty. Believing that the education of girls was important, Father Schoenmakers also recruited the missionary Sisters of Loretto who opened a companion school for Osage girls in the fall of 1847. Enrollment at the schools steadily grew. By 1860, the number of students had risen to 136 boys and 100 girls. The trauma of Civil War and its disruption greatly impacted the school, as competing armies and militia transversed southeast Kansas, alternatively burning and looting villages and homes. The sale of the Osage land between the Neosho and Verdigris (known as the Osage Ceded Lands) in 1865 and the subsequent removal of the Osage peoples first to lands west of Verdigris and then south to Oklahoma further caused the number of Osage children attending the Labor School to decrease until finally the school was transformed into an institution for the sons and daughters of white settlers who poured into the area after the Civil War.

Fr. Bax devoted himself to the sacramental ministry. As has been pointed out already, each time a French priest had visited the Osages, he had baptized their children. Many of the baptized were the children of French men and Osage women. However, as Fr. Bax toured the villages and as the lay-brothers reached out to the local population, the number of baptisms grew, both among the métis and the full-bloods. As Fr. Bax explained, the Jesuits worked hard to establish positive relationships with the Osages, "At my first visits, the children would not approach me. I dissipated their fears by giving them cakes and marbles, with which my pockets were always filled."[31] They also distributed prayer-beads and metal crucifixes to Osage men and women. Fr. Paul Ponziglione, who succeeded Fr. Bax as priest of the parish, commented on the attachment of the Osages to these gifts, "The Osage have a great respect not only for the priest, but for anything concerning our holy religion, though but simple crosses, holy pictures, medals, and above all, prayer-beads." Although the priests realized that many Osages did not understand the theology that these items expressed, they also believed in the importance of external aids and their pedagogical value in adapting Native peoples to Christian cultural ways. As Fr. Ponziglione explained, "The wearing of these is equivalent, I would say, to a profession of faith."[32]

The fact that the Jesuits had no wives and no children played an important role in helping to persuade the Osages to trust them. The large families of the Presbyterian ministers and their desire to have working farms (on Osage land) in order to feed them had offended the Osages by reminding them of the ever-persistent American settlers' demand for land. The Jesuit fathers had no children, and thus demanded no land for their families. Furthermore, the lack of familial obligations freed the Jesuit fathers to travel with the Osages in their seasonal hunts. As Fr. Bax explained, "The Indians are attached to us, principally, say they, because we have no wives and children. 'If you had,' they say, 'you would do like the missionaries (the Presbyterians) who preceded you, you would think too much of your families, and you would think too much of your families and you would neglect the red-man and his children.'"[33]

Instead of insisting that the Osages come to them, as the Presbyterians had done, the Jesuits went to them. In fact, early Jesuit priests showed an almost indefatigable willingness to travel. A story, found in the letters of

Fr. Bax, illustrates their dedication. It was evening in the autumn of 1848, when an Osage man arrived at the Mission. Looking very anxious, he begged Fr. Bax to come with him to visit his wife who was very ill. As Bax later recounted, "I had just arrived from a village called Cawva-Shinka, or Little Village, situated thirty miles from the Mission; I was exhausted with fatigue. But how could I resist an invitation so pressing and above all in circumstance so grave? After a moment of repose, I set out with the man." They rode late into the evening and arrived at the lodge around midnight. Finding it filled with weeping women and children, Bax asked them to leave and then approached the women, lying unconscious on a dirty mat. All he could do was sit by her side and wait uncomfortably. As he recalled, "I never passed such a miserable night. The women and children recommenced their clamor; the dogs of the wigwam passed back and forward over me with such steady regularity, that it would have been quite impossible for me to count the number of visits."[34] Although Fr. Bax was unable to offer medical care to this woman, and was forced to keep vigil together with her family and relatives, the fact that he was willing to sit by her side on the floor through the night could not help but impress the Osages. That this was so is evident by their reception the next time he visited the village. They presented him with twenty-five of their children to baptize.

In a letter written in 1850, Fr. Bax reported that he had baptized more than 500 and had administered last rites to 100. The manner of his untimely death, at the age of 32 two years later in 1852, underscores the depth of his compassion and care. When an epidemic of measles swept through the villages, the Osages appealed to the Jesuits for help. Using his limited medical knowledge to help relieve the suffering of the dying, Fr. Bax traveled from village to village, ministering to the sick. Over 1,500 of the Osage died; according to contemporary reports, few of them died without baptism, holy unction and communion administered by the hand of Fr. Bax. Exhausting himself, even as he exposed himself to the disease, Fr. Bax died within six weeks of the outbreak. At his funeral mass on August 5, so many Osages were in attendance that the coffin remained opened for hours after the funeral mass until 2 o'clock in the afternoon.

Fr. Bax was replaced by Fr. Paul Ponziglione, who proved himself no less dedicated and no less willing to endure the privations of ministry in southeast Kansas. One story, probably apocryphal but nonetheless revealing, is that Fr. Paul was gone so long on one of his travels that the brothers had become convinced he had died. It was only when they had gathered for the funeral mass that Fr. Paul reappeared to everyone's relief. From his base in Osage Mission, over a forty-year ministry, Fr. Paul established 180

Catholic missions, eighty-seven of which were in southern Kansas and twenty-one in the Indian Territory.[35]

A third priest to serve at Osage Mission was Fr. John Schoenmakers (1807-1883), who was assigned the task of building the school, while Fr. Bax and Fr. Ponziglione attempted to build up the parish and establish missions. Schoenmakers had left Holland at the age of twenty-six with the intention of volunteering for mission work among the Native peoples of the Americas. He was a novice in the Society of Jesus under the tutelage of Fr. Quickenborne when the society transferred to Florissant. The following story illustrates the love and respect of the Osage for Fr. Schoenmakers. In 1875, after they had left Kansas for their final destination in Oklahoma, the Osages requested that he visit them. They were having serious difficulties with the newly appointed Indian agent, Isaac T. Gibson, and Fr. Schoenmakers was the only white man that they fully trusted. It had been five years since he had seen them; thus in his visit it was necessary to visit each and every village occupied by the Osages. It took him three weeks of constant movement; when he had finally seen everyone and had negotiated a peaceful settlement between Gibson and the chiefs he prepared to leave. On August 11, the day before his intended departure, he received word that a dying Osage had requested last rites and communion. Fr. Schoenmakers immediately stopped packing and rode twenty miles to the bedside of the sick, prayed with him and prepared him for death. He then rode back to the agency to resume his packing in order to leave. During the night, he became very sick and the agency doctor was called for. As news spread among the Osages, they began to gather outside the house, down the hall and in the room in which he was lying. When the physician complained that the Osages were inhibiting his ability to care for the sick and motioned for them to leave, they interpreted his violent gestures as boding ill-will for Fr. Schoenmakers. Convinced that he was about to kill their beloved priest, they grabbed him and threatened to scalp him. It was only the intervention of Fr. Schoenmakers' traveling companion, Brother O'Donnell, that convinced them to cease and desist. The Osages, however, insisted on keeping an armed guard by the priest's bedside until he recovered. Their watch was prolonged – for it was not until September 25 that Fr. John Schoenmakers was able to return to Osage Mission.

As the story just recounted makes clear, by 1870 the Jesuit mission to the Osage peoples had ended. In 1865, the Osages agreed to sell the eastern-most portion of their land (present day Labette and Neosho counties) to the federal government, and in 1867 they sold their remaining Kansas land. By 1870, the Osages left Kansas to settle on reservation land in the Indian Territory (present-day northeast Oklahoma). Although the

Jesuit Fathers requested the right to accompany the Osages, that request was denied by the federal government and the Jesuit fathers remained stationed at Osage Mission continuing to minister to the white settlers who were pouring into southeast Kansas. The Fathers did not abandon the Osages, but rather continued to care for them despite their move south. Schoenmakers continued to agitate for them and to represent their concerns before the federal authorities; Ponziglione regularly visited the Osages on their new reservation, where he administered baptism to the newborn, extreme unction to the dying, and marriage vows to those who were living together while serving the Mass in their several villages. The Osages also did not forget the Catholics — the vast majority of Osage people still identify themselves as members of the Roman Catholic Church. But as an official mission, the Catholic outreach to the Osages came to an end in 1870.

As the Osages left, it was somewhat difficult to assess the "success" of the Jesuit mission. Fr. Ponziglione admitted as much in 1869, "Whether the labors and expenses undertaken by the Mission for the civilization have been of real utility to the Indian, I do not now intend to discuss."[36] To this day, the difficulty remains. To some extent, this is because success itself is so hard to define. If one measures success by the dedication, compassion and personal commitment of the Jesuit fathers and Loretto sisters, then undoubtedly this was a success. Conversely, if one measures success by the extent to which the fathers and sisters put aside their own cultural prejudices and embraced the cultural worldview of the Osages, then the mission was a failure. Success could be measured statistically — by the number of Osage baptisms, by the number of communicants and/or the number of times last rites were administered — but this does not address the issue of why the Osages converted and to what extent they truly became "Catholic."[37] In my opinion, each of the above-mentioned approaches is misguided and doomed to failure (or, at least, continual debate and controversy). Allan Greer is certainly right to insist that all such attempts are "ahistorical." As he writes, "Instead of trying to place them on some sort of single scale of tolerance and intolerance, we might better recognize the fundamental discontinuity between their way of thinking about cultural differences and ours."[38] So with Fr. Ponziglione, I too would say, "Whether the labors and expenses undertaken by the Mission for the civilization have been of real utility to the Indian, I do not now intend to discuss."

What I would like to do, however, in conclusion is propose that instead of looking for either "success" or "failure," our analysis should be concentrated on the manner in which Osage people and the Jesuit fathers were able to find common ground, to understand each other, and thus reach some degree of cultural accommodation. This is exactly what the

Protestant Mission was not able to do. And it was for this reason that their mission failed. The Presbyterian missionaries preferred to live within their own cultural and social environment, expecting the Osages to join them. This was even true in terms of language — in the beginning they concentrated their efforts on teaching the Osages English and did not devote time or energy to learn the Osage language. When they realized their mistake and appointed a few men to learn the language, these men were never able to master it. The reason lay in their unwillingness to adapt their cultural mindset to that of the Osages. The missionary, the Reverend Pixley, complained, "In order to learn it (the language) advantageously, we are reduced to the disagreeable necessity of living among the Indians, wandering with them, and in a manner, adopting their habits."[39] That the Osages understood the deep revulsion felt by the missionaries is revealed in their oft-repeated suggestion that perhaps the Christian religion was created for white people and did not apply to them.[40]

It is undeniable that the Jesuit Fathers were as convinced of their own cultural superiority as Pixley. Remember, it was Fr. Bax who reported upon first seeing the Osages that he had been sent to a "most savage part of the Lord's vineyard." Like the Presbyterians before them, they came with their pre-conceived plans to turn "savage Indians" into "Christian Americans." Fr. Quickenborne promoted the "Paraguay Plan" which envisioned establishing convert couples in "Christian villages" where they could raise their children on farms far from the influence of their still-pagan relatives. When the Jesuit fathers arrived in 1847, they came with a similar idea. The lay-brothers were given the responsibility of teaching Osage men how to survey individual farms and then plow, plant, and harvest the fields. In 1848, with funds supplied out of the Osage fund by the U.S. government, these brothers oversaw the construction of log-houses for individual Osage families. The homes were placed on surveyed fields, far enough apart from each other to allow for farming, and were well-stocked with European furniture and "modern" agricultural implements. The Osages responded to these efforts as they had to the previous labors of the Protestants. Osage women made a game out of moving the brothers' surveying stakes behind their backs and several Osage chiefs were able to collect valuable goods from westward bound settlers by selling all the furniture and agricultural implements in their "houses." The houses then sat empty and unused until they were destroyed one by one by the annual prairies fires that lit the sky in southeast Kansas.

It was the response of the Jesuit fathers to these "failures" that distinguished them in the eyes of the Osages and saved their mission. Instead of continuing their attempt to force the Osages to change their entire way of life to match their own, the Fathers adapted both their message and their methods. James Moore notes, "Jesuit missionaries ... were willing to accept the principle of accommodation, a principle they applied more to themselves than to the Indians."[41] In doing so, they were realistic in both their goals and aims. As Fr. Paul Ponziglione wrote, "We know this much from the perusal of ancient history, that to bring aborigines from their state of barbarism to a degree of civilization, and next make of them good Christians, has never been the work of a few years only, but of centuries." As a result, the Fathers were willing to make certain "compromises" with Native culture. They did not insist that the chiefs divorce their multiple wives, nor did they maintain that the men must take up farming or that the women must adopt European clothing. The Jesuit fathers supported the Osages in their feast making — it was Fr. Schoenmakers' habit to give them a cow or calf for their annual all-night dances. In other words, they did not expect the Osages to become "Europeanized" but were content to teach them certain basic truths and allow the Osages to come to their own understanding of the implications of those truths for their way of life. As Fr. Ponziglione explained, "We dare to say that the Mission established by the Catholic Church among the Osages in 1820 and continued to this day, has been of great benefit to humanity at large, for it has kept them from ravaging the neighboring settlements, gave them an idea, at least, of honor and righteousness, and inculcated upon their youth the importance of Christianity."[42]

Perhaps more importantly, given their organic understanding of the Church and their sacramental understanding of its theology, they did not conceive of "conversion" as only an exchange of one intellectual set of propositions for another. A Catholic Christian did not only believe a certain set of abstract propositions, but she followed an entire way of life centered in the performance of a series of external rituals. This view of religion was understandable to the Osages. For the Osages, religion was primarily a set of actions rather than a set of formulaic beliefs. This perspective rendered them culturally unable to access the Protestant worldview with its almost exclusive emphasis on propositional truths and the written "Word." As Hollings has written, "Nineteenth-century New England Protestantism ... as entirely an intellectual exercise ... had simply nothing to offer nineteenth century Osage." The Osages did, however, have points of contact with elements of Roman Catholic spiritual experiences. "Both the Osage and Roman Catholics shared a visual religious culture. They shaped their religious thoughts and beliefs visually, and expressed their spiritual beliefs with elaborate ceremony."[43] It was in the arena of this mutually shared sacramental worldview that the Osages and Catholics met.

Undoubtedly, the Osages were attracted to the external ceremonies and rituals of the Catholic faith without fully understanding their meaning; they also did not believe the adoption of Catholic rituals necessitated the rejection of their own older and more ancient rituals. The Jesuit Fathers were aware of this and frequently lamented the Osage practice of intermingling rituals and practices. At the same time, however, they also continuously looked for signs of similarities between the Osage religious traditions and their own and sought to build on these. As Peter Goddard explains, "Jesuit missionaries attempted to bridge from Indian experience to Christian truth, responding to the Ignatian injunction to find God in all things."[44] For example, the missionaries, detecting that the natives did not use "idols" in their worship, were convinced that the Osages instead practiced an ancient form of monotheism. Noting the Osage practice of regulating prayer by the hours of the day, they likened it to the Catholic Liturgy of the Hours. Fr. Paul Ponziglione even suggested that the Osages believed in a primitive expression of the doctrine of the Incarnation. Observing the ceremonial sacrifice of a bat in their annual rituals, he suggested that the ancestors of the Osages, "hearing of the coming of the Redeemer in whom were to be united two different natures," chose the bat because "as a bird it represented the Divinity; as a mammal the Humanity of Christ."[45] Obviously, he was neither a trained anthropologist nor competent zoologist, but what is striking is his intent to find parallels wherever he could. To us today, some of these attempts seem almost comical; as for example, the suggestion by Ponziglione that the Osages at one time knew the entire book of the Psalms but had lost them because they had neglected to remember the tonal system in which they had been chanted.[46] What is important, however, is that the Fathers looked for similarities and sought to find points of contact between Osage belief and practice and their own. Carole Blackburn has noted the tension in Jesuit missionary activity among Native people between "a policy of coercion" and "one of relative accommodation." The net result of this was "a complex and contradictory process, in which the distinctions between Christian civilization and savagery were identified and defined in terms that were often rigid — but were then blurred through the course of attempted conversion and the accidents of translation."[47] This is most clearly demonstrated in the Jesuit mission work among the Osage peoples.

As Richard White has reminded us, however, for an effective middle ground to develop, both parties must seek something advantageous from the relationship. It would be a fundamental mistake, and a continuation of a Eurocentric historical model, therefore, to cast the reasons for the existence of mutually beneficial negotiated relationship as being entirely dependent upon the Jesuit fathers, for there can be no doubt that the Osage were creative active agents in the developing relationship. They needed the Jesuit fathers; they realized that the changing and ever-evolving historio-cultural matrix in which they found themselves necessitated adaptation to American cultural ways. In seeking Roman Catholic rather than Protestant missionaries, they chose the route that seemed most conducive to their desire to retain as much as possible of their ancestral ways. I have already suggested a few reasons for this choice: their long and profitable relationship with the French, the celibacy of Roman Catholic priests and the sacramental spiritual cultures shared by both peoples.

In conclusion, I would like to suggest one more. The Osage were masters of the art of negotiation. Forced to live "in-between" competing European imperial powers, they had honed this mastery over centuries. They had cleverly strengthened their position vis-à-vis these powers and the surrounding Native peoples by selectively choosing (and unchoosing) alliances. Thus, as the American hegemony spread over the plains, the Osages looked to find the "in-between" position and then to exploit this to their own advantage. In the 19th century, Roman Catholicism represented their best chance to do this. Roman Catholics occupied an ambivalent social and cultural position within the predominantly Protestant world of the 19th-century United States. It was this ambivalent position that most attracted the Osages. To ally themselves with the Roman Catholic hierarchy and in a sense to come under their protection allowed them the best opportunity to continue their long-standing tradition as the "People of the Middle Waters."

NOTES

Preface

1. *Chanute Times*, April 13, 1876; *Parsons Eclipse*, April 13, 1876; *Oswego Independent*, April 15, 1876; *Southern Kansas Advance*, April 13, 1876.

2. Two cases were heard by the Supreme Court in its October 1875 session: *Leavenworth, Lawrence, and Galveston Railroad Company v. United States* (92 U.S. 733–760), and *Missouri, Kansas, and Texas Railway Company v. United States* (92 U.S. 760). The decision made by the court in the first case controls the second. In both, the court decided against the railroads in favor of the settlers.

3. *Chanute Times*, April 13, 1876.

4. *Parsons Eclipse*, April 13, 1876.

5. See Carl Johnson, "Balancing Species Protection with Tribal Sovereignty: What Does the Tribal Rights-Endangered Species Order Accomplish?" *Minnesota Law Review* (December 1998), footnote 83; Michael Newhouse, "Recognizing and Preserving Native American Treaty Usufructs in the Supreme Court: The Mille Lacs Case," *Public Land and Resources Law Review* (2000), footnote 16; Blake Watson, "The Thrust and Parry of Federal Indian Law," *University of Dayton Law Review* (Spring 1998); Carol Chomsky, "Unlocking the Mysteries of the Holy Trinity: Spirit, Letter, and History in Statutory Interpretation," *Columbia Law Review* (May 2000), footnote 195.

6. Stephen K. Williams, *Cases Argued and Decided in the Supreme Court of the United States in the October Terms, 1874, 1875–1876, in 23 Wallace, 91, 92, 193 U.S. with Others, Book 23*, Lawyers' Edition (Rochester, NY: Lawyers' Cooperative, 1901), 870–876.

7. Paul Wallace Gates, *Fifty Million Acres: Conflicts over Kansas Land Policy, 1854–1890* (Norman: University of Oklahoma Press, 1997), 152.

8. Craig Miner, *Kansas: The History of the Sunflower State, 1854–2000* (Lawrence: University Press of Kansas, 2002), 111.

9. Craig Miner and William Unrau, *The End of Indian Kansas: A Study in Cultural Revolution, 1854–1871* (Lawrence: University Press of Kansas, 1978, 1990), 131. See also Christine Klein, "Treaties of Conquest: Property Rights, Indian Treaties, and the Treaty of Guadalupe Hidalgo," *26 New Mexico Law Review 201*, 232–233.

10. Microfilmed copies of these newspapers can be found at the Kansas State Historical Society in Topeka, Kansas.

11. Brayton Harris, *Blue & Gray in Black & White* (Washington, D.C.: Batsford Brassey's, 1999), ix. See also David Dary, *Red Blood & Black Ink: Journalism in the Old West* (Lawrence: University Press of Kansas, 1998).

12. Craig Miner, *Next Year Country: Dust to Dust in Western Kansas, 1890–1940* (Lawrence: University Press of Kansas, 2006), xiii.

13. Dary, *Red Blood*, 277.

14. Jeffrey L. Pasley, "*The Tyranny of Printers*": *Newspaper Politics in the Early American Republic* (Charlottesville: University of Virginia Press, 2001), 22.

Introduction

1. L. Frank Baum, *The Wonderful Wizard of Oz* (Chicago: G.M. Hill, 1900), chapter 4.

2. Karl A. Menninger, M.D., "Bleeding Kansans," *Kansas Magazine* (1939): 5.

3. Thomas Fox Averill, "Oz and Kansas Culture," *Kansas History* 12 (Spring 1989), 10.

4. Robert W. Baughman, *Kansas in Maps*

(Topeka: The Kansas State Historical Society, 1961), 24.
5. Homer E. Socolofsky and Huber Self, *Historical Atlas of Kansas* (Norman: University of Oklahoma Press, 1972, 1988), map 13.
6. Craig Miner, *Kansas: The History of the Sunflower State, 1854–2000* (Lawrence: University Press of Kansas, 2002), 34.
7. Like Nebraska, Kansas was named for its most important river, which in turn derived its name from the dominant tribe of Native Americans living in the state when the first white men began to visit. Like many Native American names, before the name received its official spelling of Kansas, it was spelled in many different ways, including Kanzas, Kansies, Kanzon, Konza, Konzas, Kanzan, Kansaus, Cancease, Cansez, Canzas, and Canzon. See Andreas and Cutler, *History of the State of Kansas*, 33.
8. United States, *Statutes at Large X*, 283–84.
9. Albert R. Greene, "United States Land-Offices in Kansas," *Collections*, Kansas State Historical Society, VIII, 1.
10. Ibid., 3–7.
11. The original counties were Allen, Anderson, Arapahoe (in present-day Colorado), Atchison, Bourbon, Breckenridge, Brown, Butler, Calhoun, Clay, Coffey, Davis, Dickinson, Doniphan, Dorn, Douglas, Franklin, Godfrey (also spelled in some documents as Godfroy), Greenwood, Hunter, Jefferson, Johnson, Leavenworth, Linn, Lykins, Madison, Marshall, McGee, Nemaha, Pottawatomie, Richardson, Riley, Shawnee, Washington, Weller, Wilson, Wise, and Woodson.
12. On the basis of the list of countries officially recognized in section 3 of article 10 of the constitution, Wyandotte, Jackson, Wabaunsee, Osage, Chase, and Morris counties were included in the new list, and Calhoun, Richardson, Weller, and Wise were deleted. In 1860, when the official petition was presented, the state had been organized into 49 counties.
13. *Oregon Statesman*, December 2, 1831.
14. Robert W. Johannsen, "The Kansas-Nebraska Act and Territorial Government in the United States," in *Territorial Kansas: Studies Commemorating the Centennial* (Lawrence: University of Kansas Publications, 1954), 20.
15. *Congressional Globe*, 33rd Congress, 1st Session, appendix, 326.
16. J. Madison Cutts, *A Brief Treatise Upon Constitutional and Party Questions, and the History of Political Parties* (New York, 1866), 124.
17. *Congressional Globe*, 33rd Congress, 1st Session, appendix, 661.
18. Ibid., 318.
19. Ibid., 303–4.
20. Miner, *Kansas*, 35.
21. Henry Beecher, *Defense of Kansas* (Washington, D.C.: Buell and Blanchard, 1856), 5.
22. William Watson Wick to Robert M. T. Hunter, May 6, 1860, in Charles Ambler, ed., *The Correspondence of Robert M. T. Hunter, 1828–1876, Volume II* (Annual Report of the American Historical Association, 1916), 323.
23. *Cincinnati Enquirer*, June 22, 1856.
24. *Congressional Globe*, 33rd Congress, 1st Session, appendix, 338.
25. For a introduction to the debate that has raged over the motivations and intent of Douglas and his supporters, see Frank Hodder, "The Railroad Background of the Kansas-Nebraska Bill," *Mississippi Valley Historical Review* 12 (June 1925): 3–22.
26. Johannsen, "The Kansas-Nebraska Act," 23.
27. Stephen A. Douglas, "The Dividing Line between Federal and Local Authority: Popular Sovereignty in the Territories," *Harper's Magazine XIX* (September 1859), 537.
28. *Oregon Statesman*, April 4, 1854.
29. Joseph N. Prescott to Joseph Lane, July 25, 1854, Joseph Lane Papers, Oregon Historical Society (Portland).
30. Henry Bragg to Fitch [n.d.] in *the Leavenworth Kansas Territorial Register*, September 22, 1855.
31. *Leavenworth Kansas Territorial Register*, August 4, 1855.
32. *Lawrence Herald of Freedom*, April 28, 1855.
33. *Lawrence Republican*, December 23, 1858.
34. For an overview of the history of Kansas during the territorial period (1854–1861), see Thomas Goodrich, *War to the Knife: Bleeding Kansas, 1854–1861* (Mechanicsburg, PA: Stackpole Books, 1998).
35. *Anti-Monopolist*, January 19, 1871.
36. *People's Advocate*, May 11, 1871.
37. Robert W. Johannsen, "America's Golden Midcentury," in *The Frontier, the Union, and Stephen A. Douglas* (Urbana: University of Illinois Press, 1989), 288.
38. See William E. Gienapp, "'Politics Seem to Enter into Everything': Political Culture in the North, 1840–1860," in Stephen E. Maizlish and John J. Kushma, eds., *Essays on*

Antebellum Politics, 1840–1860 (College Station: Texas A & M University Press, 1982), 15.
39. Joel Sibley, "Conclusion," in Lloyd E. Ambrosius, ed., *A Crisis of Republicanism: American Politics in the Civil War Era* (Lincoln: University of Nebraska Press, 1990), 131.
40. Earl Hess, *Liberty, Virtue and Progress* (New York: New York University Press, 1988), 103.
41. My analysis follows the methodology employed by Daniel J. McInerney, *The Fortunate Heirs of Freedom: Abolition & Republican Thought* (Lincoln: University of Nebraska Press, 1994), and Bernard Bailyn, "The Central Themes of the Revolution: An Interpretation," in Stephen G. Kurtz and James H. Hutson, eds., *Essays on the American Revolution* (Chapel Hill: University of North Carolina Press, 1973).
42. *Osage Mission Transcript*, December 20, 1872.
43. *Parsons Eclipse*, August 5, 1875.
44. *Osage Mission Journal*, December 23, 1873.
45. According to geographer James Shortridge, Civil War veterans were "the dominant group" (both numerically and culturally) in the settlement of Labette and Neosho. See James Shortridge, *Peopling the Plains: Who Settled Where in Frontier Kansas* (Lawrence: University Press of Kansas, 1995), chapter 2.
46. Hess, *Liberty, Virtue, and Progress*, 109.
47. *Oswego Independent*, September 22, 1874.
48. *Labette Sentinel*, November 3, 1870.
49. *Osage Mission Journal*, September 3, 1868; *Osage Mission Journal*, September 17, 1868.
50. *Parsons Sun*, August 19, 1871.
51. See Miner, *Sunflower State*, 110–11; Gates, *Fifty Million Acres*, 197–99.
52. As reported in the *Osage Mission Journal*, January 7, 1869.
53. See Paul Cimbala and Randall Miller, eds., *Union Soldiers and the Northern Front: Wartime Experiences, Postwar Adjustments* (New York: Fordham University Press, 2002); Earl J. Hess, *The Union Soldier in Battle: Enduring the Ordeal of Combat* (Lawrence: University of Kansas Press, 1997); Reid Mitchell, *The Vacant Chair: The Northern Soldier Leaves Home* (New York: Oxford University Press, 1993); Maris A. Vinovskis, ed., *Toward a Social History of the American Civil War: Exploratory Essays* (Cambridge: Cambridge University Press, 1990).
54. Hess, *Liberty, Virtue, and Progress*, 109.

55. Bernard Bailyn, *The Ideological Origins of the American Revolution* (Cambridge: The Belknap Press of Harvard University Press, 1967), xiii.
56. Michael Holt, *The Political Crisis of the 1850s* (New York: Wiley, 1978), 134–5.
57. Gienapp, "'Politics Seem to Enter Everything,'" 66.
58. *Labette Sentinel*, December 15, 1870.
59. For two perspectives on the important political and cultural implications of 4th of July festivals, see David Waldstreicher, *In the Midst of Perpetual Fetes: The Making of American Nationalism, 1776–1820* (Chapel Hill: University of North Carolina Press, 1997), and Simon Newman, *Parades and the Politics of the Street: Festive Culture in the Early American Republic* (Philadelphia: University of Pennsylvania Press, 1997).
60. McInerney, *Fortunate Heirs*, 151.
61. William L. Barney, *The Passage of the Republic: An Interdisciplinary History of Nineteenth Century America* (Lexington, MA: D. C. Heath, 1987), 1.
62. *Osage Mission Transcript*, August 1, 1873.
63. Ruth H. Bloch, "The Gendered Meaning of Virtue in Revolutionary America," *Signs*, Vol. 13, No. 1 (1987), 41.
64. See Drew McCoy, *The Elusive Republic: Political Economy in Jeffersonian America* (Chapel Hill: University of North Carolina Press, 1980), 67–70.
65. See Charles G. Sellers, *The Market Revolution: Jacksonian America, 1815–1846* (New York: Oxford University Press, 1991).
66. Morton Keller, *America's Three Regimes: A New Political History* (New York: Oxford University Press, 2007), 69.
67. *Chetopa Advance*, February 17, 1869
68. Sven D. Nordin, *Rich Harvest: A History of the Grange, 1867–1900* (Jackson: University Press of Mississippi, 1974), 3.
69. See Alan Trachtenberg, *The Incorporation of America: Culture and Society in the Gilded Age* (New York: Hill and Wang, 1982).
70. Jane Adams, "1870s Agrarian Activism in Southern Illinois: Mediator between Two Eras," *Social Science History*, Vol. 16, No. 3 (1992), 370.
71. Ruth M. Block, "The Gendered Meaning of Virtue in Revolutionary America," *Signs*, 13 (August 1987), 37.
72. Barbara Welter, "The Cult of True Womanhood: 1820–1860," *American Quarterly* 18 (Summer 1966), 152.
73. See Linda K. Kerber, *Women of the Republic: Intellect & Ideology in Revolutionary*

America (New York: W.W. Norton, 1980); Mary Beth Norton, *Liberty's Daughters: The Revolutionary Experience of American Women, 1750–1800* (Boston: Little, Brown, 1980), and *Founding Mothers & Fathers: Gendered Power and the Forming of American Society* (New York: Alfred A. Knopf, 1996); Rosemarie Zaggari, "The Rights of Man and Woman in Post-Revolutionary America," *William and Mary Quarterly*, 3rd series, 55 (1998), 203–230; Mary R. Ryan, *Women in Public: Between Banners and Ballots, 1820–1880* (Baltimore: Johns Hopkins University Press, 1990); Elaine F. Crane, "Dependence in the Era of Independence: The Role of Women in a Republican Society," in Jack P. Greene, ed., *The American Revolution: Its Character and Limits* (New York: New York University Press, 1987).

74. See Nancy F. Cott, *The Bonds of Womanhood: Woman's Sphere in New England, 1790–1835* (New Haven: Yale University Press, 1975); Daniel S. Smith, "Family Limitation, Sexual Control, and Domestic Feminism in Victorian America," in Mary Hartman and Lois W. Banner, eds., *Clio's Consciousness Raised: New Perspectives on the History of Woman* (New York: Harper & Row, 1974). For a good review of the existing literature, see Linda Kerber, "Separate Spheres, Female Worlds, Woman's Place: The Rhetoric of Women's History," *Journal of American History*, Vol. 75, No. 1 (1988), 9–39.

75. Paula Baker, "The Domestication of Politics: Women and American Political Society, 1780–1920," *The American Historical Review*, Vol. 89, No. 3 (1984), 620.

76. Michael Barton, *Goodmen: The Character of Civil War Soldiers* (University Park: Pennsylvania State University Press, 1981), 73.

77. See Robert C. Haywood, *Victorian West: Class & Culture in Kansas Cattle Towns* (Lawrence: University Press of Kansas, 1991).

78. *Neosho Valley Dispatch*, June 29, 1869.

79. See Glenda Riley, *The Female Frontier: A Comparative View of Women on the Prairie and the Plains* (Lawrence: University of Kansas Press, 1988); Peggy Pascoe, "Western Women at the Cultural Crossroads," in Patricia Nelson Limerick, Clyde A. Milner II, and Charles E. Rankin, eds., *Trails: Toward a New Western History* (Lawrence: University Press of Kansas, 1991); Angel Kwolek-Folland, "The Elegant Dugout: Domesticity and Moveable Culture in the United States, 1870–1900," in Rita Napier, ed., *Kansas and the West: New Perspectives* (Lawrence: University of Kansas Press, 2003).

80. *Neosho County Dispatch*, July 13, 1869.

81. *Neosho Valley Eagle*, May 16, 1868.

82. Maury Klein, *Unfinished Business: The Railroad in American Life* (Hanover, NH: University Press of New England, 1994), 18–9.

83. See James A. Ward, *Railroads and the Character of America, 1820–1887* (Knoxville: University of Tennessee Press, 1986); Sarah H. Gordon, *Passage to Union: How the railroads Transformed American Life, 1829–1929* (Chicago: Ivan R. Dee, 1997); John R. Stilgoe, *Metropolitan Corridors: Railroads and the American Scene* (New Haven, CT: Yale University Press, 1983); William Cronon, *Nature's Metropolis: Chicago and the Great West* (New York: W.W. Norton, 1991); Robert F. Himmelberg, ed., *The Rise of Big Business and the Beginnings of Antitrust and Railroad Regulation, 1870–1900* (New York: Garland, 1994). The best and most comprehensive history of railroads in the United States is Albro Martin, *Railroads Triumphant: The Growth, Rejection, and Rebirth of a Vital American Force* (New York: Oxford University Press, 1992).

84. See Scott Hahn, *The Roots of Southern Populism: Yeoman Farmers and the Transformation of the Georgia Upcountry, 1850–1890* (New York: Oxford University Press, 1983); Scott Hahn and Jonathan Prude, eds., *The Countryside in an Age of Capitalist Transformation* (Chapel Hill: University of North Carolina Press, 1985); Scott McNall, *The Road to Rebellion: Class Formation and Kansas Populism, 1865–1900* (Chicago: University of Chicago Press, 1988).

85. See Charles Brooks, *Frontier Settlement and Market Revolution: The Holland Land Purchase* (Ithaca: Cornell University Press, 1996); Jamie Bronstein, *Land Reform and Working-Class Experience in Britain and America, 1800–1862* (Stanford: Stanford University Press, 1999); Allan G. Bogue, *From Prairie to Corn Belt: Farming on the Illinois and Iowa Prairies in the Nineteenth Century* (Chicago: University of Chicago Press, 1963).

86. See Stuart Banner, *How the Indians Lost Their Land: Law and Power on the Frontier* (Cambridge: The Belknap Press of Harvard University Press, 2005).

87. See Michael P. Dombeck, Christopher A. Wood, and Jack E. Williams, eds., *From Conquest to Conservation: Our Public Lands Legacy* (Washington, DC: Island Press, 2003); Reeve Huston, *Land and Freedom: Rural Society, Popular Protest, and Party Politics in Antebellum New York* (Oxford: Oxford University Press, 2000).

88. James Oberly, *Sixty Million Acres: American Veterans and the Public Lands Before the Civil War* (Kent, OH: Kent State University Press, 1990), 158.
89. *Osage Mission Journal*, January 7, 1869.
90. Paul Gates, "Why We Retained the Federal Lands," in Sterling Brubaker, ed., *Rethinking the Federal Lands* (Washington, DC: Resources for the Future, 1984), 38.
91. Donaldson, *The Public Domain*, 209–13.
92. See George R. Taylor, *Transportation Revolution, 1815–1860* (New York: Rinehart, 1951); Harry N. Scheiber, *Ohio Canal Era: A Case Study of Government and the Economy, 1820–1861* (Athens: Ohio University Press, 1969); Paul Gates, "Nationalizing Influence of the Public Domain," in *This Land Is Ours: The Acquisition and Disposition of the Public Domain* (Indianapolis: Indiana Historical Society, 1978), 102–26.

Chapter 1

1. Samuel Van Sandt claimed that his father, John Van Sandt, was immortalized by Harriet Beecher Stowe in her novel *Uncle Tom's Cabin*. John had been active in the Underground Railroad and (according to Samuel) it was he who had sheltered "Eliza" when she crossed the Ohio River.
2. http://skyways.lib.ks.us/genweb/civilwar/Van%20Sandt.htm
3. See Eleanor L. Turk, "Germans in Kansas: Review Essay," *Kansas History*, Vol. 28, No. 1 (Spring 2005), 44–71; Norman Saul, "The Migration of Russian-Germans to Kansas," *Kansas Historical Quarterly*, Vol. 40, No. 1 (Spring 1974), 38–62; Phillips G. Davies, ed. and trans., "Welsh Settlements in Kansas," *Kansas Historical Quarterly*, Vol. 43, No. 4 (Winter 1977), 448–469; Kenneth Marvin Hamilton, "The Origins and Early Promotion of Nicodemus: A Pre-Exodus, All-Black Town," *Kansas History*, Vol. 5, No. 4 (Winter 1982), 220–242; Don D. Rowlison, "An English Settlement in Sheridan County, Kansas: The Cottonwood Ranch," *Kansas History*, Vol. 12, No. 3 (Autumn 1989), 160–165; Donald M. Douglas, "Forgotten Zions: Jewish Agricultural Colonies in Kansas in the 1880s," *Kansas History*, Vol. 16, No. 2 (Summer 1992), 108–119.
4. James Shortridge, *Peopling the Plains: Who Settled Where in Frontier Kansas* (Lawrence: University Press of Kansas, 1995), 49.
5. C.E. Cory, "The Osage Ceded Lands," in George Martin, ed., *Transactions of the Kansas State Historical Society, 1903–1904, Vol. VIII* (Topeka: Geo. A. Clark, 1904), 192.
6. *Southern Kansas Advance*, January 26, 1870.
7. *Osage Mission Journal*, September 10, 1868.
8. *Neosho Valley Eagle*, May 16, 1869.
9. *Southern Kansas Advance*, January 5, 1870.
10. *Western Enterprise*, September 1872.
11. James Christianson, *A Study of Osage History prior to 1876*, Ph.D. dissertation, University of Kansas, 1968, 210–216. See also John Joseph Matthews, *The Osages: Children of the Middle Waters* (Norman: University of Oklahoma Press, 1961); Willard Rollings, *Unaffected By the Gospel: The Osage Resistance to the Christian Invasion, 1673–1906* (Albuquerque: University of New Mexico Press, 2004). For a fuller account of the Neosho Mission to the Osage peoples and its impact on settlement patterns, see the Appendix.
12. Christianson, *Osage History*, 216–20.
13. See William G. Cutler, *History of the State of Kansas* (Chicago: A. T. Andreas, 1883). Cutler's *History* can be found online at http://www.kancoll.org/books/cutler/labette/labette-co-p2.html.
14. The remainder of the Osage land in Kansas, known as the Osage Diminished Reserves, was sold to the United States government in 1868.
15. The 1862 Act can be read in its entirety at http://www.ourdocuments.gov/doc.php?doc=31&page=transcript.
16. "Antecedents of Erie: An Interview by W.W. Graves with Stephen C. Beck, June 23, 1932," Kansas State Historical Society, Manuscript Archives, Neosho County.
17. C.B. Wilber, *Mineral Wealth of Missouri. Two Lectures Delivered in the Hall of Representatives, at Jefferson City, Mo., February 17th and 18th, 1870, in Accordance with House Resolutions* (St. Louis: E.J. Crandall, 1870), 64.
18. Such was not the case in the land west of the Verdigris which was not included in the treaty of 1865. The Osage steadfastly opposed all settlement until they had negotiated a separate treaty to sell that land.
19. Mrs. J.E. Plummer, "Reminisences" (sic), 1931, 2–3, Kansas State Historical Society, Manuscript Archives, Neosho County.
20. F.M. Dinsmore, " Early Days," 1, Kansas State Historical Society, Manuscript Archives, Neosho County.

21. Jacob Beechwood claimed to have been the first white child to attend the Mission school "among the Indians."

22. As noted in footnote 18, the Osage treated settlers who had illegally moved onto the Osage Diminished Reserves (the name for the land owned by the Osage west of the Verdigris River) very differently, using a variety of means including both intimidation and violence, to keep the settlers from entering until they had signed a treaty with the government allowing settlement. See Christianson, *Osage History*, 227–35.

23. *Chetopa Advance*, June 16, 1869.
24. *Chetopa Advance*, December 29, 1869.
25. *Neosho Valley Eagle*, January 2, 1869.
26. *Neosho Valley Eagle*, September 8, 1868.
27. *Chetopa Advance*, January 20, 1869.
28. *Chetopa Advance*, July 4, 1869.
29. *Southern Kansas Advance*, August 3, 1870.
30. *The Headlight*, March 16, 1872.
31. *Chetopa Advance*, January 20, 1869.
32. *Chetopa Advance*, January 20, 1869.
33. See "Jacob Beechwood's Trip to Kansas," Kansas State Historical Society, Manuscript Archives, Neosho County.
34. Dinsmore, "Early Days," 1.
35. The following "call to arms" that appeared in the *Humboldt Union* on July 13, 1867, illustrates the attitude of many settlers: "There is scarcely a man in the west who knows the traits of the savages but that is willing to see a war of extermination enacted upon these blood-thirsty villains."
36. Dinsmore, "Early Days," 1.
37. Two stories appeared in the *Osage Mission Journal*, the first on June 24 and the second on July 8, 1869. The *Neosho Valley Dispatch*'s report was published on September 1, 1869.
38. *Chetopa Advance*, July 14, 1869.
39. *Allen County Courant*, January 11, 1868.
40. The evolving nature of the relationship between men and women in southeast Kansas and the important role played by women in the development of communities will be discussed later in Chapter 4.
41. *Neosho Valley Eagle*, April 6, 1869.
42. *Neosho County Dispatch*, September 22, 1869.
43. James Shortridge, *Peopling the Plains: Who Settled Where in Frontier Kansas* (Lawrence: University Press of Kansas, 1995), 49, 64.
44. Cory, "Osage Ceded Lands," 188.
45. William Calderhead, "The Service of the Army in Civil Life after the War," in George Martin, ed., *Collections of the Kansas State Historical Society, 1911–1912, Vol. XII* (Topeka: State Printing Office, 1912), 17. Contemporary historian John Jackson has confirmed these comments of early settlers in his investigative work in southeast Kansas cemeteries. Johnson continues to discover graves of Civil War veterans in southeast Kansas and to post them at his website: http://skyways.lib.ks.us/genweb/civilwar/civil_war_veterans.htm.

46. Phillip Shaw Paludan, *"A People's Contest": The Union and Civil War, 1861–1865* (New York: Harper & Row, 1988), 382.

47. Gerald Linderman, *Embattled Courage* (New York: The Free Press, 1987), 267.

48. Reid Mitchell, *Civil War Soldiers* (New York: Viking, 1988), 209.

49. Larry Logue, "Union Veterans and Their Government: The Effects of Public Policies on Private Lives," *Journal of Interdisciplinary History*, Vol. 22, No. 3 (Winter 1992), 434.

50. Dean May, *Three Frontiers: Family, Land, and Society in the American West, 1850–1900* (New York: Cambridge University Press, 1994), 79. For a discussion of the "wandering and tramping" that characterized some veterans, see Eric Dean, Jr., *Shook Over Hell: Post-Traumatic Stress, Vietnam and the Civil War* (Cambridge: Harvard University Press, 1997), especially 161–179. For an overview of the impact of immigrating veterans on the growth of Kansas, see Shortridge, *Peopling the Plains*. See also the pioneering work of Bruce Kahler who has suggested using the term "the Soldier State."

51. The historiography on the experiences of the "common" Civil War soldier has grown significantly in the last thirty years. In addition to the works by Paludan, Linderman, Dean and Mitchell already cited, see Phillip Paludan, "The American Civil War Considered As a Crisis in Law and Order," *The American Historical Review*, Vol. 77, No. 4 (October, 1972), 1013–1034; Earl Hess, *Liberty, Virtue and Progress* (New York: New York University Press, 1988); James McPherson, *For Cause and Comrades* (New York: Oxford University Press, 1997); Randall C. Jimerson, *The Private Civil War* (Baton Rouge: Louisiana State University, 1988).

52. Hess, *Liberty*, 3.

53. Jimerson, *Private*, 27. See the also the analysis of Michael Barton, *Goodmen: The Character of Civil War Soldiers* (University

Notes — Chapter 1

Park: The Pennsylvania State University Press, 1981), who argues, "Northerners ... hated most in other peoples, and in each other, what they feared most in themselves" (72).

54. McPherson, *For Cause*, 175. Historians debate the effect of the war on the soldiers. Gerald Linderman in *Embattled Courage* advances the thesis that by the end of the war most soldiers had become disillusioned with the republican ideology that had motivated them in the initial yeas of the war and were reduced to enduring an embittered struggle for survival; as noted in the text, James McPherson strongly disagrees. It is the position of this paper that the veterans who came to southeast Kansas fit the pattern described by McPherson and not that of Linderman.

55. Cory, "Osage Ceded Lands," 190.
56. *Neosho Valley Eagle*, May 23, 1868.
57. *Neosho Valley Eagle*, February 6, 1869.
58. Jean Baker, "From Belief into Culture: Republicanism in the Antebellum North," *American Quarterly*, Vol. 37, No. 4 (Autumn 1985), 539.
59. *Neosho Valley Eagle*, July 4, 1868.
60. In 1870, because the 4th of July fell on a Sunday, the celebration of the 4th was transferred to Monday, the 5th.
61. *Kansas Democrat*, July 7, 1870.
62. Ibid.
63. Adams' speech is found in full in the *Oswego Register*, July 8, 1870.
64. Linderman, *Embattled Courage*, 271.
65. *Labette Sentinel*, September 29, 1870.
66. *Osage Mission Journal*, February 4, 1869.
67. *Osage Mission Journal*, August 18, 1870.
68. *Chetopa Advance*, June 16, 1869.
69. *Chetopa Advance*, April 14, 1869.
70. *Kansas Democrat*, July 21, 1870.
71. *Neosho Valley Eagle*, January 23, 1869.
72. *Neosho Valley Eagle*, November 28, 1868.
73. *Southern Kansas Advance*, January 26, 1870.
74. *Southern Kansas Advance*, February 22, 1871.
75. *Kansas Democrat*, July 7, 1860.
76. *Oswego Register*, September 16, 1870.
77. *Allen County Courant*, February 22, 1868.
78. *Labette Sentinel*, October 27, 1870.
79. Julie Wilson, "Kansas Uber Alles! The Geography and Ideology of Conquest, 1870–1900," *The Western Historical Quarterly*, Vol. 27, No. 2 (Summer 1996), 186.
80. Historians have debated the meaning of the term "republicanism" in the 18th and 19th centuries. For an overview of the historiography, see Daniel Rodgers, "Republicanism: the Career of a Concept," *The Journal of American History*, Vol. 79, No. 1 (January 1992), 11–38.

81. *Osage Mission Journal*, September 22, 1870.
82. *Anti-Monopolist*, January 12, 1871.
83. *Labette Sentinel*, December 15, 1870.
84. *Neosho Valley Eagle*, June 10, 1868.
85. Quoted in the *Neosho Valley Eagle*, May 9, 1868.
86. Bruce Kahler, "Mary Ann 'Mother' Bickerdyke: A Gilded Age Icon," Virgil Dean, ed., *John Brown to Bob Dole: Movers and Shakers in Kansas History* (Lawrence: University Press of Kansas, 2006), 116.
87. *Neosho Valley Eagle*, August 22, 1868.
88. *Neosho Valley Eagle*, January 23, 1869.
89. Reynolds does not specific the nature of this "property" sacrificed by Davis. However, in light of Reynolds' commitment to the free-slavery position when he served as editor of the *Lawrence Journal World*, it is doubtful that he was referring to the slaves previously owned by Davis.
90. *Parsons Sun*, July 1, 1871.
91. Civil War veterans were not the first soldiers to insist on land as the reward for service. See James W. Oberly, *Sixty Million Acres: American Veterans and the Public Lands before the Civil War* (Kent, OH: Kent State University Press, 1990).
92. Paul Wallace Gates, *Fifty Million Acres: Conflicts Over Kansas Land Policy, 1854–1890* (Norman: University of Oklahoma Press, 1997), 145.
93. James Oakes, "From Republicanism to Liberalism: Ideological Change and the Crisis of the Old South," *American Quarterly*, Vol. 37, No. 4 (Autumn 1985), 553.
94. *Parsons Sun*, July 1, 1871.
95. *Neosho Valley Eagle*, June 15, 1868.
96. *Neosho County Dispatch*, July 27, 1869.
97. *Neosho County Dispatch*, September 29, 1869.
98. *Southern Kansas Advance*, January 5, 1870.
99. *Neosho Valley Eagle*, January 2, 1869.
100. *Parsons Sun*, July 1, 1871.
101. *Labette Sentinel*, September 29, 1870.
102. *Osage Mission Journal*, February 4, 1869.
103. Letter from R. C. Davis to John Farrel, August 23, 1869, Kansas State Historical Society, Manuscript Archives, Labette County history.

104. *Osage Mission Journal*, February 4, 1869; *Neosho Valley Eagle*, May 16, 1869.
105. C. B. Wilber, *Mineral Wealth of Missouri. Two lectures delivered in the Hall of representatives, at Jefferson City, Mo., February 17th and 18th, 1870, in Accordance with House Resolutions* (St. Louis: E. J. Crandall, 1870), 64.
106. *Osage Mission Journal*, March 4, 1869.
107. *Neosho Valley Eagle*, February 6, 1869.
108. *Southern Kansas Advance*, January 5, 1870.
109. *Parsons Sun*, July 8,1871.
110. *Neosho Valley Eagle*, June 15, 1868.
111. *Western Enterprise*, September 1871.
112. *Labette Sentinel*, October 13, 1870.
113. *Kansas Democrat*, June 8, 1870.
114. *Osage Mission Journal*, February 4, 1861.
115. Quoted in the *Osage Mission Journal*, September 17, 1868.
116. Craig Miner, "Border Frontier: The Missouri River, Fort Scott & Gulf Railroad in the Cherokee Neutral Lands, 1868–1870," *The Kansas Historical Quarterly*, Vol. 35, No. 2 (Summer 1969), 109.

Chapter 2

1. *Neosho Valley Eagle*, August 12, 1868.
2. See the comments of Larry Logue, *To Appomattox and Beyond* (Chicago: Ivan R. Dee, 1996), who has argued that veterans "developed a profound appreciation for solidarity. Most soldiers considered themselves independent individuals, but the extraordinary situations of the war had created permanent bonds with other soldiers" (142).
3. *Neosho Valley Eagle*, August 22, 1868.
4. *Neosho Valley Eagle*, September 22, 1868.
5. *Neosho Valley Eagle*, June 13, 1868.
6. As reported in the *Allen County Courant*, January 18, 1868.
7. W.W. Graves, *History of Neosho County, Vol. 1* (St. Paul, KS: Journal Press, 1959), 415.
8. *Chetopa Advance*, April 14, 1869.
9. *Chetopa Advance*, June 16, 1869.
10. Baker, "From Belief Into Culture," 543.
11. *Parsons Sun*, July 8, 1871.
12. *Southern Kansas Advance*, January 26, 1870.
13. *Labette Sentinel*, December 22, 1870.
14. *Western Enterprise*, September 1872.
15. Nelson Case, *History of Labette County, Kansas and its Representative Citizens* (Chicago: Biographical, 1901), 40.
16. *Humboldt Union*, July 13, 1867.
17. F.M. Dinsmore, "Early Days," 2, Kansas State Historical Society, Manuscript Archives, Neosho County.
18. *Chetopa Advance*, August 4, 1869.
19. Local settlers grew grape vines as well as apple and peach trees. See the *Chetopa Advance*, April 7, 1869.
20. Mrs. J.E. Plummer, Reminiscences" (*sic*), 1931, 3, Kansas State Historical Society, Manuscript Archives, Neosho County.
21. *Neosho Valley Eagle*, September 8, 1868.
22. Cory, "Osage Ceded Lands," 194.
23. *Neosho Valley Eagle*, December 12, 1868.
24. *Neosho Valley Eagle*, March 22, 1869.
25. Graves, *History of Neosho County*, 286.
26. *Neosho Valley Eagle*, August 22, 1868.
27. *Neosho County Dispatch*, August 17, 1869.
28. *Osage Mission Journal*, November 11, 1868.
29. *Southern Kansas Advance*, January 12, 1870.
30. *Osage Mission Journal*, June 17, 1869.
31. *Neosho Valley Eagle*, June 20, 1868.
32. *Osage Mission Journal*, September 17, 1868.
33. *Chetopa Advance*, August 18 and 25, 1869.
34. *Neosho County Dispatch*, August 17, 1869.
35. *Chetopa Advance*, April 7, 1869.
36. Solomon Kious to the editor of *Macomb Journal*; appeared March 20, 1879, Kansas State Historical Society, Manuscript Archives, Labette County.
37. *Neosho Valley Eagle*, September 22, 1868.
38. *Chetopa Advance*, October 13, 1869.
39. *Chetopa Advance*, November 10, 1869.
40. *Osage Mission Journal*, September 3, 1868.
41. *Osage Mission Journal*, June 17, 1869.
42. *Tioga Herald*, December 30, 1871.
43. *Oswego Register*, August 23, 1870.
44. *Neosho Valley Eagle*, February 6, 1869.
45. *Chetopa Advance*, February 3, 1869.
46. *Osage Mission Journal*, July 15, 1869.
47. *Neosho County Dispatch*, July 13, 1869.
48. *Chetopa Advance*, December 8, 1869.
49. *Osage Mission Journal*, December 30, 1869.
50. *Osage Mission Journal*, August 11, 1870.
51. The following statistics, related by the Superintendent of Public Instruction in Neosho County, give some indication of the structural problems immigration presented:

	1869	1870
Number of organized school districts	50	70
Number of children between 5 and 21 years of age	2,496	3,519
Number of school children enrolled	954	1,609
Number of school houses	22	31

Source: *Osage Mission Journal*, October 13, 1870.

52. *Neosho Valley Eagle*, December 12, 1868.
53. *Osage Mission Journal*, August 26, 1869.
54. *Osage Mission Journal*, June 24, 1869.
55. *Osage Mission Journal*, September 9, 1869.
56. *Labette Sentinel*, November 24, 1870.
57. *Neosho Valley Eagle*, June 20, 1868.
58. *Thayer News*, December 12, 1913.
59. *Thayer News*, December 21, 1917.
60. W.H. Hutchinson, "Introduction: Law, Order and Survival," *The American West*, Vol. VII, No. 1 (January 1970), 4.
61. Nelson Case, *History of Labette County, Kansas from the First Settlement to the Close of 1892*, (Topeka: Crane & Company, 1893), 49.
62. Cory, "Osage Ceded Lands," 195.
63. *Osage Mission Journal*, August 26, 1869.
64. *Neosho Valley Eagle*, March 20, 1869.
65. I also note the following notice printed in the *Osage Mission Journal* on August 4, 1870 as evidence of the attraction Kansas held for many who were seeking to flee from obligations and responsibilities incurred elsewhere: "WANTED — Information is wanted of Loren B. Holbrook, who is thought to be in Kansas. Any information regarding his whereabouts will be thankfully received by his wife at Fort Dodge, Iowa."
66. *Osage Mission Journal*, April 21, 1870.
67. *Osage Mission Journal*, August 4, 1870.
68. W.W. Graves, *Life and Letters of Fathers Ponziglione, Schoenmakers and Other Early Jesuits at Osage Mission* (St. Paul, KS: W.W. Graves, 1916), 48.
69. *Neosho Valley Eagle*, January 29, 1869.
70. The initial organizational bylaws were recorded in elaborate hand-writing and have been preserved in the Kansas State Historical Society's Neosho County manuscript collection.
71. Kansas State Historical Society, Manuscript Archives, Neosho County.
72. Cory, "Osage Ceded Lands," 195.
73. *Oswego Register*, July 30, 1869.
74. See below Dickerman's comment about "sharp lawyers" who have the ability to "bring up technical points." See also T.F. Rager's remark that all of the lawyers were young (under the age of 30) and inexperienced in his "History of Neosho County" in L. Wallace Duncan, ed., *History of Neosho and Wilson Counties* (Fort Scott, KS: Monitor, 1902), 134, 138.
75. "Address of Judge L. Stillwell," November 24, 1904, 3, Kansas State Historical Society, Manuscript Archives, Neosho County History, 4. See also KCH 14: 181, 184.
76. Nelson Case, *History of Labette County*, 48.
77. Stillwell, "Address," 5-6.
78. Ibid., 6-7.
79. *Neosho Valley Dispatch*, September 1, 1869.
80. W.W. Graves, "An Interview with A.T. Dickerman," Kansas State Historical Society, Manuscript Archives, Neosho County History.
81. Everett Dick, *The Sod-House Frontier, 1854-1890* (Lincoln: University of Nebraska Press, 1934, 1954), 20. For contrasting views on the purpose of these clubs and associations, see Benjamin Shambaugh, "Frontier Land Clubs or Claim Associations," American Historical Association, Annual Report, 1900, 2 vols. (Washington, 1901), I, 67-85; Allan G. Bogue, "The Iowa Claim Clubs: Symbol and Substance," *The Mississippi Valley Historical Review*, Vol. 45, No. 2 (September 1958), 231-253.
82. Richard Maxwell Brown, "The History of Extralegal Violence in Support of Community Values," Thomas Rose, ed., *Violence in America* (New York: Random House, 1969), 88.
83. Thomas D. Clark, *Frontier America: The Story of the Westward Movement* (New York: Scribner, 1959), 594.
84. Cory, "Osage Ceded Lands," 195.
85. Dinsmore, "Early Days," 2.
86. *Chetopa Advance*, August 4, 1869.
87. *Neosho County Dispatch*, September 29, 1869.
88. *Neosho Valley Eagle*, June 13, 1868.
89. Richard White, *"It's Your Misfortune and None of My Own": A History of the American West* (Norman: University of Oklahoma Press, 1991), 316.
90. Paludan, "The American Civil War," 1022.
91. Ibid., 1021.
92. Hess, *Liberty*, 12.
93. Hess, *Liberty*, 5.
94. Melinda Lawson, *Patriot Fires: Forging a New American Nationalism in the Civil War North* (Lawrence: University Press of Kansas, 2002), 5.

95. George Sidney Camp, *Democracy* (New York: Harper and Brothers, 1841), 100.
96. Quoted in Hugh Graham and Ted Gurr, eds., *Violence in America* (New York: F.A. Praeger, 1969), 181–182.
97. *Neosho Valley Dispatch*, September 8, 1869.
98. *Kansas Democrat*, July 21, 1870.
99. William C. Culberson, *Vigilantism: Political History of Private Power in America* (New York: Greenwood Press, 1990), 2.
100. *Chetopa Advance*, February 3, 1869.
101. Michael J. Pfeifer, *Rough Justice: Lynching and American Society, 1874–1947* (Urbana: University of Illinois Press, 2004), 3.
102. Herbert Packer, *The Limits of the Criminal Sanction* (Stanford: Stanford University Press, 1968), 158. Packer also notes that this attitude towards the criminal justice system shifted in the second half of the 19th century from concern for the safety of the community to concern for due process and the rehabilitation of the accused, especially among the elite. As an example of this shift, consider the following statement made by the editor of the *Erie Ishmaelite* in March 3, 1871. Commenting on a proposed law to limit the authority to pronounce a sentence of capital punishment to state Governors, he wrote of his wish to outlaw capital punishment altogether, arguing that "if a man has done some act which renders him dangerous to the community, and unfit to run at large, the sensible plan is to safely confine him and put him to work doing something for the benefit of the community he has wronged, and not deliberately take him out and *choke* him to death with a rope, as is the *modus operandi* of the most of the of our public executions in these days."
103. *Parsons Eclipse*, April 16, 1874.
104. *Neosho Valley Eagle*, July 4, 1868.
105. Richard Maxwell Brown, *Strain of Violence: Historical Studies of American Violence and Vigilantism* (New York: Oxford University Press, 1975), 148–150.
106. Ibid., 105.
107. Pfeifer, *Rough Justice*, 7.
108. *Neosho Valley Eagle*, July 18, 1868.
109. Dinsmore, "Early Days," 3.
110. *Neosho Valley Eagle*, June 13, 1868.
111. Cory, "Osage Ceded Lands," 192.
112. Stillwell, "Address," 8.
113. *Osage Mission Journal*, September 10, 1868.
114. *Osage Mission Journal*, June 24, 1869.
115. *Osage Mission Journal*, September 10, 1868.
116. *Osage Mission Journal*, September 17, 1868.
117. *Osage Mission Journal*, July 21, 1870.
118. *Neosho Valley Dispatch*, May 27, 1870.
119. The *Erie Ishmaelite* (February 21, 1871) furthered expressed this perspective when, in decrying the violent actions of a lynch mob in Parker, Kansas, it explained: "Mob law is unjustifiable in a settled country like that which surrounds Parker where the courts of justice are in full and successful operation."
120. *Neosho Valley Dispatch*, May 25, 1869.
121. *Osage Mission Journal*, July 21, 1870.
122. *Osage Mission Journal*, May 12, 1870.
123. *Kansas Democrat*, May 26, 1870.
124. *Osage Mission Journal*, December 22, 1870.
125. Rager, "History of Neosho County," in Duncan, ed., History of Neosho and Wilson Counties, 100.
126. *Oswego Register*, July 8, 1870.
127. *Chetopa Advance*, February 10, 1869.
128. *Neosho Valley Dispatch*, August 26, 1870.
129. *Kansas Democrat*, July 14, 1870.
130. *Tioga Herald*, November 4, 1871.

Chapter 3

1. *Humboldt Union*, April 17, 1869. The resolution to which the paper was referring was passed by Congress on April 10, 1869.
2. *Osage Mission Journal*, June 17, 1869.
3. *Osage Mission Journal*, June 21, 1869.
4. *Chetopa Advance*, August 4, 1869.
5. *Osage Mission Journal*, July 29, 1869.
6. *Osage Mission Journal*, September 9, 1869.
7. *Neosho County Dispatch*, September 22, 1869.
8. Letter to the editor, dated September 5, 1869, printed in the *Osage Mission Journal*, September 9, 1869.
9. *Neosho County Dispatch*, September 22, 1869.
10. Letter to the editor, dated September 5, 1869, printed in the *Osage Mission Journal*, September 9, 1869.
11. *Neosho County Dispatch*, September 22, 1869.
12. *Osage Mission Journal*, September 9, 1869.
13. *Neosho County Dispatch*, September 29, 1869.

14. Quoted in the *Osage Mission Journal*, June 23, 1870.
15. *Neosho Valley Eagle*, March 22, 1869.
16. This is the original meaning of the term "Little Balkans" to refer to Crawford and Cherokee Counties. Although this term would later come to refer to the presence of central and southern Europeans who came to work in the mines, its original use referred to the intra-settler violence that reminded Kansans of the ethnic, intra-tribal strife which had recently engulfed the Balkans in Europe.
17. *Neosho County Dispatch*, June 22, 1869.
18. *Chetopa Advance*, July 14, 1869.
19. *Neosho County Dispatch*, August 3, 1869.
20. *Southern Kansas Advance*, February 9, 1870.
21. *Kansas Democrat*, July 14, 1870.
22. *Southern Kansas Advance*, February 9, 1870.
23. For example, A.T. Dickerman who had served as secretary of an early Labette County Vigilant Committee became the first county clerk of Labette.
24. *Chetopa Advance*, August 4, 1869.
25. *Osage Mission Journal*, January 6, 1870 (emphasis added by author).
26. As reported in the *Neosho Valley Eagle*, April 20, 1869. A similar decision was made by the doctors of Neosho and Labette County in May of 1870. See *Osage Mission Journal*, May 19, 1870.
27. Diary of W.J. Haughawout, January 3, 1870, printed in the *Southern Kansas Advocate*, January 26, 1870.
28. *Chetopa Advance*, March 10, 1869.
29. *Neosho Valley Eagle*, May 16, 1868.
30. *Chetopa Advance*, February 17, 1869.
31. *Osage Mission Journal*, September 22, 1870.
32. Quoted in the *Southern Kansas Advance*, February 9, 1870.
33. *Osage Mission Journal*, February 11, 1869.
34. For example, Fr. John Schoenmakers reported that "ten churches have been erected in this portion of Kansas, within one year, and others are under construction" (*Osage Mission Journal*, September 29, 1870).
35. *Southern Kansas Advance*, January 5, 1870.
36. *Oswego Register*, July 22, 1870.
37. *Southern Kansas Advance*, January 18, 1871.
38. *Oswego Register*, September 16, 1870.
39. Note the references to the "established old towns of the East" in the *Advance* and "many older towns" in the *Journal*.
40. *Osage Mission Journal*, January 20, 1870.
41. *Southern Kansas Advance*, February 9, 1870 (emphasis is in the original).
42. *Labette Sentinel*, January 5, 1871.
43. *Labette Sentinel*, March 2, 1871.
44. *Kansas Democrat*, July 28, 1870.
45. *Neosho Valley Eagle*, March 22, 1869; *Chetopa Advance*, September 15, 1869; *Chetopa Advance*, October 27, 1869.
46. *Neosho County Dispatch*, June 22, 1869.
47. *Southern Kansas Advance*, January 5, 1870.
48. *Southern Kansas Advance*, February 16, 1870.
49. *Osage Mission Journal*, April 14, 1870.
50. *Osage Mission Journal*, December 22, 1870
51. *Erie Ishmaelite*, April 21, 1871.
52. *Neosho Valley Dispatch*, September 16, 1870.

Chapter 4

1. In fact, so firm was their allegiance to the Republican Party that there was no organized Democratic Party in either Labette or Neosho County in the 1860s.
2. *Parsons Sun*, November 11, 1871.
3. There is much discussion among historians about "republicanism" and its enduring legacy in the 19th century. For an overview of the debate, see Linda Kerber, "The Republican Ideology of the Revolutionary Generation," *American Quarterly*, Vol. 37, No. 4 (Autumn 1985), 474–495.
4. *Neosho Valley Eagle*, June 13, 1868.
5. Clifford Gertz, "Ideology as a Cultural System," in *The Interpretation of Cultures* (New York: Basic Books, 1973), 220.
6. J.H. Hexter, "Republic, Virtue, Liberty and the Political Universe of J. G. A. Pockock," in J.H. Hexter, ed., *On Historians: Reappraisals of Some of the Makers of Modern History* (Cambridge: Harvard University Press, 1974), 293.
7. Kerber, "Republican Ideology," 485.
8. *Neosho Valley Eagle*, July 4, 1868.
9. *Neosho Valley Eagle*, July 18, 1868.
10. *Neosho Valley Eagle*, August 1, 1868.
11. *Oswego Register*, August 19, 1870.
12. *Oswego Register*, November 4, 1870.
13. *Labette Sentinel*, November 3, 1870.
14. Nelson Case, *History of Labette County* (Topeka: Crane & Company, 1893), 251.

15. *Oswego Register*, November 4, 1870.
16. *Kansas Democrat*, May 26, 1870.
17. Ibid.
18. *Erie Ishmaelite*, March 24, 1871.
19. *The Anti-Monopolist*, January 12, 1871.
20. *Southern Kansas Advance*, August 13, 1873
21. *Osage Mission Transcript*, August 22, 1873.
22. *Parsons Sun*, August 3, 1872.
23. Ibid.
24. *Parsons Sun*, May 11, 1872.
25. *Thayer Headlight*, September 23, 1874.
26. *Thayer Headlight*, October 21, 1874.
27. *Osage Mission Transcript*, June 18, 1872.
28. For an overview of the existing historiography, see Richard Allen Gerber, "The Liberal Republicans of 1872 in Historiographical Perspective," in *The Journal of American History*, Vol. 62, No. 1 (June 1975), 40–73. The fact that this article is twenty-two years old and yet still remains the standard overview of the Liberal Republicans is an indication of the need for contemporary research into this important movement in the 1870s.
29. *Parsons Sun*, March 9, 1872.
30. See the *Parsons Sun*, August 31, 1872, and the *Neosho County Journal*, September 7, 1872.
31. *Neosho County Journal*, August 24, 1872.
32. *Labette Sentinel*, December 15, 1870.
33. Editors routinely used the term "frontier" to describe their communities of Anglo-American settlers. Recent scholarship has drawn attention to the ethnocentric nuances of the term; see Patricia Limerick, *The Legacy of Conquest: the Unbroken Past of the American West* (New York: W.W. Norton, 1987), 24–5. In reality, the term "border" or "borderlands" more adequately describes southeast Kansas, for the settlers were living between regions controlled by indigenous peoples (the Indian Territory) and those controlled by Anglo-Americans. The emerging, Anglo-American settlements in the Osage Ceded Lands were therefore contested places.
34. For an overview of the struggle of immigrant families to preserve the ideology they had brought with them to Kansas, see Lyn Ellen Bennett, *Living on the Edge: Families in Crisis in Nineteenth-Century Kansas*, dissertation, University of Kansas, 1996, especially chapter 2, "Great Expectations: Nineteenth-Century Gender and Familial Roles," 38–90.
35. *Chetopa Advance*, June 16, 1870.
36. *Osage Mission Journal*, February 4, 1869.
37. *Thayer Headlight*, December 16, 1874.
38. *Kansas Democrat*, July 21, 1870.
39. For more on the gender expectations of westward bound immigrants, see John Mack Faragher, *Women and Men on the Overland Trail* (New Haven: Yale University Press, 1979), and Julie Roy Jeffrey, *Frontier Women: The Trans-Mississippi West, 1840–1880* (New York: Hill and Wang, 1979).
40. *Western Enterprise*, September 1872.
41. *Osage Mission Journal*, September 3, 1868.
42. *Chetopa Advance*, February 3, 1869.
43. *Labette Sentinel*, October 17, 1870.
44. *Osage Mission Journal*, December 8, 1869.
45. Laura F. Edwards, "Gender and the Changing Roles of Women," in William Barney, ed., *A Companion to 19th-Century America* (Malden, MA: Blackwell, 2001), 224.
46. Richard Farrell, "Advice to Farmers: The Content of Agricultural Newspapers, 1860–1910," *Agricultural History* 51, no. 1 (1977), 209–217.
47. Lisa Miles Bunkowski, *The Butler County Kansas Vigilantes: An Examination of Violence and Community, 1870*, dissertation, University of Kansas, 2003, 50. For an overview of the scholarship on the ideology of the separate spheres and the cult of domesticity, see Barbara Welter, "The Cult of True Womanhood, 1820–1860," *American Quarterly* 18 (1966), 151–74; Linda K. Kerber, "Separate Spheres, Female Worlds, Woman's Place: The Rhetoric of Women's History," *Journal of American History* 75, no. 1 (June 1988), 9–39. For a broad analysis of the evolution of the cultural understanding of masculinity, see E. Anthony Rotundo, *American Manhood: Transformations in Masculinity from the Revolution to the Modern Era* (New York: HarperCollins, Basic Books, 1993).
48. Bennett, *Living on the Edge*, 56.
49. *Osage Mission Journal*, December 4, 1868.
50. The evolution of the "domestic sphere" and the discursive nature of the discussion over "women's work" in the 19th century have been noted by many historians. As Edwards comments, "The ideology of separate spheres, with its sharp distinction between men and women's work, did not just reflect the results of economic and political change. It was also a powerful political tool that different groups of people marshaled to shape the course of historical events" ("Gender," 236). To be clear, my argument in this chapter depends upon

the theory that frontier conditions expanded the traditional notion of the women's sphere by challenging middle class ideals (including gender ideals). See Robert C. Haywood, *Victorian West: Class & Culture in Kansas Cattle Towns* (Lawrence: University Press of Kansas, 1991), Bruce Dorsey, *Reforming Men and Women: Gender in the Antebellum City* (Ithaca: Cornell University Press, 2002). For an overview of the scholarship on the ideology of the separate spheres and the cult of domesticity, see Barbara Welter, "The Cult of True Womanhood, 1820–1860," *American Quarterly* 18 (Summer 1966): 151–74; Linda K. Kerber, "Separate Spheres, Female Worlds, Woman's Place: The Rhetoric of Women's History," *Journal of American History* 75 (June 1988): 9–39. For a broad analysis of the evolution of the cultural understanding of masculinity, see E. Anthony Rotundo, *American Manhood: Transformations in Masculinity from the Revolution to the Modern Era* (New York: HarperCollins, Basic Books, 1993). For a counter argument that rural households up to about 1930 operated with flexible gender roles as both men and women bent gender ideals in order to deal with the necessities of earning a living from the land, see Joan Cashin, *A Family Venture: Men and Women on the Southern Frontier* (New York: Oxford University Press, 1991), and Sally McMurry, *Transforming Rural Life: Dairying Families and Agricultural Change, 1820–1885* (Baltimore: Johns Hopkins University Press, 1995).

51. *Oswego Independent*, October 5, 1872.
52. *Osage Mission Journal*, February 24, 1870.
53. *Southern Kansas Advance*, July 27, 1870.
54. *Oswego Register*, November 25, 1870.
55. *Oswego Register*, July 30, 1869.
56. *Southern Kansas Advance*, April 5, 1871.
57. Bruce Dorsey, *Reforming Men and Women: Gender in the Antebellum City* (Ithaca: Cornell University Press, 2002), 4.
58. Simone de Beauvoir, *The Second Sex* (New York: Vintage Books, 1989), xxii.
59. *Register*, May 2, 1872.
60. *Neosho Valley Eagle*, May 16, 1868.
61. *Neosho Valley Eagle*, May 9, 1868.
62. *Neosho Valley Eagle*, May 16, 1868.
63. For an overview of how historians have interpreted the struggle to define gender in Kansas, see Carol K. Coburn, "Women and Gender in Kansas History. Review Essay," *Kansas History Journal* 26 (Summer 2003): 126–151.
64. *Neosho Valley Eagle*, June 20, 1868.

65. *Neosho Valley Eagle*, July 11, 1868.
66. Ibid.
67. This is the argument of Michael Goldberg in *An Army of Women: Gender and Politics in Gilded Age Kansas* (Baltimore: Johns Hopkins University Press, 1997). For a contrary argument, see Robert Smith, *Prohibition in Kansas: A History* (Lawrence: University Press of Kansas, 1986).
68. Nancy G. Garner, "'A Prayerful Public Protest': The Significance of Gender in the Kansas Woman's Crusade of 1874," *Kansas History* 20 (Winter 1977–78): 217, 229.
69. *Chetopa Advance*, February 17, 1869.
70. It is interesting to note that, according to my research among the newspapers of southeast Kansas in the late 1860s and '70s, the papers published close to the border between Kansas and the Indian Territory tended to emphasize the negative 19th century stereotypes of Native Americans males as perpetual "drunks" more so than those that were published further north.
71. *Osage Mission Journal*, June 29, 1870.
72. *Labette Sentinel*, February 9, 1871.
73. *Tioga Herald*, May 27, 1871.
74. *Tioga Herald*, February 17, 1872.
75. *Neosho Valley Eagle*, June 20, 1868.
76. See Nancy Garner, "'A Prayerful Public Protest': The Significance of Gender in the Kansas Woman's Crusade of 1874," *Kansas History: A Journal of the Central Plains* 20 (Winter 1997–1998): 215–29.
77. *Transcript*, July 19, 1872. The paper did not record the response of Joseph Pittman, but from later stories, it appears that he did not heed their "request."
78. *Southern Kansas Advance*, November 26, 1873. The saloon keeper complained to the local law authorities and Justina was fined three dollars for her aggressive behavior.
79. *Osage Mission Journal*, March 4, 1874.
80. *Oswego Independent*, March 7, 1874.
81. *Oswego Independent*, May 9, 1874.
82. For a discussion of the Crusades' impact on the development of the Women Christian Temperance Union in the late 1870s, see Nancy Garner, *For God and Home and Native Land: The Kansas Woman's Christian Temperance Union, 1878–1938*, dissertation, University of Kansas, 1994, especially chapter 1, "The Women's Crusade in Kansas: Prelude to the Formation of the Kansas WCTU," 25–91.
83. *Parsons Eclipse*, May 21, 1874.
84. *Oswego Independent*, April 4, 1874.
85. *Parsons Eclipse*, June 11, 1874.
86. *Oswego Independent*, May 9, 1874.

87. *Oswego Independent*, April 25, 1874

88. In her examination of the Temperance movement in northeast Kansas, Nancy Garner observed a similar response among the men of the communities she studied. See Nancy Garner, *For God and Home and Native Land: The Kansas Woman's Christian Temperance Union, 1878–1938*, dissertation, University of Kansas, 1994. It is be hoped that as more analyses of local Temperance movements in particular Kansas communities are completed by scholars it will be possible to determine the larger, more region-wide patterns of response among Kansas men in general (and specifically veterans of the Civil War) to this movement.

89. For more on the role of newspaper editors as "boosters," see Don W. Wilson, "Barbed Words on the Frontier: Early Kansas Newspaper Editors," *Kansas History* 1 (Autumn 1978): 147–154; David Dary, *Red Blood & Black Ink: Journalism in the Old West* (Lawrence: University Press of Kansas, 1998); Jeffrey L. Pasley, *"The Tyranny of Printers" Newspaper Politics in the Early American Republic* (Charlottesville: University of Virginia Press, 2001), Jeffrey L. Pasley, *"The Tyranny of Printers" Newspaper Politics in the Early American Republic* (Charlottesville: University of Virginia Press, 2001).

90. *Neosho Valley Eagle*, May 9, 1868.
91. *Neosho Valley Eagle*, May 16, 1868.
92. *Osage Mission Journal*, September 17, 1868.
93. *Neosho Valley Dispatch*, June 29, 1869.
94. *Neosho Valley Eagle*, November 21, 1870.
95. *Southern Kansas Advance*, February 16, 1870.
96. *Oswego Independent*, November 2, 1872.
97. *Tioga Herald*, March 2, 1872.
98. *Osage Mission Journal*, September 2, 1869; *Southern Kansas Advance*, January 26, 1870; *Southern Kansas Advance*, February 2, 1870; *Southern Kansas Advance*, December 7, 1870; *Neosho County Dispatch*, January 20, 1871; *Oswego Register*, January 27, 1871; *Tioga Herald*, June 24, 1871.
99. *Osage Mission Journal*, December 4, 1868.
100. *Transcript*, October 4, 1872.
101. *Erie Ishmaelite*, March 17, 1871.

Chapter 5

1. *Neosho Valley Eagle*, July 11, 1868.
2. *Osage Mission Journal*, December 10, 1868.
3. *Neosho Valley Register*, June 2, 1869.
4. *Neosho Valley Eagle*, January 2, 1869.
5. *Neosho County Dispatch*, July 13, 1869.
6. *Chetopa Advance*, February 17, 1869.
7. *Chetopa Advance*, December 8, 1869.
8. James Shortridge, *Cities on the Plains: The Evolution of Urban Kansas* (Lawrence: University Press of Kansas, 2004), 118.
9. This decision was supported by J.D. Cox, the secretary of the interior, in a report to President Grant in a May 21, 1870, memo.
10. *Chetopa Advance*, March 24, 1869.
11. *Chetopa Advance*, September 29, 1869.
12. *Southern Kansas Advance*, January 26, 1870.
13. *Osage Mission Journal*, August 11, 1870.
14. *Southern Kansas Advance*, April 13, 1870.
15. *Neosho Valley Register*, June 2, 1869.
16. Letter from an unnamed correspondent to the *Chetopa Advance*, published December 15, 1869.
17. *Osage Mission Journal*, June 20, 1870.
18. *Parsons Sun*, June 17, 1871.
19. *Parsons Sun*, July 1, 1871.
20. *Tioga Herald*, June 3, 1871.
21. *New Chicago Transcript*, May 10, 1872.
22. *Oswego Register*, October 17, 1873.
23. Masterson, *The Katy*, 89, footnote 2.
24. Letter of Levi Parsons, to Robert Stevens, dated August 29, 1872 (Stevens Family Papers #1210, Division of Rare and Manuscript Collections, Cornell University Library, Ithaca, NY).
25. Quoted by V.V. Masterson, *The Katy Railroad and the Last Frontier* (Columbia: University of Missouri Press, 1952, 1978), 27.
26. Letter of Robert Stevens to Levi Parsons, dated September 22, 1871 (Stevens Family Papers #1210, Division of Rare and Manuscript Collections, Cornell University Library, Ithaca, NY).
27. Letter of Robert Stevens to Levi Parsons, dated May 14, 1872 (Stevens Family Papers #1210, Division of Rare and Manuscript Collections, Cornell University Library, Ithaca, NY).
28. Letter of Robert Stevens, to George Denison, dated June 9, 1873 (Stevens Family Papers #1210, Division of Rare and Manuscript Collections, Cornell University Library, Ithaca, NY). There is no record that anything was ever made of this suggestion.
29. Letter of Robert Stevens, to George Denison, dated February 13, 1872 (Stevens Family Papers #1210, Division of Rare and Manuscript Collections, Cornell University Library, Ithaca, NY).

30. Letter of Robert Stevens, to George Denison, dated February 13, 1872 (Stevens Family Papers #1210, Division of Rare and Manuscript Collections, Cornell University Library, Ithaca, NY).
31. Letter of Robert Stevens, to Levi Parsons, dated February 15, 1872 (Stevens Family Papers #1210, Division of Rare and Manuscript Collections, Cornell University Library, Ithaca, NY).
32. Letter of Robert Stevens, to Levi Parsons, dated May 7, 1872 (Stevens Family Papers #1210, Division of Rare and Manuscript Collections, Cornell University Library, Ithaca, NY).
33. Letter of Robert Stevens, to Levi Parsons, dated May 14, 1872 (Stevens Family Papers #1210, Division of Rare and Manuscript Collections, Cornell University Library, Ithaca, NY).
34. *Southern Kansas Advance*, June 2, 1870.
35. *Osage Mission Journal*, June 16, 1870.
36. *Osage Mission Journal*, June 30, 1870.
37. *People's Advocate*, May 25, 1871.
38. As reported in the *Kansas Democrat*, July 21, 1870.
39. As reported in the *Kansas Democrat*, July 28, 1870.
40. *Labette Sentinel*, October 27, 1870.
41. *Labette Sentinel*, February 2, 1871.
42. *Erie Ishmaelite*, May 12, 1871.
43. "The Osage Ceded Lands. Who Owns Them? The Settlers vs. the Railroads. Views of Judge Lawrence of Ohio" (n.d., n.p.). A copy of this pamphlet is in the Newberry Library. The entire letter was printed in the *Parsons Sun*, July 15, 1871.
44. *Tioga Herald,* November 11, 1872.
45. *Tioga Herald*, April 6, 1872.
46. Letter of Robert Stevens, to Levi Parsons, dated May 15, 1872 (Stevens Family Papers #1210, Division of Rare and Manuscript Collections, Cornell University Library, Ithaca, NY).
47. Letter of Robert Stevens, to Levi Parsons, dated May 18, 1872 (Stevens Family Papers #1210, Division of Rare and Manuscript Collections, Cornell University Library, Ithaca, NY).
48. Letter of Robert Stevens, to Randolph Parsons, dated May 22, 1872 (Stevens Family Papers #1210, Division of Rare and Manuscript Collections, Cornell University Library, Ithaca, NY).
49. For an introduction to the political career of Stevens, see Robert C. Stevens and Betty Adams, *Thunderbolt from a Clear Sky: the Irrepressible Life of Robert W.S. Stevens* (Rochester, NY: WME Books, 2006), especially chapters 3–9.
50. Letter of Robert Stevens, to Levi Parsons, dated November 4, 1872 (Stevens Family Papers #1210, Division of Rare and Manuscript Collections, Cornell University Library, Ithaca, NY).
51. Quoted by Gates, *Fifty Million Acres*, 214–15.
52. *Parsons Sun*, April 20, 1872.
53. Gates, *Fifty Million Acres*, 216.
54. *Tioga Herald*, April 6, 1872.
55. Gates, *Fifty Million Acres*, 217.
56. *Parsons Sun*, May 4, 1872.
57. *New Chicago Transcript*, July 19, 1872.
58. *Parsons Weekly Herald*, May 29, 1873.
59. Letter of Robert Stevens, to Levi Parsons, dated September 17, 1873 (Stevens Family Papers #1210, Division of Rare and Manuscript Collections, Cornell University Library, Ithaca, NY).
60. *Oswego Independent*, July 19, 1873.
61. *Osage Mission Transcript*, July 18, 1873.
62. *Osage Mission Transcript*, July 25, 1873.
63. *Osage Mission Transcript*, August 1, 1873.
64. *Osage Mission Transcript*, October 10, 1873.
65. *Oswego Independent*, May 30, 1874.
66. Ibid.
67. See McCrary 610, 26 F.Cas. 901, 1 Cent. L.J. 425, No. 15, 582.
68. *Oswego Independent*, August 22, 1874.
69. The court cases can be found in 92 U.S. (page 733 for the Leavenworth, Lawrence, and Galveston decision and page 760 for the Katy decision).
70. Gates, *Fifty Million Acres*, 220–21.
71. *Chanute Times*, April 13, 1876.
72. *Oswego Independent*, April 15, 1876.
73. *Parsons Eclipse*, April 13, 1876.
74. *Southern Kansas Advance*, April 13, 1876.
75. Nelson Case, *History of Labette County*, 373.

Appendix

1. Bax to DeSmet, June 1, 1850. *Western Mission*, 354–355.
2. The story of the Osage Mission to the Osage peoples is recounted in Gilbert J. Garraghan, *The Jesuits of the Middle United States* (New York: America Press, 1938), chapter 27 (493–593). See also Mary I. McCarthy, *The Influence of the Osage Mission Upon Catholic*

Development in Southern Kansas, 1847–1883, Masters thesis, Notre Dame University, 1930.

3. See Richard White, *The Middle Ground: Indians, Empires and Republics in the Great Lakes Region, 1650–1815* (New York: Cambridge University Press, 1991).

4. Robert Liebert, *Osage Life & Legends* (Happy Camp, CA: Naturegraph, 1987), 73–96.

5. Stephen Aron, *American Confluence: The Missouri Frontier from Borderland to Border State* (Bloomington: Indiana University Press, 2006), 8–10.

6. This relationship is explored in detail by James Christianson, *A Study of Osage History Prior to 1876*, unpublished Ph.D. Dissertation, University of Kansas, 1969, chapters 2 and 3. See also Garrick Alan Bailey, *Changes in Osage Social Organization: 1673–1906* (Eugene: University of Oregon Press, 1973), 33–46.

7. Fred Voget, *Osage Indians I: Osage Research Report* (New York: Garland, 1974), 339–340.

8. See Colin Calloway, *The Scratch of a Pen: 1763 and the Transformation of North America* (New York: Oxford University Press, 2006), 122–149.

9. Willard Hughes Rollings, *Unaffected by the Gospel: Osage Resistance to the Christian Invasion 1673–1906* (Albuquerque: University of New Mexico Press, 2004), 32; Voget, *Osage Indians I*, 114–115.

10. Hollings, *Unaccepted*, 32.

11. See Arrell Morgan Gibson, *The American Indian* (Lexington, MA: D.C. Heath, 1980), 269–276; Stuart Banner, *How the Indians Lost Their Land* (Cambridge: The Belknap Press of Harvard University Press, 2005), 112–149; Roger Nichols, *American Indians in U.S. History* (Norman: University of Oklahoma Press, 2003), 81–124.

12. Bailey, *Changes*, 49–56.

13. Ibid., 56–59; Voget, *Osage Indians I*, 349–356.

14. James Muldoon, ed., *The Spiritual Conversion of the Americas* (Gainesville: University Press of Florida, 2004), 2–3.

15. Aron, *Confluence*, 24.

16. The story of DuBourg's life and ministry is recounted in Annabelle M. Melville, *Louis William DuBourg, 1766–1833, Vols. 1 and 2* (Chicago: Loyola University Press, 1986). For an overview of the Jesuit missionary effort in North America, see Calloway, *Scratch*, 157–164.

17. Quoted by Hollings, *Unaffected*, 132.

18. The full story of the Osage visit to the Bishop is given by Melville, *DuBourg*, 611–13.

19. Christianson, "Osage History," 18–19.

20. It was the inability of the Roman Catholic hierarchy to meet their needs that opened the door for the Protestant missionaries to step in. Using their established political connections and reaching into the deeper pockets of their members, the United Missionary Society successfully convinced the government to back their endeavors. Between 1820 and 1830 the Mission, staffed mainly by Presbyterians, established five missionary stations among the tribe. The story of the failed Presbyterian effort is recounted in Hollings, *Unaffected*, 45–128.

21. De La Croix, June 18, 1822, quoted in Fitzgerald, *Beacon*, 242.

22. DuBourg was part of the resurgent missionary movement among French Catholics in the 19th century. See Lawrence Nemer, *Anglican and Roman Catholic Attitudes on Missions* (St. Augustin: Studia Instituti Missiologici Societatis Verbi Divini, 1981), 25–27.

23. Quoted by Hollings, *Unaffected*, 136.

24. The concordat relative to the rights and obligations of the Society of Jesus and the Bishop of New Orleans was signed on March 19, 1823.

25. There is an oft-repeated "legend" by early settlers to southeast Kansas that Fr. Quickenborne was the "Black Robe Chief" mentioned in Longfellow's poem *Evangeline*.

26. Quoted by Fitzgerald, *Beacon*, 54.

27. Local clergy complained of Quickenborne's bad temperament, describing him as gloomy, secretive and not easy to work with. "Hard on himself, hard on others" was the standard description (see Hollings, *Unaffected*, 142).

28. "Osage Chiefs to the President of the United States," June 14, 1843, quoted by Hollings, *Unaffected*, 145.

29. Letter of Father John Bax to Father John De Smet, June 1, 1850, quoted in Graves, *Letters*, 224.

30. Quoted in Graves, *Letters*, 231.

31. Graves, *Letters*, 252.

32. Quoted by Hollings, *Unaffected*, 158.

33. Graves, *Letters*, 241.

34. Ibid., 238.

35. Ponziglione was the first Catholic priest to serve in thirty of the counties of Kansas. He also served in the Indian Territory (present-day Oklahoma), and established missionary stations at the Indian agencies and military posts as far south as Fort Sill, near the Texas

border. The following is a summary list of his missionary labors:
- 1854: 3 missions in Bourbon and Franklin counties among the "Five Nations" and the Chippewas and Appanoose;
- 1855 and 1856: 3 missions among the Native peoples in Bourbon Country and Franklin County; 1 mission in Crawford County among the "whites";
- 1858: 15 missions in the following places: Mound City, Greeley, Anderson County; Burlington, Leroy, Humboldt, Elizabethtown and Iola, Allen County; 2 missions in Wilson; 2 missions in Greenwood Counties; 1 mission in Franklin, Crawford, Cherokee and Woodson Counties;
- 1859: 1 mission in Little Osage, Bourbon County; Pleasant Grove, Greenwood County; Granby, Missouri; Defiance, Woodson County; and Emporia, Lyon County;
- 1860: 2 missions were organized, one in Marion and one in Allen Counties;
- 1863: 1 Church in Ft. Scott;
- 1866: the first stone Church edifice in southeast Kansas in Humboldt;
- 1869: 6 new missions in Winfield, Hutchinson and Council Grove;
- 1870: 1 mission in Eldorado, Greenwood and Independence; 1 church in Wichita (where the Cathedral now stands);
- 1872: 1 mission in Wellington;
- 1873: 1 mission in Oxford (Sumner County), Sedan and Elgin (Chautauqua County);
- 1889: 1 mission to the Crow tribe in Montana.

36. "Origin of the Osage Mission," published in the *Osage Mission Journal*, July 1, 1869.

37. This is the criticism raised by Rollings in *Unaffected*. While not denying that many Osage received baptism and the sacraments, he insists that they never accepted Catholic doctrine.

38. Allan Greer, ed., *The Jesuit Relations: Natives and Missionaries in Seventeenth-Century North America* (Boston: Bedford/St. Martin's, 2000), 17.

39. Quoted by Rollings, *Unaccepted*, 81.

40. Montgomery, "Great Osage Mission: Extracts of Letters, December 3, 1821," *American Missionary Register* 2 (March 1822), 351.

41. James Moore, *Indian and the Jesuit: A Seventeenth Century Encounter* (Chicago: Loyola University Press, 1982), xi.

42. Fr. Paul Ponziglione, "Origin of the Osage Catholic Mission."

43. Hollings, *Unaffected*, 156.

44. Peter Goddard, "Two Kinds of Conversions among the Hurons," in Muldoon, *Spiritual Conversion*, 70.

45. *Missionary Chronicle*, II: 58–59, quoted by Fitzgerald, *Beacon*, 25.

46. *Western Missionary Journal*, Vol. 7: 4–5, quoted by Fitzgerald, Beacon, 27.

47. Carole Blackburn, *Harvest of Souls: The Jesuit Mission and Colonialism in North America, 1632–1650* (Montreal: McGill-Queen's University Press, 2000), 131, 133.

BIBLIOGRAPHY

Primary Sources

Newspapers
Anti-Monopolist (Parsons)
Chanute Times (Chanute)
Chetopa Advance (Chetopa)
Chetopa Herald (Chetopa)
Enterprise (Parsons) *Southern*
Erie Ishmaelite (Erie)
Kansas Advance (Chetopa)
Kansas Democrat (Oswego)
Labette Sentinel (Labette)
Neosho County Dispatch (Erie)
Neosho County Journal (Osage Mission)
Neosho County Record (Erie)
Neosho Valley Eagle (Jacksonville)
New Chicago Times (New Chicago)
New Chicago Transcript (New Chicago)
Osage Mission Journal (Osage Mission)
Osage Mission Transcript (Osage Mission)
Oswego Independent (Oswego)
Oswego Register (Oswego)
Parsons Eclipse (Parsons)
Parsons Sun (Parsons) *Western*
Parsons Surprise (Parsons)
Parsons Weekly Herald (Parsons)
People's Advocate (Osage Mission)
Thayer Criterion (Thayer)
Thayer Headlight (Thayer)
Tioga Herald (Tioga)
Weekly Anti-Monopolist (Osage Mission)

Manuscript Collections
William White Graves Personal Papers, Kansas Collection, Spencer Library, University of Kansas, Lawrence, KS.
Robert S. Stevens Family Papers #1210, Division of Rare and Manuscript Collections, Cornell University Library, Ithaca, NY.

Government Documents
2 *U.S. Stat.*, 729–30.
3 *U.S. Stat.*, 332.
9 *U.S. Stat.*, 125–6, 520.
10 *U.S. Stat.*, 701.
11 *U.S. Stat.*, 8.
12 *U.S. Stat.*, 392.
Leavenworth, Lawrence, and Galveston Railroad Company v. United States (92 U.S. 733–760).
Missouri, Kansas, and Texas Railway Company v. United States (92 U.S. 760).
McCrary 610, 26 F. Cas. 901, 1 Cent. L.J. 425, No. 15, 582.
Worthington, C. Ford, ed. *Journals of the Continental Congress, Vol. V.* Washington, DC: United States Government Publishing Office, 1907–37.

Archival
Beechwood, Jacob. "Jacob Beechwood's Trip to Kansas." Kansas State Historical Society, Manuscript Archives, Neosho County.
Calderhead, William. "The Service of the Army in Civil Life after the War." George Martin, ed., *Collections of the Kansas State Historical Society, 1911–1912, Vol. XII.* Topeka: State Printing Office, 1912.
Cory, C.E. "The Osage Ceded Lands." George Martin, ed., *Transactions of the Kansas State Historical Society, 1903–1904, Vol. VIII.* Topeka: Geo. A. Clark, 1904.

Davis, R.C. "Letter to John Farrel." August 23, 1869. Kansas State Historical Society, Manuscript Archives, Labette County history.

Dinsmore, F.M. "Early Days." Kansas State Historical Society, Manuscript Archives, Neosho County.

Graves, W.W. "Antecedents of Erie: An Interview by W.W. Graves with Stephen C. Beck, June 23, 1932." Kansas State Historical Society, Manuscript Archives, Neosho County.

———. "An Interview with A.T. Dickerman." Kansas State Historical Society, Manuscript Archives, Neosho County history.

Kious, Solomon. Letter to the editor of *Macomb Journal*; appeared March 20, 1879. Kansas State Historical Society, Manuscript Archives, Labette County.

Plummer, Mrs. J.E. "Reminisences" (*sic*) 1931. Kansas State Historical Society, Manuscript Archives, Neosho County.

Stillwell, Judge L. "Address," November 24, 1904, 3. Kansas State Historical Society, Manuscript Archives, Neosho County history, 4. See also KCH 14: 181, 184.

"The Osage Ceded Lands. Who Owns Them? The Settlers vs. the Railroads. Views of Judge Lawrence of Ohio" (n.d., n.p.) A copy of this pamphlet is in the Newberry Library.

Wilber, C.B. *Mineral Wealth of Missouri. Two Lectures Delivered in the Hall of Representatives, at Jefferson City, Mo., February 17th and 18th, 1870, in Accordance with House Resolutions*. St. Louis: E.J. Crandall, 1870.

Secondary Sources

Adams, Jane. "1870s Agrarian Activism in Southern Illinois: Mediator Between Two Eras." *Social Science History*, Vol. 16, No. 3 (1992). 370.

Ambrosius, Lloyd E., ed., *A Crisis of Republicanism: American Politics in the Civil War Era*. Lincoln: University of Nebraska Press, 1990.

Appleby, Joyce. *Capitalism and a New Social Order: The Republican Vision of the 1790s*. New York: New York University Press, 1984.

———. *Liberalism and Republicanism in the Historical Imagination*. Cambridge: Harvard University Press, 1992.

Armitage, Susan and Elizabeth Jameson, eds., *The Women's West*. Norman: University of Oklahoma Press, 1987.

Bailyn, Bernard. *The Ideological Origins of the American Revolution*. Cambridge: The Belknap Press of Harvard University Press, 1967.

Baker, Jean. "From Belief into Culture: Republicanism in the Antebellum North." *American Quarterly*, Vol. 37, No. 4 (1985), 532–50.

Baker, Paula. "The Domestication of Politics: Women and American Political Society, 1780–1920." *The American Historical Review*, Vol. 89, No. 3 (1984), 620–47.

Banner, Stuart. *How the Indians Lost their Land: Law and Power on the Frontier*. Cambridge: The Belknap Press of Harvard University Press, 2005.

Banning, Lance. "Jeffersonian Ideology Revisited: Liberal and Classical Ideas in the New American Republic." *William and Mary Quarterly*, 3rd Series, 43 (January 1983), 3–19.

———. *The Jeffersonian Persuasion: Evolution of a Party Ideology*. Ithaca: Cornell University Press, 1978.

Barney, William L., ed. *A Companion to 19th-Century America*. Malden, MA: Blackwell, 2001.

———. *The Passage of the Republic: An Interdisciplinary History of Nineteenth Century America*. Lexington, MA: D.C. Heath, 1987.

Barton, Michael. *Goodmen: The Character of Civil War Soldiers*. University Park: Pennsylvania State University Press, 1981.

Bell, Sharon. "Osages, Iron Horses and Reversionary Interests: The Impact of *United States v. Atterberry* on Railroad Abandonments." *20 Tulsa Law Journal* (1984), 255–285.

Ben-Atar, Doron S. "Republicanism, Liberalism, and Radicalism in the American Founding." *Intellectual History Newsletter* 14 (1992), 47–59

Bennett, Lyn Ellen. *Living on the Edge: Families in Crisis in Nineteenth-Century Kansas*. Dissertation, University of Kansas, 1996.

Block, Ruth M. "The Gendered Meaning

of Virtue in Revolutionary America." *Signs*, 13 (1987), 37–58.

Bogue, Allan G. *From Prairie to Corn Belt: Farming on the Illinois and Iowa Prairies in the Nineteenth Century*. Chicago: University of Chicago Press, 1963.

———. "The Iowa Claim Clubs: Symbol and Substance." *Mississippi Valley Historical Review* 45 (1959), 231–53.

Bordin, Ruth. *Women and Temperance: The Quest for Power and Liberty, 1873–1900*. Philadelphia: Temple University Press, 1981.

Boylan, Anne M. *Sunday School: The Formation of an American Institution, 1790–1880*. New Haven: Yale University Press, 1988.

Breen, T. H. *The Marketplace of Revolution: How Consumer Politics Shaped American Independence*. Oxford: Oxford University Press, 2004.

Bronstein, Jamie. *Land Reform and Working-Class Experience in Britain and America, 1800–1862*. Stanford: Stanford University Press, 1999.

Brooks, Charles. *Frontier Settlement and Market Revolution: The Holland Land Purchase*. Ithaca: Cornell University Press, 1996.

Brown, Ray. "The Indian Problem and the Law." *Yale Law Review* (January 1930), 307–331.

Brown, Richard Maxwell. *Strain of Violence: Historical Studies of American Violence and Vigilantism*. New York: Oxford University Press, 1975.

Brubaker, Sterling, ed. *Rethinking the Federal Lands*. Washington, DC: Resources for the Future, 1984.

Bunkowski, Lisa Miles. *The Butler County Kansas Vigilantes: An Examination of Violence and Community, 1870.* Dissertation, University of Kansas, 2003.

Butler, Jon. "Jack-in-the-Box Faith: The Religion Problem in Modern American History." *The Journal of American History*, Vol. 90, No. 4 (2004), 1357–1378.

Camp, George Sidney. *Democracy*. New York: Harper and Brothers, 1841.

Carlson, Theodore L. "The Illinois Military Tract: A Study in Land Occupation, Utilization and Tenure." *University of Illinois Studies in the Social Sciences*, Vol. 32, No. 2 (1951).

Carstensen, Vernon, ed.. *The Public Lands: Studies in the History of the Public Domain*. Madison: University of Wisconsin Press, 1963.

Case, Nelson. *History of Labette County, Kansas and its Representative Citizens*. Chicago: Biographical, 1901.

Chomsky, Carol. "Unlocking the Mysteries of the Holy Trinity: Spirit, Letter, and History in Statutory Interpretation." *Columbia Law Review* (May 2000), 901–56.

Christianson, James. "A Study of Osage History prior to 1876." Dissertation, University of Kansas, 1968, 210–216.

Cimbala, Paul, and Randall Miller, eds., *Union Soldiers and the Northern Front: Wartime Experiences, Postwar Adjustments*. New York: Fordham University Press, 2002.

Clark, Christopher. *The Roots of Rural Capitalism: Western Massachusetts, 1780–1860*. Ithaca: Cornell University Press, 1990.

Clark, Thomas D. *Frontier America: The Story of the Westward Movement*. New York: Scribner, 1959.

Clawson, Marion. *Uncle Sam's Acres*. New York: Dodd, Mead, 1951.

Coburn, Carol K. "Women and Gender in Kansas History. Review Essay." *Kansas History Journal* 26 (2003), 124–149.

Cohen, Lester H. *The Revolutionary Histories: Contemporary Narratives of the American Revolution*. Ithaca: Cornell University Press, 1980.

Cott, Nancy F. *The Bonds of Womanhood: Woman's Sphere in New England, 1790–1835*. New Haven: Yale University Press, 1975.

Countryman, Edward. "Of Republicanism, Capitalism, and the American Mind." *The William and Mary Quarterly*, 3rd Series, Vol. 44, No. 3, The Constitution of the United States (July 1987), 556–562.

Cronon, William. *Nature's Metropolis: Chicago and the Great West*. New York: W.W. Norton, 1991.

Culberson, William C. *Vigilantism: Political History of Private Power in America*. New York: Greenwood Press, 1990.

Culhane, Paul J. *Public Lands Politics: Interest Group Influence on the Forest Service and the Bureau of Land Management*. Baltimore: Johns Hopkins University Press, 1981.

Cutler, William G. *History of the State of Kansas*. Chicago: A.T. Andreas, 1883.

Dary, David. *Red Blood & Black Ink: Journalism in the Old West*. Lawrence, KS: University Press of Kansas, 1998.

Davies, Phillips G., ed. and trans. "Welsh Settlements in Kansas." *Kansas Historical Quarterly*, Vol. 43, No. 4 (1977), 448–469.

Dean, Eric, Jr. *Shook Over Hell: Post-Traumatic Stress, Vietnam and the Civil War*. Cambridge: Harvard University Press, 1997.

Dean, Virgil, editor. *John Brown to Bob Dole: Movers and Shakers in Kansas History*. Lawrence: University Press of Kansas, 2006.

Deverell, William. *Railroad Crossing: Californians and the Railroad, 1850–1910*. Berkeley, CA: University of California Press, 1994.

Dick, Everett. *The Lure of the Land: A Social History of the Public Lands from the Articles of Confederation to the New Deal*. Lincoln: University of Nebraska Press, 1970.

———. *The Sod-House Frontier, 1854–1890*. Lincoln: University of Nebraska Press, 1934, 1954.

Diggins, John Patrick. *The Lost Soul of American Politics: Virtue, Self-Interest, and the Foundations of Liberalism*. New York: Basic Books, 1984.

Dombeck, Michael P., Christopher A. Wood, and Jack E. Williams, eds., *From Conquest to Conservation: Our Public Lands Legacy*. Washington, DC: Island Press, 2003.

Donaldson, Thomas. *The Public Domain: Its History with Statistics*. Washington, DC: Government Publishing Office, 1884.

Dorsey, Bruce. *Reforming Men and Women: Gender in the Antebellum City*. Ithaca: Cornell University Press, 2002.

Douglas, Donald M. "Forgotten Zions: Jewish Agricultural Colonies in Kansas in the 1880s." *Kansas History*, Vol. 16, No. 2 (1992), 108–119.

Earle, Jonathan. *Jacksonian Antislavery & the Politics of Free Soil, 1824–1854*. Chapel Hill: University of North Carolina Press, 2004.

Ellis, David, ed. *The Frontier in American Development: Essays in Honor of Paul Wallace Gates*. Ithaca: Cornell University Press, 1969.

———, Richard C. Overton, Robert E. Riegel, Herbert O. Brayer, Chester M. Destler, Stanley Pargellis, Fred A. Shannon, and Edward C. Kirkland. "Comments on 'The Railroad Land Grant Legend in American History Texts.'" *The Mississippi Valley Historical Review*, Vol. 32, No. 2 (1945), 171–194.

Entz, Gary R. "Religion in Kansas. Review Essay." *Kansas History Journal* 28 (2005), 120–145.

Evans, Paul Demund. *The Holland Land Company*. Buffalo: Buffalo Historical Society, 1924.

Faragher, John Mack. *Women and Men on the Overland Trail*. New Haven: Yale University Press, 1979.

Farrell, Richard. "Advice to Farmers: The Content of Agricultural Newspapers, 1860–1910." *Agricultural History* 51, no. 1 (1977), 209–217.

Finke, Roger, and Rodney Stark. *The Church of America, 1776–1990: Winners and Losers in our Religious Economy*. New Brunswick, NJ: Rutgers University Press, 1992.

Fitzpatrick, John C., ed. *The Writings of George Washington from the Original Manuscript Sources, 1745–1799, Vol. 6*. Washington, DC: United States Government Publishing Office, 1931–44.

Flynn, Roger. "The 1872 Mining Law as an Impediment to Mineral Development on the Public Lands: A 19th Century Law Meets the Realities of Modern Mining." *Land and Water Law Review* (1999), 301–78.

Foner, Eric. *Free Soil, Free Labor, Free Men: The Ideology of the Republican Party Before the Civil War*. New York: Oxford University Press, 1980.

Ford, Amelia C. "Colonial Precedents of Our National Land System as it Existed in 1800." *Bulletin of the University of Wisconsin*, no. 352, History Series, vol. 2, no. 2 (1909–10), 103–7.

Garner, Nancy. *For God and Home and Native Land: the Kansas Woman's Christian Temperance Union, 1878–1938*. Dissertation, University of Kansas, 1994.

Gates, Paul Wallace. *Fifty Million Acres:*

Conflicts Over Kansas Land Policy, 1854–1890. Norman: University of Oklahoma Press, 1997.
_____. *History of Public Land Law Development.* Washington, DC: Government Publishing Office, 1968.
_____. *The Illinois Central Railroad and its Colonization Work.* Cambridge: Harvard University Press, 1934.
_____. *This Land Is Ours: The Acquisition and Disposition of the Public Domain.* Indianapolis: Indiana Historical Society, 1978.
Gerber, Richard Allen. "The Liberal Republicans of 1872 in Historiographical Perspective." *The Journal of American History*, Vol. 62, No. 1 (1975), 40–73.
Gertz, Clifford. *The Interpretation of Cultures.* New York: Basic Books, 1973.
Glaab, Charles N. *Kansas City and the Railroads: Community Policy in the Growth of a Regional Metropolis.* Lawrence: University Press of Kansas, 1993.
Goldberg, Michael. *An Army of Women: Gender and Politics in Gilded Age Kansas.* Baltimore: Johns Hopkins University Press, 1997.
_____. "Non-Partisan and All-Partisan: Rethinking Women's Suffrage and Party Politics in Gilded Age Kansas." *The Western Historical Quarterly*, Vol. 25, No. 1 (1994), 21–44.
Goodman, Paul. *Towards a Christian Republic: Antimasonry and the Great Transition in New England, 1826–1836.* New York: Oxford University Press, 1988.
Gordon, Sarah H. *Passage to Union: How the Railroads Transformed American Life, 1829–1929.* Chicago: Ivan R. Dee, 1997.
Graham, Hugh, and Ted Gurr, eds. *Violence in America.* New York: F.A. Praeger, 1969.
Graves, William White. *History of Neosho County, Vol. 1.* St. Paul, KS: Journal Press, 1959.
_____. *Life and Letters of Fathers Ponziglione, Schoenmakers and Other Early Jesuits at Osage Mission.* St. Paul, KS: W.W. Graves, 1916.
Greene, Jack P., ed., *The American Revolution: Its Character and Limits.* New York: New York University Press, 1987.
Greever, William. *Arid Domain: The Santa Fe Railway and its Western Land Grant.* Stanford: Stanford University Press, 1954.
Gribbon, William. "Republicanism, Reform, and the Sense of Sin in Antebellum America." *Cithara* 14 (December 1974), 25–41.
Gross, Robert A. "Culture and Cultivation: Agriculture and Society in Thoreau's Concord." *Journal of American History* 69 (1982), 42–61.
Hahn, Scott. *The Roots of Southern Populism: Yeoman Farmers and the Transformation of the Georgia Upcountry, 1850–1890.* New York: Oxford University Press, 1983.
_____, and Jonathan Prude, eds. *The Countryside in an Age of Capitalist Transformation.* Chapel Hill: University of North Carolina Press, 1985.
Hamilton, Kenneth Marvin. "The Origins and Early Promotion of Nicodemus: A Pre-Exodus, All- Black Town." *Kansas History*, Vol. 5, No. 4 (1982), 220–242.
Harris, Brayton. *Blue & Gray in Black & White.* Washington, DC: Brassey's, 1999.
Hartman, Mary, and Lois W. Banner, eds. *Clio's Consciousness Raised: New Perspectives on the History of Woman.* New York: Harper & Row, 1974.
Hatch, Nathan O. *The Democratization of American Christianity.* New Haven: Yale University Press, 1989.
_____. *The Sacred Cause of Liberty: Republican Thought and the Millennium in Revolutionary New England.* New Haven: Yale University Press, 1977.
Haywood, Robert C. *Victorian West: Class & Culture in Kansas Cattle Towns.* Lawrence: University Press of Kansas, 1991.
Hedges, James. *Building the Canadian West: the Land and Colonization Policies of the Canadian Pacific Railway.* New York: Macmillan, 1939.
Hess, Earl. *Liberty, Virtue and Progress.* New York: New York University Press, 1988.
_____. *The Union Soldier in Battle: Enduring the Ordeal of Combat.* Lawrence: University of Kansas Press, 1997.
Hexter, J.H., ed. *On Historians: Reappraisals of Some of the Makers of Modern History.* Cambridge: Harvard University Press, 1974.

Higham, John, and Paul K. Conkin, eds., *New Directions in American Intellectual History*. Baltimore: Johns Hopkins University Press, 1979.

Himmelberg, Robert F., ed. *The Rise of Big Business and the Beginnings of Antitrust and Railroad Regulation, 1870–1900*. New York: Garland, 1994.

Hoffert, Sylvia D. *When Hens Crow: The Woman's Rights Movement in Antebellum America*. Bloomington: Indiana University Press, 1995.

Holt, Michael F. *The Political Crisis of the 1850s*. New York: John Wiley & Sons, 1978.

_____. *The Political Crisis of the 1950s*. New York: Wiley, 1978.

Howe, Daniel Walker. *The Political Culture of the American Whigs*. Chicago: University of Chicago Press, 1979.

Huston, Reeve. *Land and Freedom: Rural Society, Popular Protest, and Party Politics in Antebellum New York*. Oxford: Oxford University Press, 2000.

Hutchinson, W.H. "Introduction: Law, Order and Survival." *The American West*, Vol. VII, No. 1 (1970), 4.

Hutchinson, William T. "Military Bounty Lands of the American Revolution in Ohio." Dissertation, University of Chicago, 1927.

Jeffrey, Julie Roy. *Frontier Women: The Trans-Mississippi West, 1840–1880*. New York: Hill and Wang, 1979.

Jimerson, Randall C. *The Private Civil War*. Baton Rouge: Louisiana State University, 1988.

Johannsen, Robert W. "America's Golden Midcentury." *The Frontier, the Union, and Stephen A. Douglas*. Urbana and Chicago: University of Illinois Press, 1989.

Johnson, Carl. "Balancing Species Protection with Tribal Sovereignty: What does the Tribal Rights-Endangered Species Order Accomplish?" *Minnesota Law Review* (December 1998), 523–64.

Johnson, Russell. "The Civil War Generation: Military Service and Mobility in Dubuque, Iowa, 1860–1870." *Journal of Social History*, Vol. 32, No. 4 (1999), 791–820.

Jurdjevic, Mark. "Virtue, Commerce, and the Enduring Florentine Republican Moment: Reintegrating Italy into the Atlantic Republican Debate." *Journal of the History of Ideas*, Vol. 62, No. 4 (October 2001), 721–743.

Kaestle, Carl F. *Pillars of the Republic: Common Schools and American Society, 1780–1860*. New York: Hill and Wang, 1983.

Keller, Morton. *America's Three Regimes: A New Political History*. New York: Oxford University Press, 2007.

Kerber, Linda K. "The Republican Ideology of the Revolutionary Generation," *American Quarterly*, Vol. 37, No. 4 (1985), 474–495.

_____. "Separate Spheres, Female Worlds, Woman's Place: The Rhetoric of Women's History." *Journal of American History*, Vol. 75, No. 1 (1988), 9–39.

_____. *Women of the Republic: Intellect & Ideology in Revolutionary America*. New York: W.W. Norton, 1980.

Klein, Christine. "Treaties of Conquest: Property Rights, Indian Treaties, and the Treaty of Guadalupe Hidalgo," *26 New Mexico Law Review*, 201, 232–233.

Klein, Maury. *Unfinished Business: The Railroad in American Life*. Hanover, NH: University Press of New England, 1994.

Kleppner, Paul. *The Third Electoral System, 1853–1892: Parties, Voters, and Political Cultures*. Chapel Hill: University of North Carolina Press, 1979.

Kloppenberg, James T. "The Virtues of Liberalism: Christianity, Republicanism, and Ethics in Early American Political Discourse." *Journal of American History* 74 (June 1987), 9–33.

Kramnick, Isaac. *Republicanism and Bourgeois Radicalism: Political Ideology in Late Eighteenth Century England and America*. Ithaca: Cornell University Press, 1990.

Kulikoff, Allan. *The Agrarian Origins of American Capitalism*. Charlottesville: University Press of Virginia, 1992.

_____. "The Transition to Capitalism in Rural America." *The William and Mary Quarterly*, 3rd Series, Vol. 46, No. 1 (1989), 120–144

Kurtz, Stephen G., and James H. Hutson, eds. *Essays on the American Revolution*. Chapel Hill: University of North Carolina Press, 1973.

Latta, Leroy, Jr. "Public Access over Alaska

Public Lands as Granted by Section 8 of Lode Mining Act of 1866." *Santa Clara Law Review* (Fall 1988), 811–40.

Lawson, Melinda. *Patriot Fires: Forging a New American Nationalism in the Civil War North.* Lawrence: University Press of Kansas, 2002.

Limerick, Patricia Nelson. *The Legacy of Conquest: The Unbroken Past of the American West.* New York: W.W. Norton, 1987.

———, Clyde A. Milner II, and Charles E. Rankin, eds., *Trails: Toward a New Western History.* Lawrence: University Press of Kansas, 1991.

Logue, Larry. *To Appomattox and Beyond.* Chicago: Ivan R. Dee, 1996.

———. "Union Veterans and Their Government: The Effects of Public Policies on Private Lives." *Journal of Interdisciplinary History*, Vol. 22, No. 3 (1992), 411–34.

Linderman, Gerald. *Embattled Courage.* New York: The Free Press, 1987. Maier, Pauline. *From Resistance to Revolution: Colonial Radicals and the Development of American Opposition to Britain, 1765–1776.* New York: Knopf, 1972.

Maizlish, Stephen E., and John J. Kushma, eds. *Essays on Antebellum Politics, 1840–1860.* College Station: Texas A & M University Press, 1982.

Martin, Albro. *Railroads Triumphant: The Growth, Rejection, and Rebirth of a Vital American Force.* New York: Oxford University Press, 1992.

Masterson, V. V. *The Katy Railroad and the Last Frontier.* Columbia, MO: University of Missouri Press, 1952, 1978.

Matson, Cathy D., and Peter S. Onuf. *A Union of Interests: Political and Economic Thought in Revolutionary America.* Lawrence: University Press of Kansas, 1990.

Matthews, John Joseph. *The Osages: Children of the Middle Waters.* Norman: University of Oklahoma Press, 1961.

May, Dean. *Three Frontiers: Family, Land, and Society in the American West, 1850–1900.* New York: Cambridge University Press, 1994.

McConnell, Stuart. *Glorious Contentment: The Grand Army of the Republic, 1865–1900.* Chapel Hill: University of North Carolina Press, 1992.

McCoy, Drew R. "Commercial Farming and the 'Agrarian Myth' in the Early Republic." *The Journal of American History*, Vol. 68, No. 4 (March 1982), 833–849.

———. *The Elusive Republic: Political Economy in Jeffersonian America.* Chapel Hill: University of North Carolina Press, 1980.

McInerney, Daniel J. *The Fortunate Heirs of Freedom: Abolition & Republican Thought.* Lincoln: University of Nebraska Press, 1994.

McNall, Scott. *The Road to Rebellion: Class Formation and Kansas Populism, 1865–1900.* Chicago: University of Chicago Press, 1988.

McPherson, James. *For Cause and Comrades.* New York: Oxford University Press, 1997.

Miner, Craig. "Border Frontier: The Missouri River, Fort Scott & Gulf Railroad in the Cherokee Neutral Lands, 1868–1870." *The Kansas Historical Quarterly*, Vol. 35, No. 2 (1969), 105–29.

———. *Kansas: The History of the Sunflower State, 1854–2000.* Lawrence: University Press of Kansas, 2002.

———. *Next Year Country: Dust to Dust in Western Kansas, 1890–1940.* Lawrence: University Press of Kansas, 2006.

———, and William Unrau. *The End of Indian Kansas: A Study in Cultural Revolution, 1854–1871.* Lawrence: University Press of Kansas, 1978, 1990.

Mitchell, Reid. *Civil War Soldiers.* New York: Viking, 1988.

———. *The Vacant Chair: The Northern Soldier Leaves Home.* New York: Oxford University Press, 1993.

Morrison, Michael A. "Westward the Course of Empire: Texas Annexation and the American Whig Party." *Journal of the Early American Republic* 10 (Summer 1990), 221–49.

Napier, Rita, editor, *Kansas and the West: New Perspectives.* Lawrence: University of Kansas Press, 2003.

Newhouse, Michael. "Recognizing and Preserving Native American Treaty Usufructs in the Supreme Court: the Mille Lacs Case." *Public Land and Resources Law Review* (2000), 169–200.

Newman, Simon. *Parades and the Politics of the Street: Festive Culture in the Early American Republic.* Philadelphia: University of Pennsylvania Press, 1997.

Nordin, Sven D. *Rich Harvest: A History of the Grange, 1867–1900*. Jackson: University Press of Mississippi, 1974.

Norton, Mary Beth. *Founding Mothers & Fathers: Gendered Power and the Forming of American Society*. New York: Alfred A. Knopf, 1996.

———. *Liberty's Daughters: The Revolutionary Experience of American Women, 1750–1800*. Boston: Little, Brown, 1980.

Oakes, James. "From Republicanism to Liberalism: Ideological Change and the Crisis of the Old South." *American Quarterly*, Vol. 37, No. 4 (1985), 551–71.

Oberly, James W. *Sixty Million Acres: American Veterans and the Public Lands before the Civil War*. Kent, OH: Kent State University Press, 1990.

Orsi, Richard J. *Sunset Limited: the Southern Pacific Railroad and the Development of the American West*. Berkeley: University of California Press, 2005.

Overton, Richard. *West: A Colonization History of the Burlington Railroad*. Cambridge: Harvard University Press, 1941.

Packer, Herbert. *The Limits of the Criminal Sanction*. Stanford: Stanford University Press, 1968.

Paludan, Phillip Shaw. "The American Civil War Considered as a Crisis in Law and Order." *The American Historical Review*, Vol. 77, No. 4 (1972), 1013–1034.

———. *"A People's Contest": The Union and Civil War, 1861–1865*. New York: Harper & Row, 1988.

Pasley, Jeffrey L. *"The Tyranny of Printers": Newspaper Politics in the Early American Republic*. Charlottesville: University of Virginia Press, 2001.

Paulson, Ross Evans. *Women's Suffrage and Prohibition: A Comparative Study of Equality and Social Control*. Glenview, IL: Scott, Foresman, 1973.

Peskin, Lawrence A. "How the Republicans Learned to Love Manufacturing: The First Parties and the "New Economy," *Journal of the Early Republic*, Vol. 22, No. 2 (Summer 2002), 235–262.

Pfeifer, Michael J. *Rough Justice: Lynching and American Society, 1874–1947*. Urbana: University of Illinois Press, 2004.

Pitkin, Hannah F. *Fortune Is a Woman*. Berkeley: University of California Press, 1984.

Pocock, J.G.A. *The Machiavellian Moment: Florentine Political Thought and the American Republican Experience*. Princeton, NJ: Princeton University Press, 1975.

———. *Three British Revolutions: 1614, 1688, 1776*. Princeton, NJ: Princeton University Press, 1980.

———. *Politics, Language, and Time: Essays on Political Thought and History*. New York: Antheneum, 1971.

Prude, Jonathan. *The Coming of Industrial Order: Town and Factory Life in Rural Massachusetts, 1810–1860*. New York: Cambridge University Press, 1985.

Riley, Glenda. *The Female Frontier: A Comparative View of Women on the Prairie and the Plains*. Lawrence: University of Kansas Press, 1988.

Robbins, Roy. *Our Landed Heritage: The Public Domain, 1776–1936*. Princeton, NJ: Princeton University Press, 1942.

Rodgers, Daniel T. "Republicanism: The Career of a Concept." *Journal of American History* 79 (June 1992), 11–28

Rodgers, Thomas E. "Billy Yank and G. I. Joe: An Exploratory Essay on the Sociopolitical Dimensions of Soldier Motivation." *The Journal of Military History*, Vol. 69, No. 1, (2005), 93–121.

Rollings, Willard. *Unaffected by the Gospel: the Osage Resistance to the Christian Invasion, 1673–1906*. Albuquerque: University of New Mexico Press, 2004.

Rose, Thomas, ed. *Violence in America*. New York: Random House, 1969.

Ross, Steven J. "The Transformation of Republican Ideology." *Journal of the Early Republic* 10 (Fall 1990), 324–35

Rothenberg, Winifred Barr. *From Market-Places to a Market Economy: The Transformation of Rural Massachusetts, 1750–1850*. Chicago: University of Chicago Press, 1992.

Rotundo, E. Anthony. *American Manhood: Transformations in Masculinity from the Revolution to the Modern Era*. New York: Harper Collins, Basic Books, 1993.

Rowlison, Don D. "An English Settlement in Sheridan County, Kansas: The Cottonwood Ranch." *Kansas History*, Vol. 12, No. 3 (1989), 160–165.

Ryan, Mary R. *Civic Wars: Democracy and Public Life in the American City during the Nineteenth Century*. Berkeley: University of California Press, 1997.

———. *Women in Public: Between Banners and Ballots, 1820–1880*. Baltimore: Johns Hopkins University Press, 1990.

Saul, Norman. "The Migration of Russian-Germans to Kansas." *Kansas Historical Quarterly*, Vol. 40, No. 1 (1974), 38–62.

Scheiber, Harry N. *Ohio Canal Era: A Case Study of Government and the Economy, 1820–1861*. Athens: Ohio University Press, 1969.

Schwantes, Carlos A. *Railroad Signatures across the Pacific Northwest*. Seattle: University of Washington Press, 1993.

Sellers, Charles G. *The Market Revolution: Jacksonian America, 1815–1846*. New York: Oxford University Press, 1991.

Shalhope, Robert E. "Toward a Republican Synthesis: The Emergence of an Understanding of Republicanism in American Historiography." *William and Mary Quarterly*, 3rd series, 29 (January 1972), 49–80

Shambaugh, Benjamin. "Frontier Land Clubs or Claim Associations." American Historical Association, *Annual Report*, 1900, Volume 1, Washington, 1901.

Shortridge, James. *Cities on the Plains: The Evolution of Urban Kansas*. Lawrence: University Press of Kansas, 2004.

———. *Peopling the Plains: Who Settled Where in Frontier Kansas*. Lawrence: University Press of Kansas, 1995.

Sklar, Kathryn K. *Catherine Beecher: A Study in American Domesticity*. New Haven: Yale University Press, 1973.

Smith, Henry Nash. *Virgin Land: The American West as Symbol and Myth*. Cambridge: Harvard University Press, 1950, 1978.

Smith, Rogers M. "The 'American Creed' and American Identity: The Limits of Liberal Citizenship in the United States." *The Western Political Quarterly* Vol. 41, No. 2 (1988), 225–251.

Smith, Wilma M. "A Half-Century of Struggle: Gaining Women's Suffrage in Kansas." *Kansas History* 2 (1981), 74–95.

Stevens, Robert C., and Betty Adams. *Thunderbolt from a Clear Sky: the Irrepressible Life of Robert W. S. Stevens*. Rochester, NY: WME Books, 2006.

Stilgoe, John R. *Metropolitan Corridors: Railroads and the American Scene*. New Haven: Yale University Press, 1983.

Stourzh, Gerald. *Alexander Hamilton and the Idea of Republican Government*. Stanford: Stanford University Press, 1970.

Streifford, David M. "The American Colonization Society: An Application of Republican Ideology to Early Antebellum Reform." *Journal of Southern History* 45 (May 1979), 201–20.

Taylor, George R. *Transportation Revolution, 1815–1860*. New York: Rinehart, 1951.

Thelen, David. *Paths of Resistance: Tradition and Dignity in Industrializing Missouri*. New York: Oxford University Press, 1986.

Trachtenberg, Alan. *The Incorporation of America: Culture and Society in the Gilded Age*. New York: Hill and Wang, 1982.

Turk, Eleanor L. "Germans in Kansas. Review Essay." *Kansas History*, Vol. 28, No. 1 (2005), 44–71.

Valencius, Conevery Bolton. *The Health of the Country: How American Settlers Understood Themselves and Their Land*. New York: Basic Books, 2002.

Vinovskis, Maris A., ed. *Toward a Social History of the American Civil War: Exploratory Essays*. Cambridge: Cambridge University Press, 1990.

Waldstreicher, David. *In the Midst of Perpetual Fetes: The Making of American Nationalism*, 1776–1820. Chapel Hill: University of North Carolina Press, 1997.

Wallace, Duncan, L., ed. *History of Neosho and Wilson Counties*. Fort Scott, KS: Monitor, 1902.

Ward, James A. *Railroads and the Character of America, 1820–1887*. Knoxville: The University of Tennessee Press, 1986.

Watson, Blake. "The Thrust and Parry of Federal Indian Law." *University of Dayton Law Review* (Spring 1998), Appendix.

Watson, Henry L. *Liberty and Power: The Politics of Jacksonian America*. New York: Hill and Wang, 1990.

Welter, Barbara. "The Cult of True Womanhood: 1820–1860." *American Quarterly 18* (Summer), 151–74.

White, Richard. *"It's Your Misfortune and None of My Own": A History of the American West*. Norman: University of Oklahoma Press, 1991.

Wiley, Bell Irvin. *The life of Billy Yank: The Common Soldier of the Union*. Indianapolis: Bobbs-Merrill, 1952; reprint, Garden City, NY: Doubleday, 1971.

———. *The Life of Johnny Reb: The Common Soldier of the Confederacy*. Indianapolis: Bobbs-Merrill, 1943; reprint, Garden City, NY: Doubleday, 1971.

Williams, Stephen K. *Cases Argued and Decided in the Supreme Court of the United States October Terms, 1874, 1875, 1876, in 23 Wallace, 91, 92, 193 U.S. with Others, Book 23*, Lawyers' Edition. Rochester, NY: Lawyers' Cooperative, 1901.

Wilson, Julie. "Kansas Uber Alles! The Geography and Ideology of Conquest, 1870–1900," *The Western Historical Quarterly*, Vol. 27, No. 2 (1996), 186.

Wood, Gordon S. *The Creation of the American Republic, 1776–1787*. Chapel Hill: University of North Carolina Press, 1969.

———. *The Radicalism of the American Revolution*. New York: Knopf, 1992.

———. "Republicanism in the History and Historiography of the United States." *American Quarterly* 37 (Fall 1985).

———. "The Virtues and the Interests." *The New Republic* (11 February 1991), 32–35.

Zaggari, Rosemarie. "The Rights of Man and Woman in Post-Revolutionary America." *William and Mary Quarterly*, 3rd Series, 55 (1998), 203–230.

Zahler, Helene Sara. *Eastern Workingmen and National Land Policy, 1829–1862*. New York: Columbia University Press, 1941.

Index

Abbot, F. M. 68–69
Adams, Henry J. 46–47
African Americans 51, 112, 115, 125–27
Ammerman, Maia 130
Applegate, Jesse 12
aristocracies, opposition to 13, 16, 18, 23, 27, 45, 47, 54, 82, 113, 115, 119; *see also* monopolies, opposition to

Barker, Joseph 105
Barrett, James 89–90
Bax, Fr. John 163, 171, 174–77
Beck, Stephen 36
Beecher, Henry Ward 13
Bennett, William 113–14, 122
Big Elk 40
Bookter, Justina 130–31
Buchanan, James 13, 156

Calhoun, John 10, 169
Campbell, Bob 72–73
Canville (Kansas) 60–61, 68
capitalists 113–15, 117
Case, Nelson 62, 74, 160
cattle thieves 69
Chanute (Kansas) 5, 32, 68, 75; *see also* New Chicago; Tioga
Cherokee Neutral Lands 96–98, 139
Chetopa (Kansas) 5, 37, 49, 65, 67, 89–90, 100, 102, 104, 115, 127–28, 139, 144, 148
Civil War 1, 3, 15–16, 23–24, 27–29, 32–34, 42, 47, 110–11, 113–15, 132, 155, 157, 161, 172
Clarke, Sidney 41, 43–45, 51, 57–58, 96, 100, 156–57
Constitution of the United States 12–16, 60, 117, 156

Corey, T.C. 154
Cory, C.E. 33, 42, 62–63, 69, 73, 77, 82
courts 73–76, 90, 101, 105–106, 108, 157–58; *see also* Supreme Court
Crawford, T. Hartley 171
Cunning, A.D. 69

Dalson, E.G. 88
Dash, Charles 87
Davies, R.A. 70
Davis, David 158, 160
Davis, R.C. 56
Davis, Willard 52
Dawson, William 13
Declaration of Independence 14–15, 46
de Coronado, Francisco Vasquez 8
De La Coix, Fr. Charles 169
Dement, Hiddie 130
Democratic Party 13, 28, 111–14, 117–19
Denison, Eleanor D. 142
Denison, George 142, 144
Denison, J.L. 48
De Theux, Fr. Theodore 170–71
Dickerman, Austin Thomas 76
Dinsmore, Francis M. 37, 39–40, 77, 82
Disbro, Sarah 105–06
Douglas, Stephen 11–14
DuBourg, Louis William Valentine 168–70

Ebert, Barberry 123
Ebert, Jacob 123
Elm Creek (Kansas) 105
Elston (Kansas) 84
Erie (Kansas) 5, 22, 60, 74, 84, 92, 96, 105, 126, 155

210 Index

Farel, John 56
farming 8, 21, 23, 33–34, 46, 49–51, 55–56, 62, 64–65, 67, 84, 120–21, 137, 141, 152; farmers' wives 122–23
fire 49, 65, 67–68, 121, 177; *see also* natural disasters
floods 57, 62, 66–67; *see also* natural disasters
Fort Roach (Kansas) 20
Fort Scott (Kansas) 37, 61

gender construction 23–25, 119–36
Goodnow, Isaac 142, 144–45, 151, 153
Graham, George 19
Grant, Ulysses S. 58, 60, 111–12, 114, 118, 135–36
grasshoppers 62–63; *see also* natural disasters
Graves, W.W. 60–62, 77

Hale, Edward Everett 9–10
Harper's Magazine 14
Harper's Weekly 53
Harvey, James M. 19, 152
Haughawout, W.J. 101
Haynes, Enoch 19
Herd Law 99
Hill, John 18
Holbrook, Loren B. 70
Homestead Act of 1862 27, 36, 93, 97, 149
Horne, Taylor 107–08
Horner, John 22, 37–39, 48–49, 61, 66–67, 77, 80, 98, 100–01, 103–04, 120, 124, 133, 138–40, 144–45
horse thieves 75–76, 82–83, 85
Humboldt (Kansas) 36, 61, 74, 94, 141
Hutchinson, D.C. 147–48

Indian Territory 3, 56, 77, 127, 137–38, 142, 175
insects 62–64

Jackson, Andrew 9, 166
Jacksonville (Kansas) 5, 33, 45, 60, 81–82, 92, 95–96, 100, 130
Jefferson, Thomas 9, 11, 154–55, 166
Joy, James F. 96–98, 138
July 4th celebrations 21, 36, 40, 45–46, 52, 81, 92, 108, 146–47, 160

Kansas Balkans 6
Kansas-Nebraska Act 9–12, 149
Kerns, James 107–08
Kious, Solomon 65

Labette City (Kansas) 5, 71,. 104
Ladore (Kansas) 60, 86–87, 89, 96, 108, 128, 147
Land, B.K. 59
land office(s) 10, 36, 41, 74, 92, 94–96, 107–08, 141–42, 145
Lawrence, William 145, 148–50, 156, 158
Leavenworth, Lawrence, and Galveston railroad company 4, 138, 142, 150–53, 158
Liberal Republican Party 28, 117–18
Lincoln, Abraham 36, 110, 112
Little Beaver 40
Livingstone, Clay 87

Markham, Solomon 60
McCrary, George W. 157
McMillen, G.W. 14–48
Medill, William 172
Missouri, Kansas, and Texas railroad company 4, 27, 138, 142, 150–53, 158
Mitchell, D.T. 60
Moaks, Kiziah 130
monopolies, opposition to 17–18, 19, 21–22, 41, 43–44, 50–52, 59, 78, 85, 94–95, 98, 100, 114, 118–19, 137–38, 146, 148, 156–57, 160–61; *see also* aristocracies, opposition to
Mosher, Jane 106
Moss, James 69
Mound Valley (Kansas) 147

natural disasters 49, 62; *see also* fire; floods; grasshoppers; weather
Neilson, Soren 106
Neola (Kansas) 92
Neosho River 8, 37, 64, 66–67, 75, 121, 171–72
New Chicago (Kansas) 5, 75; *see also* Chanute

Oden, Thomas 88–89
Oden, William 89
Osage Ceded Lands 2–3, 27–28, 34, 36–37, 39, 41, 92, 94, 96–99, 138–39, 145, 148–53, 160
Osage indigenous peoples 28, 34–37, 39, 40–41, 56, 60, 77, 148–49, 155, 163–180
Osage Mission (Kansas) 5, 37, 52, 70, 74–75, 83–85, 90, 96, 101–02, 107–08, 118, 122, 140, 156
Oswego (Kansas) 5, 45, 48, 60, 66, 88, 90, 96, 99, 128, 131, 144

Index

Parker, William 89
Parsons (Kansas) 4–5, 52, 110, 115, 131, 142, 144, 154, 156–58
Parsons, Levi 142, 144, 151–52, 155
Parsons, Randolph 151–52
Parsons Town Company 142, 144
Peck, G.R. 158
Phelps, William 89
Phillips, S.F. 158
Pierce, Franklin 10
Pierrepont, Edward 158
Plummer, Margaret 37, 62
Pomeroy, Samuel C. 94–95
Ponziglione, Fr. Paul 70, 173–76, 178
popular sovereignty 11–12, 14–15

Quickenborne, Fr. Charles 170–71

Rager, T.F. 88, 90
Reed, Enos 71
religion and religious communities 37, 102–04, 128, 131, 163
Republican Party 28, 45, 110, 112–114, 116–19
republicanism (political theory) 2, 12–13, 17, 20, 22–23, 27, 43–45, 50, 54, 59, 61, 95, 95, 98, 110–11, 162
Revolutionary War 17, 19, 20, 22, 26, 47, 166–67; *see also* 1776
Reynolds, Milton 19, 52, 54–55, 110, 116, 131, 141–42, 153, 157
Rhodes, William 68
Rich, George 123
Roach, I.N. 86
Robinson, Charles 22, 155–56
Rome 17, 46

Schoenmakers, Fr. John 172, 175–76
self-government 2, 11–16, 27, 61, 78–79
Settlers' Clubs (Committees) 28, 71–72 77, 80–83, 89, 99–100, 105, 109; *see also* Vigilance Committees
Settlers' Protective Association 29, 77, 109, 145, 147, 150, 156, 160
1776 17–18, 116, 156, 161; *see also* Revolutionary War
Seward, Harrison 105
Shannon, Wilson 156, 160

Sharp, F. 120
Sisters of Loretto 37, 172, 176
slavery 18–20, 23, 26–27, 34, 36, 38, 44–43, 48, 51, 57, 60, 85, 95, 101, 110–14, 117, 161
Snow Creek (Kansas) 65–66, 106
soldiers 18–20, 23, 26–27, 34, 36, 38, 42–43, 48, 51, 57, 60, 85, 95, 101, 110–114, 117, 161; *see also* veterans of the Civil War
Stevens, E.B. 144
Stevens, Robert S. 4, 142, 144, 151–52, 155
Stillwell, Leander 74–75, 82
Sturges Treaty 20
Supreme Court 2, 158, 160; *see also* courts

Taylor, J.G. 51
temperance movement 29, 126–28, 130–31
Texas cattle trade 83–85, 89–90, 138, 142
Thayer (Kansas) 5, 68, 155
Tioga (Kansas) 5, 90; *see also* Chanute
Topeka (Kansas) 15, 60, 118
Toucey, Isaac 13
Tyler, John 171

Van Sandt, Samuel 31–33
veterans of the Civil War 1, 3–4, 16, 18, 20–21, 26, 32–33, 36, 41–43, 47–48, 52, 54 59, 78, 110, 114, 132, 138, 161; *see also* soldiers
Vigilance Committees 28, 77, 80–81, 88–89, 97, 99–100, 105, 107, 109; *see also* Settlers' Clubs (Committees)

Wall, Francis 69
Washington, George 12, 56, 154–55, 166
Washington, D.C. 12, 31, 33, 60, 156, 162, 169, 172
weather 62, 65–66, 71–72, 125; *see also* natural disasters
White Hair, George 171
Wickard, Samuel 90
Wilber, C.B. 37, 56
Williams, W.H. 19

www.ingramcontent.com/pod-product-compliance
Lightning Source LLC
Chambersburg PA
CBHW032054300426
44116CB00007B/731